Social History of Canada

Michael Bliss, general editor

A.I. Silver is a member of the Department of History at Glendon College, York University, and the co-author of *The Northwest Rebellion*.

Sheila Fischman is well known as a translator of Quebec literature.

In his frankly separatist and religious novel *Pour la patrie*, Jules-Paul Tardivel expressed in an extreme way what the majority of nineteenth-century Quebeckers would have expressed more moderately.

Pour la patrie was originally published in 1895, and reiterates two central themes of Tardivel's writing: the Catholicism of French Canada and its unique social and political implications, and the Quebec-centred need of French Canada for its own separate state. Tardivel wrote this book to help Quebec become 'a new France, whose mission it will be to continue on this American soil the work of Christian civilization that the old France pursued for so many hundreds of years.'

Though set in the mid-twentieth century, *Pour la patrie* represents Tardivel's vision of his own times. He was a man of his time and of his society, and both as editor of the widely-read newspaper *La Vérité* and in his many other political writings, his influence on that society was great.

If Tardivel was more extreme than most of his contemporaries in Quebec, it was more in his politics than his ideology: his underlying notions of religion, society, and the relations of men to each other and to God were in harmony with those of his province, and indeed, as the international circulation of his writings suggests, with the extreme Catholicism – the militantly defensive Catholicism – of his age.

'POUR LA PATRIE'

AN 1895 RELIGIOUS AND SEPARATIST
VISION OF QUEBEC
IN THE MID-TWENTIETH CENTURY

For my country

JULES-PAUL TARDIVEL

INTRODUCED BY A. I. SILVER
TRANSLATED BY SHEILA FISCHMAN

UNIVERSITY OF TORONTO PRESS
Toronto and Buffalo

© University of Toronto Press 1975
Reprinted in 2018
Toronto and Buffalo
Printed in Canada

Library of Congress Cataloging in Publication Data

Tardivel, Jules Paul, 1851-1905
  For my country — 'Pour la patrie'

  (Social History of Canada; 27 ISSN 0085-6207)
  Includes bibliographical references.
  I. Title.
  PZ3.T1737Fo15 [PQ3919.T3] 843 75-6862
  ISBN 0-8020-2183-2
  ISBN 978-0-8020-6267-3 (paper)

This book has been published with the assistance of a grant from the Canada Council. It was originally published in French under the title *Pour la patrie: roman du XXe siècle* in 1895 by Cadieux & Derome of Montreal. The book was republished in Montreal in 1935 by La Croix and in Montreal in 1974 by Editions HMH.

An introduction

BY A. I. SILVER

Introduction

THE LAST THIRD OF THE NINETEENTH CENTURY was a period of crisis for Catholicism. Throughout the European world a series of reversals was driving it out of the last traditional positions which the liberal revolutions had left it. The execution of the emperor Maximilian in Mexico in 1867 marked the final defeat of the last attempt to establish a Catholic empire. In 1870 the success of Italian unificationists deprived the papacy of temporal authority in the central Italian states it had ruled for more than a millenium and left Pope Pius IX a self-styled 'prisoner' in the Vatican. The same year saw the downfall of Napoleonic France, succeeded by a Third Republic that would drive religious orders into exile and secularize the nation's school system in a burst of radical anti-clericalism. Other governments too were chasing the Church from their schools, and fierce conflicts over education were waged in Germany as in New Brunswick, in Switzerland as in Manitoba. Everywhere Catholic conservatism was forced back by liberalism, secularism, modernism.

One of the few successes which Catholicism enjoyed in this period was the creation, by the British North America Act of 1867, of the Province of Quebec. Forming what French Canada's largest newspaper, *La Minerve*, called 'a state within the state,'[1] Quebec provided a French-Canadian homeland, whose Catholic majority would be able, through its own provincial parliament, to give itself legislation consistent with its own Catholic ideology. According to the pro-Confederation press, 'everything connected in any way with our national and religious institutions will be under the jurisdiction of our provincial legislature.'[2]

The French-Canadian advocates of Confederation repeatedly stressed, between 1864 and 1867, when the great constitutional scheme was being debated, that its chief advantage lay in the degree of independence French Canadians would enjoy in their autonomous province. The federal parliament would only concern itself with matters of a very general nature, material questions of common interest to all provinces and unaffected by ideology. On a more important level, Quebec would be separated from Ontario (with

Introduction vii

which it had been merged in 1840) and would receive a parliament of its own to deal with 'the sacred heritage of our traditions,'[3] with 'all those questions which involve our religion or our nationality.'[4] Jules-Paul Tardivel was to write in 1882 that 'Confederation has given to us, inhabitants of the province of Quebec, a relatively complete autonomy.'[5] And this autonomy was precious, for it was to Quebec, and not to Ottawa, that French Canadians must look for legislation in the most important areas:

Our highest interests are not centred at Ottawa; for us, who are French-Canadian and Catholic, they are centred at Quebec, where we make our own laws on education, civil rights, property, municipal institutions, the administration of justice, charitable institutions, etc. – in fact, all those things which make up the intimate and real life of a nation.[6]

But appreciation of political autonomy did not mean a feeling of isolationism. As Catholics in the last third of the nineteenth century, French Quebeckers were aware of events outside their province, and they saw themselves as engaged in the same struggle between Catholic conservatism and the modern liberal ideology as was raging elsewhere. Indeed, if Quebec's autonomy was important, it was at least partly because that autonomy would enable the French-Canadian nationality to act as a vital agent of the Catholic cause. Intellectuals had been saying for some time that God had raised up this nation to embody and advance Catholic principles in the world. Quebec, according to *La Minerve,* would now become 'the avenue of Catholic principles, the beacon light of the New World.'[7] Another Conservative newspaper was more emphatic: 'The French Canadians will disappear as a political influence the day they cease to be the active champions of Catholic interests.'[8]

In designating themselves the champions of Catholic interests, French Canadians were modelling their national mission on that of Catholic France. It was France which, in 1863, used its army to back up the establishment of a Mexican Empire under the Austrian Archduke Maximilian. As early as 1861 Napoleon III had intervened in Mexico to check the anticlerical government of the revolutionary Juarez, and had appealed to Catholic opinion to support the intervention as an act for the restoration of religion and order, of government based on Christian principles. This caught French-

Canadian attention; some young men went off to join the French forces in Mexico, while newspapers in Quebec followed, most of them with sympathy, the progress of Maximilian's Catholic empire. In the end, American hostility frightened Napoleon III away. The freeing of the Union army after the civil war hastened the withdrawal of French troops and made Maximilian's downfall inevitable. In Montreal, *La Minerve* expressed regret that the French flag was once more retreating across the Atlantic, but went on to announce:

Nevertheless, just because an empire on which we had counted as an ally is falling, that does not mean we are discouraged. The struggle against the invasion of republican ideas will continue with no less ardour on this small corner of earth which we occupy in America.[9]

The Mexican affair was highly symbolic. Behind Maximilian and Juarez were the real protagonists: on the one hand, Napoleonic France, eldest daughter of the Church, champion of order and the conservative principles that held society together; on the other hand, the United States, mother of revolutions, embodiment of republicanism, secularism, and conscienceless individualism. Now that the empire had fallen, predicted *Le Journal des Trois-Rivières*, foreseeing Maximilian's death before a revolutionary firing squad, Mexico would 'fall once more into its old state of anarchy and troubles under the government of Juarez.'[10] And standing by to pick up the pieces were the United States, ready to exploit the situation to their own advantage.

Mexico was neither the last nor the worst reversal for Napoleon III and his French-Canadian sympathizers. The Franco-Prussian war of 1870 destroyed him completely. In that war too the issue was symbolic, for France could still be seen as agent of the Catholic cause. Thus, *Le Nouveau Monde* of Montreal:

God has made of the French people (despite all its faults still the most Catholic in Europe) His instrument in the past; and it is reasonable to see in this war a struggle on which will depend the future of Europe, whether or not predominance will go to the Prussian principle – tyrannic, protestant, rationalist, and Hegelian.

As for us, we say it with a legitimate pride, regardless of all considerations of material interest or of fanaticism: our sympathies are

Introduction ix

with France, our old mother-country, whose flag has always protected, all over the world, the cause of the weak, the cause of justice, and Truth.[11]

The Franco-Prussian war thus caused universal excitement in Quebec. Some men went overseas to join the French forces. At home, popular subscriptions raised money to send food and medical supplies to France, and, in the tense autumn of 1870, crowds were known to stand all night in front of newspaper offices, where the latest bulletins from the battlefront were posted as they arrived.[12]

That same autumn saw an even greater defeat for the Catholic cause. Since the 1830s Italian nationalists had been campaigning to unite the various kingdoms, principalities, and duchies of their peninsula into one democratic nation-state. One obstacle to the accomplishment of such a program was the papacy, for the Pope was himself the ruler of states in central Italy, and he insisted on retaining the independence which this position gave him. In 1848 a revolution expelled him from his seat at Rome, but he was eventually returned to it by the intervention of Napoleon III. During the 1850s and 1860s, the Pope, supported by forces which Napoleon III kept in Rome to appease Catholic opinion in France, remained a chief opponent of Italian unification.

Crisis built up in the late 1860s, when the colourful nationalist leader, Garibaldi, led his forces against Rome. In the English and liberal world, where papal temporal power was seen as retrograde and reactionary, Garibaldi was considered a hero (British Columbia was to set up a Garibaldi Provincial Park). But throughout the Catholic world opinion rallied behind Pope Pius IX. From near and far Catholic volunteers flocked to join the French Zouave regiment defending Rome.

This movement could not leave Quebec unaffected. Between 1867 and 1870, detachments of more than 600 men, trained and equipped in Quebec by popular subscription and clerical leadership, were despatched to Europe to join the Zouaves. 'Soldiers of Truth and Justice' they were called by the Quebec Catholic press,[13] and 'champions of the rights of God.'[14] Huge crowds turned out to see them off, and to welcome them when they came back; special masses were celebrated and special sermons preached for their departures and arrivals. This impressive French-Canadian exertion on behalf of world-wide Catholicism had a great impact on Quebec opinion. When, in 1882, the French general de Charette, under whom the Canadians had served at Rome, visited Canada, he was greeted at Montreal by a vast crowd of cheering people, and accompanied from the station to his hotel by the greatest procession ever seen in that city.[15]

Despite such support, the temporal power of the papacy was destroyed in 1870. It was only one of a series of disasters which French Canadians had to brood over in the second half of the nineteenth century – the revolutions of 1848, the Mexican disaster, the crushing of the national aspirations of Catholic Poland in 1863, the defeat of France, the triumph of secularism in the schools of the Third Republic, of Germany, Switzerland, and closer to home, of New Brunswick and Manitoba. It hardly seemed possible that such a continuous succession of defeats could have been brought about by purely natural causes, and it was not surprising that many Catholics began to believe in secret conspiracies working to overthrow the Good Cause by devious and underhanded means.

Two elements in particular came to symbolize the secret forces which were thought to be working underground against Catholicism and order: the Jews and the Freemasons. Both groups were (at least in western countries) supporters of that secular individualism to which Catholic conservatives were opposed. Freemasonry was, too, a secret society, which, in some repressive countries, had been associated with liberal revolutions. The Jews, for their part, were necessarily outsiders in any society that defined itself as Catholic, and for that reason, they had in modern times fought for a liberal society whose members would be considered as independent individuals regardless of their racial or religious background. To Catholic conservatives, who believed that society was not just a collection of autonomous individuals, but an organic unity whose members were held together by common language, institutions, and traditions and given purpose and strength by a Catholic religion, Jews necessarily appeared as an alien and dissolving element. Thus, in 1883, commenting on the secular school laws of France, *L'Etendard* of Montreal complained of 'the horde of atheists, free-thinkers, Jews, and other foreigners, who are trampling upon the disfigured body of our unfortunate mother-country, insulting everything we hold most dear.'[16] The next year, in an article

Introduction					xi

'exposing' a masonic conspiracy to take over the world, the same paper claimed:

> By ingenious manipulations, by various astute manoeuvres, Freemasonry has little by little enabled the State to become so powerful that it has gobbled up all the belongings of its constituent elements, dropping them in turn into the voracious belly of the Jews. This is proved by the gradual impoverishment of all the peoples of the world, and, in contrast, the excessive wealth of the Hebrews.[17]

In the late 1880s and 1890s the idea of Jewish and masonic conspiracies became increasingly current. In his novel, *Les Caves du Vatican*, André Gide has given us a picture of some fervent Catholics of the period, ready to believe even that the Pope himself was a secret prisoner of the Freemasons, held in chains in the cellars beneath the Vatican, while the man who sat openly on the papal throne was only a masonic puppet, placed there to bring about from within the downfall of the Catholic Church. The late 1880s saw the publication of a number of 'exposés' that played on such credulity. Edouard Drumont's *La France juive* (which was well reviewed in Quebec) claimed to document the secret Jewish take-over of France, while a number of books by the ex-anti-clerical, Léo Taxil, who had noisily converted to Catholicism in 1885, described in horrifying detail the machinations of the ultra-secret top-level lodges of Freemasonry, said to be commanded by Satan himself and relentlessly pursuing the worship and work of Lucifer throughout the world.[18]

The Dreyfus affair, which tormented France for more than a decade after 1894, was also seen as a sign of secret Jewish and masonic control in France. 'Poor France is completely in the hands of cosmopolitan Jewry,' lamented *La Revue canadienne* (Quebec's respectable, conservative monthly journal), on hearing of Dreyfus' arrest. France ought to recognize in this affair 'the underground work being carried out by Jewry to destroy her.'[19] Nor was Jewish control confined to France, for the international sympathy which the defenders of Dreyfus had acquired by the end of the 1890s was to be attributed to 'the despatches of the wire agencies, which are controlled by the Jews.'[20] In any case, though foreign opinion might support Dreyfus, French-Canadian conservatives remained convinced that the Dreyfusards represented 'everything which is most impious, most revolutionary, most anti-French,' while 'all our friends in France, the Catholic press, the most respectable writers' were opposed to him.[21]

But it was not only in foreign lands that the struggle raged between Catholic conservatism and modern liberal individualism. For while Confederation had created an autonomous Catholic province of Quebec, it had federated that province with others whose English and Protestant majorities tended to prize the modern ideology. And if Quebeckers felt bound to support the Catholic cause abroad, so much the more were they bound to act as its defenders within Confederation. When New Brunswick ended tax support to Catholic schools in 1871 and established a compulsory neutral school system, Quebec, styling itself 'the defender of the oppressed,'[22] campaigned for a restitution of Catholic school support. Quebeckers were 'the defenders of our faith in Confederation,'[23] with a 'noble' and 'elevated mission'[24] to defend 'civil and religious order' as perceived by Catholicism.[25]

It was frequently given to Quebeckers to pursue this mission during the first decades of Confederation. The New Brunswick schools affair, the harassment of French Catholics at Red River during the 1870s and in the events leading up to and following the North-West Rebellion of 1885, the disestablishment of the French language in Manitoba and the North-West and the destruction of the Manitoba separate school system in 1890 – all these occasioned campaigns by the Quebec press and attempts by Quebec politicians to defend the French and Catholic cause in these other parts of the dominion.

But so little success did these attempts achieve, so regular were the victories of the anti-Catholic cause, that within Canada as without, many Quebeckers began to see conspiracies operating against them. 'One is tempted to believe,' complained Le Canadien of Quebec, in 1875, 'that there is an immense conspiracy against the French race in the dominion. Trampled underfoot in Manitoba, crushed in New Brunswick, we are threatened with annihilation.'[26]

It was, after all, a credulous age. People believed things which today seem ludicrous to us. In 1866 a number of Quebec newspapers[27] carried a story about a man from a Gulf of St Lawrence south shore community who one day, while out rowing, saw a sleeping whale, rowed up to it and climbed onto its back. The whale, according to the report, woke up, and before the man could get back to his boat, swam off at great speed into the middle of the gulf. A devout Catholic, this unwilling passenger on the whale's back began to pray and sing hymns. The whale, for his part, swam ever northward all that day, until at night he reached the north shore. This was not where the man wanted to be, so he continued to pray and sing hymns, till the whale turned around and swam through the night to the south shore. Still far from his village, the man continued to sing and pray while the whale swam along the shore. He finally deposited his pious passenger safe and sound at the dock of his own home town, perhaps a little hoarse, but grateful to heaven for its protection and eager to tell the world about his adventure. Perhaps even more outlandish was the 1871 report that Louis Riel had been killed by a poison-pen letter: the poisoned ink had apparently entered his body through the pores of his fingers as he picked up the letter to read it.[28] People who believed this could only believe the worst about the deviousness, the secret underhandedness of the enemies of Catholicism and its chosen nation. Were there not secret societies in Canada as in Europe: Freemasonry and its particularly virulent relation, the Orange Lodge? Was not Sir John A. Macdonald himself said to have been an ex-master of the latter? It was hardly surprising, then, to read in the papers, shortly after the execution of Louis Riel, that Macdonald, whose party had enjoyed the support of the French Canadians since the 1850s, was really a secret enemy of their cause, a participant in devious cabals that conspired their ruin. George-Étienne Cartier, the great French-Canadian leader and longtime colleague of Macdonald, had, on the verge of death, tried to warn against him; but it had been too late.[29]

The repeated need for Quebeckers to defend the French and Catholic cause against those with whom they were united in a federal partnership gave rise to frequent expressions of doubt about the validity or durability of Confederation. 'It would be better for Confederation to break up than for us to go on being mistreated in this way by a band of wild fanatics,' complained the *Courrier de St-Hyacinthe* after a case of harassment of a Catholic Métis.[30] Such actions were 'a proof that the English population does not possess that spirit of justice and conciliation which is necessary for the maintenance of Confederation.'[31]

If, then, the common material interests of French and English Canadians militated in favour of the federal union, ideological, national, or religious differences appeared to urge separation. Confederation itself had been seen as a way to reconcile those common interests with the differences by the creation of a common federal government to promote the former and separate provincial governments to protect the latter. But there were many in Quebec who continued to look forward to the day when Quebec's material interests could be promoted without the help of English Canada, and when her autonomy would be in all respects complete. This aspiration was particularly cherished by the most conservative and Catholic elements of the province, those most eager to build a thoroughly French and thoroughly Catholic society on the banks of the St Lawrence, uncontaminated by that modernism which so plagued other parts of the world. It was the ultra-Catholic Oscar Dunn who wrote that French Canada 'naturally hopes to achieve national independence sooner or later,'[32] the Conservative *Courrier de St-Hyacinthe* that foretold the day 'when, on the banks of the St Lawrence as on those of the Seine the flag of independence will proudly fly,'[33] and still another Conservative paper that asserted: 'We [French Canadians] are certain to form one day an independent State in a second Europe.'[34]

Meanwhile, it was not only necessary to fight the enemies without the province, but also to guard against those within. For alas, the Catholicism and conservatism of the province were not complete. Not only was there a strong English-Protestant minority with language and school privileges and political guarantees of its autonomy, but even among French Canadians themselves the virus of modernism was present. At Montreal, the small but prominent Institut Canadien continued into the 1870s to maintain a library with books and papers banned by the Church's *Index*, and to discuss, despite episcopal censure and even excommunication, liberal ideas condemned by Pius IX's 1864 *Syllabus of Errors*. Worse than that, there were even French-Canadian Freemasons, and in 1896 they established the first thoroughly French-Canadian lodge, affiliated not with the moderate British lodges but with the militantly atheistic orders of France and Italy.[35] Moreover, new attempts were constantly being made, by people who insidiously spoke French, to teach wicked ideas to the French Canadians, to convert them away from their noble cause. In 1871 such an attempt led to violence when a Swiss Protestant minister entered a militia camp near Lévis and was ejected by an angry mob of militiamen (nearly murdered, according to the Protestant press of Montreal) after he tried to preach in French. The same year a riot occurred when the apostate ex-priest Chiniquy tried to preach in Quebec. The first appearance of the Salvation Army on the streets of Quebec City provoked a similar riot in 1887. The ideological purity of Quebec was not to be tainted with impunity, nor were the ideological sensitivities of its majority to be offended without protest. The defence of Catholic conservatism would be maintained at home as in New Brunswick or at Rome.

It was in such a province and at such a time that Jules-Paul Tardivel wrote his religious and nationalist novel, *Pour la patrie*. The fears, hopes, and beliefs of Catholic conservatives were expressed in it, concentrated in it, amplified in it. Modern critics seem to agree that from a literary point of view the novel can make no great claims to our admiration – André Laurendeau even called it 'unreadable'[36] – and modern readers may find it hard to accept that its diabolical plots, miraculous conversions, lofty discourses, and melodramatic laments really represent what was believed or hoped by the majority of literate Quebeckers in 1895. Nevertheless, if Tardivel's writing was untypical, it was not because his ideology was different from that of the majority, but because Tardivel expressed in an extreme way what the majority would have put more moderately, because he applied his ideological premises to real situations with more rigour than others would have done, and fought their battles with more zeal than many others who equally accepted their truth. 'Thoroughgoing' was the word that he himself used to describe his own zealous approach, and it was, in fact, the typical approach of a convert. For Tardivel was, after all, a convert to French Canadianism. Born in Kentucky of European parentage, he never saw Canada nor spoke a word of French until his eighteenth year.

Tardivel's father had emigrated from France to the United States in 1848; his mother was the daughter of an Englishman who had settled in the American Midwest in 1832 and whose family had converted to Catholicism after his death that same year. When Jules-Paul was three, his mother died, and his father soon moved farther west, leaving him to the care of a maternal aunt and her brother. The latter was a priest whose large parish and its responsibilities left him little time at home.

In 1868, at the age of seventeen, Tardivel was sent by his uncle to obtain a classical education at the seminary of St-Hyacinthe. It was not uncommon, at that time, for American Catholics to attend Quebec colleges, whose classical courses were held in high repute, and while Tardivel was at St-Hyacinthe, about a fifth of his fellow students were Americans.

He performed brilliantly at college. In four years he mastered the French language and completed an eight-year course, carrying off an impressive number of prizes in the process. Here, too, he became acquainted with the great political and religious concerns of French Canadians. In the year of his enrolment nineteen St-Hyacinthe students went off with the Zouaves, to the applause of professors and fellow students alike. In 1870, the papacy was the subject of the public composition contest whose prize was keenly sought by students, and in 1871 the contest was cancelled because of 'the captivity of Pius IX' (according to the *Courrier de St-Hyacinthe*), and the 'wicked treatment he has been subjected to.'[37] As for the college curriculum, it stressed orthodox Catholicism and French-Canadian patriotism: the pagan writers of Greece and Rome were banned; the Church Fathers and French-Canadian history were emphasized.

So much was Tardivel affected by this environment that when, at the end of his studies, he returned to his homeland, he was no longer able to feel at ease there. By the beginning of 1873 he was back in St-Hyacinthe, feeling now more a French Canadian than an American. He soon found a job with the *Courrier de St-Hyacinthe*, one of the Conservative party organs. (In that age most papers survived only by the open patronage of political parties whose views they expressed.) Within a few months his talents had brought him to the attention of important party journalists, and he was offered a position at the more important *La Minerve* in Montreal. Although Tardivel's stay in Montreal was not an unpleasant one (he married there early in 1874), his job involved mainly the tedious work of translating, and he was glad enough to move to *Le Canadien*, another Conservative paper at Quebec City, where he was given more opportunity to write. His work soon filled the paper's columns, and by the end of the decade, two of his pieces had been published in book form: a biography of Pius IX and a polemic on behalf of the purity of the French language.

Introduction xvii

In 1881 Tardivel left *Le Canadien,* and that summer he founded his own paper, *La Vérité,* which he was to publish weekly, almost without interruption, until his death in 1905. It was to be an independent newspaper, expressing no party 'line' but only the opinions and interests of a thorough-going Catholicism. To maintain his independence, Tardivel had to forsake the party patronage which provided the financial life of other papers. He would never become a wealthy man, and would have to work as writer, editor, proofreader, and printer for *La Vérité.* Nevertheless, he made it into a noted and notable journal, read not only in Quebec but by Catholics in other countries as well, whose newspapers translated and reprinted its articles in their own columns.

Two central themes repeat themselves again and again in *La Vérité* as in Tardivel's other writings. The first is the Catholicism of French Canada and its unique social and political implications; the second is the Quebec-centred need of French Canada for its own separate state.

For Tardivel, as for Pius IX or any orthodox Catholic of his time, Catholicism was not just a Sunday mass but a way of life, a divinely revealed philosophy of the Good, the Just, and the moral ordering of society. To them society was not just a collection of individual people, each pursuing his own welfare, but an organic whole, consisting of classes or communities, each with its own function and position, and working toward a common Good established by God and interpreted by religion. It followed that all social, and even political, questions must be settled by religious principles. In *Pour la patrie,* the political action turns on a religious happening, and this, as one of the characters tells us late in the novel, is inevitably so:

> You may say what you will, but religion, the bond which unites us with God, will always have a preponderant influence on politics, the bond which unites men among themselves. The man who truly believes in God, the beginning and the end of all things; the man who truly believes in Jesus Christ, the Son of God, who descended into this world to redeem mankind and open the gates of heaven to us; the man who truly believes in the Holy Catholic Church ... cannot envisage politics in the same way as one who does not believe.[38]

Every religion influenced its adherents according to its own inspiration, which could be good in some respects, or bad. Only one religion, though, was thoroughly true and truly good: Catholicism.

A curious illustration of Tardivel's notions about the influence of religion on peoples' behaviour can be seen in an 1883 commentary in *La Vérité* on the trial of some Hungarian Jews for an alleged 'ritual' murder. There were Jews in Quebec, wrote Tardivel, and it hardly seemed possible to believe them capable of such monstrous crimes. It was necessary, however, to distinguish between the western Jew found in Canada and the Jew of eastern Europe. The former, living in a largely secularized society in which religion had lost its primordial place, had also lost the religious fervour of his ancestors. 'He is a financier or a dealer in drugs, with a keen eye for profit, sly, not very scrupulous in business. He may amass millions by shady means, but he no longer spills blood.' Such, after all, was corrupt man, left on his own in a society without religion to guide and order its conduct.

But the Jews of eastern Europe lived among pious Christian populations whose lives still expressed the proper influence of their religion. In such a milieu the Jews too retained their orthodoxy. But it was a corrupt orthodoxy, for the refusal of the Jews to acknowledge Christ had meant that the torch of divine truth had passed from their nation to the Christian Church, and they, left without the guidance of divine revelation, had easily been led astray by rabbis and Talmudists with false and perverse teachings. So it was that a portion of the Talmud, dealing with the slaughter of the lamb at Passover, had been corrupted in many editions to say that the blood of a Christian child was more pleasing to God than that of a lamb! 'The Talmud,' concluded Tardivel, 'has really provoked murders in the past. This has been proven unquestionably!'[39]

The grace of revelation and of mission which God had withdrawn from the Jews had passed to the Catholic Church. It, therefore, was the only real source of Truth in the world. Men must be guided by it alone. However intelligent, tolerant, and good-willed they might be, they would inevitably go astray without the spiritual guidance of the Church whose head was the Vicar of Christ. Thus, in *Pour la patrie*, the Archbishop of Montreal tells the hero not to depend on the good will of Protestant friends, for 'true faith is the necessary basis for all true good. Where faith exists, there is a solid foundation. ... Building where there is no faith is like building on sand.'[40]

Introduction

For Tardivel, then, no true and lasting social order was possible unless it was a Catholic order. And the ritual murder cases made clear what danger there was for such an order to allow error to flourish in its midst. Thus, Tardivel defended the rioters who, in 1887, tried to stop the Salvation Army ('that scandalous and grotesque organization') from parading in Quebec City. 'In a country such as ours,' he wrote, 'and we've admitted this often enough already, an official tolerance of the different cults is necessary; it is a sad necessity imposed on us by the evil character of our times.' But such tolerance could hardly extend to the *public* manifestation of such cults:

But for this band of mountebanks to invade our streets at all hours of the day and night, to deafen us with its vocal and instrumental cacophony, to scandalize our youth with its grossness and promiscuity, that is something which cannot be tolerated, even here, where we tolerate so many intolerable things.[41]

The essential quality, goals, and conduct of French-Canadian society must be Catholic, and this could hardly remain the case if corrupt and corrupting elements were allowed to operate openly, even to attempt to proselytize, to influence French Canadians away from a Catholic conduct.

Tardivel's insistence on maintaining the purity of Catholic thought and action in Quebec naturally made him an advocate of censorship. He was hardly departing from the spirit of the *Syllabus of Errors*, of the Bishop of Montreal's war against the Institut Canadien, or of the St-Hyacinthe seminary's curriculum, when he wrote:

A bad book is only fit to be burned. Nobody can read it with impunity, unless he has received special dispensation. Otherwise, you might as well say that a man, because he is in good health, can eat poison without danger. Reading is the nourishment of the mind; it must be healthy if it is to give life instead of death.[42]

Among bad books Tardivel was inclined to list virtually all novels. The novel form itself was an invention of the devil. 'The novels one reads in the newspapers, as a general rule, are veritable pulpits of Satan, nothing more nor less. In them, the Demon advocates all possible sins and mocks all virtues.'[43] Strange words from a man who was to write a novel himself! Yet, as he explained in the preface, it was only because 'it is permitted to capture the enemy's war machines and to use them to assault his own ramparts'[44] that he was able to bring himself to compose *Pour la patrie*. The way in which authors used literary forms and their own talents was the essential thing. Thus, in the novel, Tardivel tells us that the writer-editor of a certain newspaper 'had gone into journalism without moral preparation, without having sufficiently purified his intention,'[45] and we are, therefore, not surprised to see him and his paper inflicting harm upon the Catholic cause. Similarly, Tardivel complained, when Sarah Bernhardt and her French theatrical company visited Montreal, of spectators who praised her talents when they should be condemning the use to which she put them. The plays she presented were vehicles of diabolical notions, and the Bishop of Montreal was right in warning Catholics to stay away from them.[46] Indeed, Quebeckers ought to make such shows 'physically impossible' by the use of whistles, rotten eggs, and cabbages.[47]

Against the agencies of error, then, Catholics must constantly fight. 'It is not only the *right* but also the *duty* of Catholics to unite in order to cause the teachings of the Church to prevail in social life.'[48] It was particularly their duty because of the constant war which the modern world was waging against Catholicism in country after country, and because of the insidious ways in which that war was waged. As a journalist, Tardivel was particularly aware of the setbacks which the Catholic cause was undergoing, and, like so many others, he came to see organized conspiracies behing those setbacks: 'a united Freemasonry, that *powerful* sect which wages a *furious* war *everywhere* against the Catholic Truth, sometimes openly, sometimes in secret ... the terrible attacks made by the huge army of evil, *in all countries,* against everything Christian.'[49]

If the war against Christianity was being waged in all countries, there were, nevertheless, certain ones that provided powerful bases for the enemy. Not least of these was France, for alas, modern France was no longer the thoroughly Catholic eldest daughter of the Church that she had been of old, and with the new France French Canadians could feel little sympathy. Tardivel was expressing a common attitude when he made this distinction in *Le Canadien:*

We love the France of olden times, powerful, great, and glorious France, France the eldest daughter of the Church; we also love the

Catholic France of our own times. But modern France as the Revolution has made her, France stripped of her ancient splendours, impious France, republican France, only fills us with feelings of horror and pity.[50]

There were, then, two Frances: 'the Catholic France and the impious France, the France that prays and the France that blasphemes, the France that suffers and the France that persecutes, the France that weeps and the France that jeers.'[51] It was the former France that Montrealers cheered in their 1882 reception of General de Charette; it was the latter that they complained of in 1880, when 3000 of them paraded to protest against the expulsion of the Jesuits. It was the former that *La Revue canadienne* referred to as 'all our friends in France'; the latter that it called 'everything which is most impious, most revolutionary, most anti-French.'

With Christian France – with the Catholic elements of the motherland – Tardivel maintained correspondence and felt sympathy. But, since 1870, these were no longer the establishment of France, for the 'official France' was 'Jewish and Masonic,'[52] and a source of infection for the Catholic world. Here was a first triumph for Freemasonry, which had 'undertaken to de-Christianize France' by devious means, and largely succeeded because of 'that satanic cleverness that makes it so dangerous.'[53]

Tardivel's attitude toward 'official France' led him to oppose contacts between Quebec and the mother country, and to fear French emigrants to Quebec as carriers of the disease of modernism, agents of the Masonic infection. In *Pour la patrie,* Paris (which Tardivel compared unfavourably with Babylon) was the origin of the danger that threatened Catholic Quebec; it was a Frenchman who carried to Canada the Satanic orders which were to be carried out in the secret lodges of this country.

Undoubtedly, the literal acceptance of Satanism in this novel will appear ridiculous to modern English readers. Indeed, at the time of its publication, many people thought it worse than that. The Liberal Montreal newspaper *La Patrie* called the book 'the product of a sick mind,' while the English Protestant *Witness* of Montreal considered it a 'libel' in its association of both Freemasonry and Protestantism with Satanism.[54] Nevertheless, there were respectable Catholic elements with reason to believe in the true basis of the book's accusations. The summer of 1895, which saw publication of

Tardivel's novel, was also a time when the 'revelations' of Léo Taxil were receiving their widest attention.

Tardivel had followed the Taxil affair closely from the beginning. In 1887 he had carried Taxil's *Confessions of an Ex-Freethinker* in *La Vérité*, and in 1888 he met Taxil on a trip to France. He accepted literally the truth of statements published under Taxil's name and others[55] about Satan's direct influence on the actions of the highest levels of Freemasonry, and in 1894 he informed his readers of Taxil's revelation that Satanism was rampant in Canada, with important centres in Montreal and Hamilton. It was clear to Tardivel that 'Freemasonry is the cult of Satan,'[56] and when, later that year, an Italian journalist published a new book about the world-wide organization of 'High-Masonry,' Tardivel was confirmed in his worst fears:

There is no longer any doubt about it: Montreal is a centre of High-Masonry, of Palladism, of neo-Manichaeism, of Luciferism — of Satanism, to call this horror by its true name. It will be denied; it will be called absurd; but the proof is there. ... Freemasonry is clearly a unified, world-wide organization, run by High-Masonry or Palladism, which is nothing more nor less than Manichaeism or the cult of Lucifer.[57]

This was the premise of *Pour la patrie*, and it was widely enough accepted in the Catholic world of the time for the novel to be republished, in serial form, in several Catholic papers in Europe. It was just about the time of *Pour la patrie*'s appearance that there occurred in France the remarkable conversion of a certain Diana Vaughan, whose existence had been made known to the public some time before by Léo Taxil. Miss Vaughan was said to have been a member of the Palladium, the highest and most intimate circle of Freemasonry, and her conversion (brought about by the direct intervention of Saint Joan and the Virgin Mary, and despite the combined opposition of Beelzebub, Astaroth, Moloch, and Asmodeus) was followed by new revelations about the role of Satan and other devils in Masonic meetings and projects. She herself was reported to have called Tardivel's novel an 'admirable book, shining with truth,' and, in a series of monthly confessions about her Masonic past, which she began publishing in July 1895, she went on to praise Tardivel's newspaper, warning that 'all North America is

Introduction xxiii

infected with Masonry' and that 'the conspiracy against the Catholicism of the French Canadians is particularly strong.'[58]

The following year, with the Freemason scare running even more wildly through Catholic circles, an international anti-Masonic congress was organized at the north Italian town of Trent, site of the famous sixteenth-century Church Council. Tardivel was invited to speak to the congress, and a group of Quebec Catholics raised the money to pay for his trip. He travelled under a false name, with false initials stamped onto his luggage, and with his life heavily insured against accidents – for, as he wrote to a friend, 'as you know, accidents happen rather often to the enemies of Freemasonry.'[59]

The congress was attended by more than 1500 laymen and clerics (from a cardinal down to ordinary priests), including seven French Canadians, one of them a bishop. Tardivel's speech was a success, but his attendance at the congress made him uneasy on another score, for strong doubts were raised there about the authenticity of Léo Taxil's revelations, and in particular, about the existence of Miss Diana Vaughan. No one, in fact, had ever seen the young lady. Taxil claimed she was in hiding in a French convent; he couldn't say which one, for if the Luciferians knew where she was, they would certainly seek vengeance against her for having revealed their secrets. But many Catholics, including the theologians of the Jesuit order, were unwilling to accept his assertions. In the end, the congress agreed to set up a commission to investigate the matter.

Despite the doubts of the congress, Tardivel returned to Canada still convinced of Miss Vaughan's existence. He had met Taxil again in Europe and received his personal reassurances on the matter. His embarrassment, therefore, was all the greater when the commission reported, in early 1897, that although it had found no proof that Diana Vaughan did not exist, neither had it found any evidence that she did. Two months later, at a stormy public lecture, Taxil announced that the whole thing had been a fraud, that Diana Vaughan and all the 'revelations' about the Satanic workings of Freemasonry, from beginning to end, had been a colossal 'April fool's joke' perpetrated for the 'delicious pleasure ... the sheer joy of playing a good prank on an adversary, just for fun, for a good laugh.'[60]

Tardivel was dismayed, but, like many other thorough-going Catholics in Europe as here, not completely undeceived. Clearly, he wrote, Taxil was a villain. Nevertheless, there must still be some basis in truth for all the Satanism stories that had been circulating for the past decade; where there was smoke, there surely was fire. Was it not likely, in fact, that the Masonic Luciferians had purposely circulated the false Diana Vaughan stories in order, by revealing their falsehood, to discredit the anti-Masonic elements and cover their own trail?[61]

Commanded by Satan or not, Freemasonry was still, like all secret societies, condemned by the Church, and Tardivel was far from alone in his continued war against it. Secret lodges he saw as responsible for defeat after defeat of the Catholic cause in Canada. Had not the Orange Order secretly worked up the North-West Rebellion in 1885, in order to have an excuse to suppress the French-Catholic Métis?[62] Was not the federal government pursuing a relentless program of centralization aimed at suppressing the autonomy of the Catholic province of Quebec, in accordance with a long-prepared plan unfolded secretly in the lodges of the Freemasons?[63]

That Tardivel saw the lodges as enemies of Quebec's autonomy brings us to the second principal theme of his writing: French-Canadian independence. Because Catholicism involved a whole social and political program, or, at any rate, a unique perception of social and political questions, it was necessary for the French Canadians, the only coherent Catholic population in America, to have their own state. Only a formal French-Canadian government, with a wide range of competence, would be able to apply such a program or such a perception. For a Catholic society would certainly be materially different from those around it. It would be agricultural in a world of industry, and stable in a world of progress. (Early in *Pour la patrie* Tardivel observes that the countryside is the last bastion of Christian morality, while later in the novel the wreck of a train symbolizes the fate of technological man, rushing headlong in his arrogance toward the abyss. The Eiffel Tower, symbol of industrial progress, was to him a modern Tower of Babel.)

While the identification of Catholicism with agriculture was characteristic of nineteenth-century Quebec, it was also rather ineffective. The inability (from a number of causes) of the old rural parishes to support the rapidly increasing French-Canadian population was compelling thousands of young men, by mid-century, to

Introduction   xxv

leave their homes in search of jobs in the industrial towns of New England. It was natural enough that for men of that time the extension of agriculture into new areas of the province should appear as the proper method for stemming this flow. Yet, by the mid-1850s, there were men who realized that colonization was an ineffective answer to the problem, and that the only way to stop emigration was to create, in Quebec itself, the sort of jobs that French Canadians were seeking abroad. But this meant co-operation with English-Canadian businessmen, both inside Quebec and in the other provinces, to build the kind of commercial and industrial economy that French Quebeckers were not able, on their own, to create. Confederation itself was the result of this perception of Quebec's needs. The province's autonomous government was expected to promote the national interests of French Canada, while the federal association with the other provinces, together with the special privileges granted to English Protestants in Quebec, seemed necessary for the promotion of her material interests.

To Tardivel it seemed at first that Confederation was a considerable advantage to French Canada. Quebec seemed to have been given a government with sufficient constitutional authority and independence to build a truly Catholic society:

The province of Quebec, with its almost-complete political autonomy, its immense majority of Catholic inhabitants, could not only have governed itself always according to the laws of the Church, but could also have formed a centre of Catholicism in North America, a dam against the flood of modern errors.[64]

Unfortunately, the possibilities which Confederation had offered were not being exploited by French Canada's leaders. Too conscious of material questions and not enough of national and religious ones, they tended too much to open French Canada to English-Canadian influences, to principles the very opposite of those for which French Canadians ought to stand.

Within the province Tardivel found excessive the presence of Protestantism and of the English language. Recently, he complained in an 1881 editorial, he had rented a post office box in Quebec City. The post office had issued its receipt entirely in English – 'to me, owner of a French newspaper in an essentially French city!' Nor was this all. Telegraph companies in Quebec used English only, and French messages were usually garbled or not delivered at all. The fault belonged to Quebec politicians too eager to co-operate with the English:

We see our politicians running around the other provinces to win the good will of the English. That is all very well, but they should not forget that they also represent the French Canadians, and that they have a duty to make sure our language is respected.[65]

In the long run, excessive tolerance of English language and institutions would only lead to the destruction of French Canada. Tardivel, therefore, opposed all notions of bilingualism as a 'trap' for the French-Canadian nationality. 'Do you know of many bilingual peoples?' he asked. 'I haven't heard of any. But I do know of a people that lost its national language because it was forced to learn another.' It was all right for a few individual French Canadians to learn English if they *had* to. 'But let them learn French first, and let French always remain their mother tongue, their *real* language.'[66]

Like bilingualism, the idea of a pan-Canadian nationality was also to be opposed as destructive of the uniquely French-Canadian identity. In 1887 Tardivel criticized Quebec's prime minister, Honoré Mercier, for a speech that called for 'the creation of a truly Canadian feeling, transcending all questions of race and religion.' To Tardivel, this sounded too much like the English-Quebec newspapers, or 'all those who dream of God-knows-what mixture of the different races living in this country. This is a wicked idea. The French-Canadian race must remain what it is now, with its own language, institutions, traditions, and distinct autonomy.'[67]

The danger of anglicization within Quebec and the danger of pan-Canadianism went together with the danger represented by centralizing tendencies within the Canadian confederation. The British North America Act had given Quebec 'a relatively complete autonomy'; but, warned Tardivel, it was necessary to 'watch out constantly to preserve the true character of the federal pact. Let us not, by our negligence, permit the federal system to degenerate into a unitary state.'[68] If there was any province that had a particular interest in maintaining provincial autonomy, it was Quebec, for her unique religion and nationality set her apart from all the others. The unification of Canada through the increasing dominance of the federal government was a particular threat to French-Canadian Catholicism.

Introduction   xxvii

Yet a program of centralization was being pursued at Ottawa by government after government, whatever party was in power. It was the Liberals who, in 1875, had established the Supreme Court of Canada, giving jurisdiction to a federally appointed, English-majority court over Quebec's distinctive French-Catholic laws and autonomy. Such a court, Tardivel feared, would bring about 'the demolition of our provincial institutions and the anglicization of our French laws.'[69] Unfortunately, the return of the Conservatives to power in 1878 had not led to the elimination of the Supreme Court (although Quebec Conservatives had opposed its creation on the same grounds as Tardivel), and by 1883 *La Vérité* was complaining that 'since the Supreme Court was set up, we have been marching with giant steps toward centralization. ... The Supreme Court is out to kill the provinces. The provinces must, therefore, kill the Supreme Court.'[70]

Not surprisingly, Tardivel's complaints about anglicization and centralization led him, eventually, to doubt the advantage of maintaining Confederation. In the final analysis, it was probable that 'the province of Quebec can do without Confederation more easily than Confederation can do without her.'[71] In fact, as far as Quebec was concerned, 'a simple customs and postal union would be a definite improvement over the federal government.'[72] This would certainly get rid of the 'capital fault' of the confederation, which was 'too great a centralization of power.'[73]

By 1883, the willingness of Quebec's Conservative party to co-operate with English-Canadian interests that favoured anglicization, centralization, and industrialization had led Tardivel and other Ultramontanes to open expressions of discontent with this party that had traditionally been favoured by the Catholic Church. These discontented Conservatives were described by Tardivel as men who were involved in politics (like the hero of *Pour la patrie*) 'not to make a fortune but to serve their country.' They were, he wrote, 'convinced of the need to break openly with the dishonest organization that has taken power, with the Conservative party, with the so-called conservative press.' Not that they were ready to throw their support behind the Liberals, 'whose political and social principles are inadmissible.' But these '*true* conservatives are determined to give the country an honest government that would get rid of the present clique and prevent the triumph of liberal and radical ideas.'[74]

It was with this discontent in its ranks that the Conservative party had to face the tremendous wave of anger that shook Quebec after the hanging of Louis Riel. Riel had led a group of Saskatchewan District Indians and half-breeds in a short-lived rebellion during the spring of 1885. That summer he had been tried and convicted of high treason by an all-English jury at Regina. Despite serious doubt about his sanity, and despite a universal demand from French Canada that his sentence be moderated, the federal government allowed the law to take its course, and he was hanged that November.

Tardivel's reaction to the Riel affair was a typical French-Quebec one. As a Catholic, he felt that rebellion 'could not be condemned too severely' since it violated the duty of obedience to legitimate authority. On the other hand, in the irresponsibility of Ottawa's native policy he saw extenuating circumstances which, while not justifying the rebellion, should at least impose moderation in the punishment of its authors.[75] By the end of Riel's trial, Tardivel was convinced that he was 'a madman who cannot be held responsible for his own acts.'[76] When he was hanged nevertheless, Tardivel joined his protests to those of other Quebeckers. 'Throughout the province of Quebec,' he wrote, 'there is not a single man who dares to affirm that Louis Riel was in possession of all his mental faculties to the point of being responsible for his acts in the eyes of the law.' Why, then, had he been hanged? It was because he had been French and Catholic. 'If Riel had not had French blood in his veins and if he had not been Catholic; if he had been English and Protestant – or even Turkish – there would never have been any question of hanging him.'[77] Quebec had not wanted any special treatment for Riel. Most French Canadians had had little sympathy for him personally. But they had insisted that he not be made an exception to the rule that madmen not be hanged for acts which, because of their mental state, they could not be held responsible for. He *had* been made an exception, and it was perfectly clear to Tardivel that the reason for this was to be found in the secret influence of the Orange Lodge. Like Freemasonry, this secret society pursued a relentless war against the principles represented by French Canada, and Tardivel believed that French Canadians must unite to resist its efforts, which, otherwise, might succeed in destroying the Catholic nation.

Introduction   xxix

Tardivel's fear of Orangism, as well as his belief in French-Canadian national unity, led him to support Quebec's Liberal leader, Honoré Mercier, who, in the winter of 1885-6, attempted to direct the Riel agitation toward specific political ends. Mercier told Quebeckers that in the face of concerted anti-Catholic and anti-French action in English Canada, they must abandon their old party divisions to form a single National party that would represent the French-Canadian nation through its natural political expression, the government of Quebec. Exploiting the discontent that had existed in the Conservative party even before the Riel affair, Mercier was able to win over enough of its members (particularly among the Ultramontanes) to bring him to power in Quebec after the 1886 elections.

To Tardivel, Mercier's appeal to abandon partisan politics in the formation of a united National party was consistent with a healthy attitude toward politics. Political parties, he felt, were expressions of greed, egotism, and decadence, concerned with the gaining of power and material wealth for their members, rather than with the true welfare of the nation. Their existence was in direct opposition to Catholic principles; for, he wrote, 'the spirit of Catholicism comes from God; it vivifies and unites; the party spirit comes from Man and from the Demon; it disunites and kills.'[78]

The national unity advocated by Mercier's movement naturally focused within the province of Quebec, where French Canadians saw the greatest chances for the flourishing of their national life. Tardivel advocated this point of view strongly, but it was opposed by those French Catholics who already lived outside Quebec and who feared being isolated in an Anglo-Protestant world if Quebec turned its back upon them. In April 1886, for example, the French-language newspaper, *Le Manitoba*, criticized the Quebec press for not encouraging French Quebeckers to go and settle in the West, where they might reinforce the already-established French-Catholic community. Tardivel responded fiercely in *La Vérité:*

> There is one thing which *Le Manitoba* does not seem to realize, and which ought to be perfectly obvious to it: recent events have hardly been likely to attract our compatriots to the West.
> What, after all, do we see there?

Those of our compatriots who have already settled in these immense territories are mistreated, pushed to revolt by the civil authorities; and then, instead of being treated with justice, they are massacred, hanged, imprisoned.[79]

This reference to the North-West Rebellion and its aftermath, however, was not Tardivel's principal argument. 'When you get right down to it,' he admitted, 'those events really have little to do with the question. Even if they had not occurred, we would be no less hostile ... to any idea of French-Canadian emigration, either to the West or to the South.'[80] Here was the essential point: no matter where it was directed to, 'emigration is a curse upon our province.'[81] Quebec had huge resources and vast spaces, requiring all its population to occupy and exploit them. Moreover, the French-Canadian nation could not expect to flourish if it did not concentrate its forces within this province, which had been designed to give it a political dimension:

It should be obvious to anyone who thinks about it, that the French race in America will never have any real influence for good unless it is solidly based in the province of Quebec, as in a fortress. We must occupy the territory of this province, which belongs to us by every sort of title. We must develop and strengthen ourselves here, under the protection of the Church which watched over our beginnings and whose magnificent institutions are still our greatest strength.

We must remain united in the province of Quebec, and not dissipate our force and vitality here and there on all parts of the North American continent.[82]

This did not mean that Tardivel was opposed to *all* French-Canadian expansion. 'Later, once we have taken possession of all the territory of this province, and solidly established ourselves here, maybe then we'll gradually extend our domain by a peaceful and legitimate expansion into the surrounding regions.'[83] By a peaceful and legitimate expansion Tardivel meant a movement of Quebeckers into regions adjacent to Quebec itself. By moving, for example, into the eastern counties of Ontario, northwestern New Brunswick, or the northern fringes of New England, they would remain a compact and coherent group, always retaining contact with the heartland of French Canada. 'This expansion into neighbouring territory must be a natural development, a gradual outward movement along our borders and into contiguous regions, and not a matter of great

Introduction xxxi

migrations to distant countries.' The maintenance of a solid area of French-Canadian population would pay off in the end. For, like many other French-Canadian intellectuals in the 1890s, Tardivel believed not only 'that Confederation is a fragile arrangement without political stability or permanence,'[84] but also that there was 'nothing to make us believe that the neighbouring republic will exist forever' either. 'On the contrary,' he wrote, 'everything leads us to expect profound upheavals. As early as 25 years ago that republic was almost split in two.' In time, would the United States not inevitably break up into a number of independent countries? And with the break-up both of the United States and of the Canadian confederation, would one not see the establishment of an independent French-Canadian state, whose territory would include the old province of Quebec as well as the neighbouring regions of eastern Ontario, northwestern New Brunswick, and northern New England?[85]

In fact, the achievement of such a state (whether it included Quebec only or the surrounding areas as well) would only be the realization of French Canada's perennial dream, the 'goal,' as the hero of *Pour la patrie* puts it, toward which 'our people have aspired ... as long as we have existed,' the goal toward which 'Divine Providence has led us ... across a thousand obstacles.'[86] Even the acceptance of Confederation had only been a step toward that goal, a way of preserving the integrity of the French-Canadian nation until the day when it would be able to stand alone. Hence the need for the never-ending vigilance over Quebec's autonomy, the eternal resistance against the centralizing schemes of Ottawa. Even the Riel affair had had its greatest significance, for Tardivel, in what it showed about the degree of Quebec's subservience to Ottawa. For, as champion of Catholic interests in America, and particularly in Canada, had not Quebec's government been duty-bound to stand up in defence of that poor madman who was being hanged only for his French blood and Catholic religion? That it had not done so was surely a sign that its autonomy had been eroded, that it had allowed itself to become the mere 'instrument and accomplice of the federal cabinet.'[87] This was why the first aim of the Mercier government, founded out of the Riel agitation, must be to champion Quebec's autonomy as a French and Catholic province.

It did not take Tardivel long, however, to become disenchanted with the National party, and to see the same petty partisanship, the same advance of centralization under Mercier as under his predecessors. In the end, English and French Canada simply could not continue to live together, but must separate. This was the idea that Tardivel was to express in his novel. 'We hope,' says one of his characters, 'that English and French Canadians can get along as neighbours, joined by a simple customs and postal treaty. ... There are too many basic differences between the two races who inhabit this country to be able to make them into a truly united nation.'[88] Quebec, therefore, must seek to become what Confederation had failed to make it: 'a New France, whose mission it will be to continue on this American soil the work of Christian civilization that the old France pursued so gloriously for so many hundreds of years.'[89] It was to help on this aspiration that *Pour la patrie* was written.

It is, no doubt, always tempting with political novels to try to identify their characters and circumstances with real-life people and events. While it is not possible to give, for *Pour la patrie*, the sort of 'key' or exact table of equivalents between novel characters and real political figures that one finds, for example, with Disraeli's *Coningsby*, one can, at least, see certain characteristics of the fictional people that were shared by real ones of Tardivel's world. Tardivel himself can probably be found in two characters, the hero, Lamirande, and his journalistic sidekick, Leverdier. Certainly, Lamirande's ideas are Tardivel's, while Leverdier's newspaper, *La Nouvelle-France*, bears a close resemblance to *La Vérité*. Moreover, Leverdier shares Tardivel's own first name.

Other newspapers and journalists may also be tentatively identified. *Le Mercure* is a pretty thinly disguised *La Minerve*. Its name, its political affiliation, and its interest in commerce are all clues. Moreover, the tactics followed by *Le Mercure* during the period of crisis following Lamirande's denunciation of the first Marwood bill are pretty much the same as those followed by *La Minerve* and other ministerial papers during the Riel crisis. Less obvious are the inspirations for *La Libre Pensée* and its director, Ducoudray. They may well, however, have been *La Patrie*, and that controversial poet-journalist, Louis Fréchette. Certainly Fréchette was a bête noire for Tardivel, as indeed Tardivel was to him. There was constant editorial warfare between *La Patrie* and *La Vérité*, and a continual trading of insults between the two men, the one a liberal and the other a 'thorough-going' Catholic. If Fréchette was, at least in part, the model for Ducoudray, then we must at least praise Tardivel's charity toward a bitter adversary, for whose soul (at least in the novel) he obtained divine grace and eternal salvation.

Certain resemblances can be found between Lawrence Houghton and Edward Blake, who had led the federal Liberal party at the time of the Riel affair. Like Houghton in the novel, Blake had separated himself from the majority of English Canadians to condemn the federal Conservative government for an action which French Canadians had taken as an attack on their nationality. Furthermore, Blake had opposed the incorporation of the Orange Order, and, just as Houghton opposed the legislative union of English and French Canada, with the cry 'No Ireland in America!' so Blake ended his career as an advocate of Irish Home Rule, of the break-up of the legislative union of Great Britain and Ireland.

Easier to guess at is the original for Sir Henry Marwood. In that ugly face with the big nose, in the famous appellation, 'the old fox,' can we not recognize Sir John A. Macdonald himself? Both Marwood and Macdonald were federal premiers who introduced new constitutions; both were brilliant political tacticians, wily diplomats, shrewd manoeuvrers. Both were leaders of the Conservative party, which enjoyed the electoral support of French Canada, and just as Marwood was the secret enemy of his French-Canadian followers, a member of the Masonic lodge that conspired against them, so Macdonald was accused by Ultramontanes of being an Orangeman and secret enemy of Quebec.

Sir Vincent Jolibois could be any of the federal cabinet ministers from French Canada. The interview in which Lamirande asks him to take on the leadership of the separatist movement is reminiscent of Honoré Mercier's 1885 invitation to Adolphe Chapleau to lead the Parti National. On the other hand, unlike Chapleau in the Riel affair, Jolibois resigns from the cabinet after Lamirande's denunciation of the first Marwood bill. The actions and reasonings of his colleagues, however, who do keep their portfolios, are those of Chapleau and his two colleagues, Hector Langevin and Adolphe Caron.

Not only characters but also circumstances in the novel seem to be drawn from nineteenth-century Canadian political life. The debate in the Commons on the Marwood plan very much resembles that which was held in the Canadian legislature of 1865 about the project for a Confederation of British North America. Lamirande's criticism is very much along the lines of what the Rouges of 1865 had to say against Confederation, and indeed, of what Tardivel himself complained: that despite its name, the inherent centralizing tendencies of Confederation led it inexorably toward legislative union. On the other hand, Marwood's defence of the project very much resembles the ministerial arguments of 1865, even to the contention that the silence of the bishops signified their approval of the plan.

Many small, specific references in the novel remind us again that *Pour la patrie* represents, for all its futuristic setting, Tardivel's vision of his own times. Lamirande is accused of wanting to reintroduce the Inquisition – an accusation which Tardivel's opponents had brought against him too. Montarval, the Satanist leader, repeatedly asserts that he wants freedom, that Lucifer is the god of liberty – assertions that represent Tardivel's conception of the evil nature of liberalism. In the identification of Montarval's lodge with the Carbonari we see again the Quebec Catholic attitude toward the Italian unificationists against whom the Zouaves had fought, and in the revelation that the Satanists' physician is a Dr Cohen we have the common association of Jews with Freemasonry. References in the novel to parental and religious authority in educational matters remind us that the time of publication of *Pour la patrie* was a period of crisis in Canadian politics provoked by the Manitoba schools question. Catholics in Manitoba and in Quebec were rallying in opposition to a Manitoba law that abolished separate schools and established one compulsory common school system. According to the Catholic argument, education was a parental and religious responsibility with which the state had no right to interfere.

Finally, it is interesting to note that the issue of separatism arises, in *Pour la patrie*, at the moment of Canada's separation from the British Empire – a separation, by the way, brought about by the secret influence of the Masons. Tardivel, in fact, took it for granted that only the continuance of British imperial authority made Confederation possible, and that when that authority disappeared, Confederation would have to give place to some new arrangement. For in his view, Anglo-Saxon aggression was not to be feared in the form of British imperialism so much as in the form of English-Canadian nationalism. 'As for us,' he wrote, 'inhabitants of the

Introduction   xxxv

province of Quebec, we fear English fanaticism a lot less at London than at Ottawa.'[90] In fact, the imperial authorities could be seen as protectors of French-Canadian identity against the assimilating projects of English Canadians. 'We can be sure that the political ties which unite us to England protect us, in some measure, against the enterprises of our "brothers" of Ontario, the West and the Maritimes.'[91] Because of his view of the metropolis as a fair referee ensuring just dealing between English and French Canada, Tardivel opposed Canadian independence from the Empire. 'We would have nothing to gain from that kind of independence,' he wrote; 'for we would continue to be the minority in an independent Canada.' Far better to have the empire without Canada than vice versa. 'The best idea for us would be to get the province of Quebec out of Confederation while remaining a British colony.'

It may seem strange to us today, when we have become accustomed to the idea of French-Canadian hostility to the British Empire, and have so often been told that what French Canadians most disliked in their English-speaking compatriots was their pro-British tendency, to see Tardivel expressing such contrary notions. But at the time, there was nothing extraordinary about them. Most French Canadians agreed that the imperial power was necessary both to protect all Canadians against American annexationism and to act as a fair arbitrator in disputes against English-Canadian assimilationists. In the 1860s, the opponents of Confederation had urged that rather than associate itself with the English-speaking provinces, Quebec ought to seek a complete separation under the protection of the British Empire.[92] In 1875, Quebec's conservative press was unanimous in protesting against the establishment of a Supreme Court of Canada, which, it feared, might some day cut French Canadians off from their right of final appeal to the imperial Privy Council.[93] Indeed, it was in considerable measure such fears that maintained the Privy Council as Canada's highest court of appeal until as late as 1949.

Tardivel, then, was far from alone in his view of the empire as a defender of his people against English Canada, and in his consequent fear of independence for the existing Confederation. 'To entrust our destinies to an English-Canadian majority, without any counterbalance from the other side of the Atlantic, is a terrible danger, to which the French-Canadian nationality must never expose itself,' according to the prestigious *Revue Canadienne*.[94] And just as Tardivel, in his novel, assumed that the end of imperial authority would make necessary a replacement of Confederation by something else, so in the 1920s, when the break-up of the empire was actually coming about, many French Canadians expected that Confederation would have to be changed, and began casting about to find replacements.[95]

What Tardivel put into *Pour la patrie*, then (apart from the Satanism, perhaps), was not untypical of what French Canadians were thinking in his time. Indeed, his whole program was consistent with the mainstream of French-Quebec thought.[96] His writings were to be found in all the presbyteries, seminaries, and colleges of the province;[97] his works were given out as prizes in schools; for his main aims were those of Quebec. The struggle for the principle of Catholic education, which he claimed was *La Vérité*'s main purpose,[98] preoccupied French-Canadian politicians for decades, played an essential part in the federal elections of 1874 and 1896, and kept Quebec itself from having a secular ministry of education before the 1960s. The fear of modern progress and development which led Tardivel to criticize American life and values throughout his career also inspired the French-Canadian fathers of Confederation, and remained a main theme in French-Canadian politics until our own times. In particular, the doctrine of liberalism,' the exclusion of God from politics,'[99] which is so completely rejected by *Pour la patrie*, with its theme of the unity of religion and politics, was also continually rejected by the Quebec church during the nineteenth century and, indeed, by the papacy in its *Syllabus of Errors*. It has been maintained, in fact, that it was only by abandoning liberalism that the Liberal party was able to get itself elected in Quebec![100]

However shocking, then, his ideas may seem to us today, it cannot be denied that Tardivel was a man of his time and of his society, nor that his influence on that society was considerable. When he died in 1905, his funeral was attended by a crowd that included three ministers of the Quebec government, and services were conducted by the Archbishop of Quebec, the Rector of Laval University, the principal of Laval's École normale, and the superior of the Franciscan order of Quebec. He had fought battles against such notable French Canadians as Sir Wilfrid Laurier, Henri Bourassa, and Archbishop Taschereau, but he cannot, on that

Introduction xxxvii

account, be thought to have opposed the main currents of French-Canadian thought. The differences were usually more of strategy than of fundamental values, and if he was more extreme than most of his contemporaries in Quebec, it was more on a political than on an ideological level. His underlying notions of religion, society, the relations of men to each other and to God, were in harmony with those of his province, and indeed, as the international circulation of his writings suggest, with the extreme Catholicism – the militantly defensive Catholicism – of his age.

NOTES

1 *La Minerve* (Montreal) 1 July 1867
2 *Le Courrier de St-Hyacinthe* (St-Hyacinthe) 23 Sept. 1864
3 *Contre-poison: La Confédération c'est le salut du Bas-Canada* (Montreal: Senécal 1867) 3
4 *La Minerve* 30 Dec. 1864
5 *La Vérité* (Quebec) 8 July 1882
6 Ibid., 15 Jan. 1888
7 *La Minerve* 28 June 1880
8 *L'Union des Cantons de l'Est* (Arthabaskaville) 6 June 1872
9 *La Minerve* 11 Sept. 1866
10 *Le Journal des Trois-Rivières* (Trois-Rivières) 31 Aug. 1866
11 *Le Nouveau Monde* (Montreal) 18 July 1870
12 N.H.E. Faucher de Saint-Maurice, 'Le Canada et les Canadiens-français pendant la guerre franco-prussienne,' in his *La Question du jour: Resterons-nous français?* (Quebec: Belleau 1890)
13 *L'Union des Cantons de l'Est* 14 Apr. 1870
14 *La Minerve* 23 Apr. 1870
15 Pierre Savard, *Jules-Paul Tardivel, la France et les États-Unis* (Quebec: Les Presses de l'université Laval 1967) 61
16 *L'Etendard* (Montreal) 3 Feb. 1883
17 Ibid. 3 May 1884
18 Taxil's 'revelations' are described in Eugen Weber, *Satan Franc-Maçon* (np: René Julliard 1964).
19 *La Revue canadienne* (Montreal) XXX (1894) 778-9
20 Ibid. XXXIV (1898) 220

21 Ibid. XXXVI (1899) 66
22 *La Minerve* 1 June 1872
23 *L'Union des Cantons de l'Est* 6 June 1872
24 *Le Nouveau Monde* 1 June 1874
25 *Le Canadien* (Quebec) 17 Mar. 1875
26 Ibid. 3 Feb. 1875
27 Including the prestigious *La Minerve* 27 Jan. 1866
28 *Le Journal de Quebec* (Quebec) 14 Jan. 1871
29 [Joseph Bellerose], *L'Orangisme et le catholicisme* (Montreal: l'Etendard 1886) 10-12
30 *Le Courrier de St-Hyacinthe* 29 Oct. 1874
31 *Le Nouveau Monde* 4 Nov. 1874
32 Oscar Dunn, *L'Union des partis politiques dans la province de Québec* (Montreal: G.E. Desbarats 1874) 25
33 *Le Courrier de St-Hyacinthe* 6 July 1880
34 *Le Courrier du Canada* (Quebec) 9 Aug. 1871
35 Savard 428
36 André Laurendeau, 'Sur une Polémique entre Bourassa et Tardivel' in *L'Action nationale* XLIII 2 (Feb. 1954) 248
37 *Le Courrier de St-Hyacinthe* 6 July 1871, quoted in Savard 16
38 *Pour la patrie* 196 (paging corresponds to this reprint)
39 *La Vérité* 4 Aug. 1883
40 *Pour la patrie* 126
41 *La Vérité* 1 Oct. 1887
42 Tardivel, *Mélanges religieux*, III 158, quoted in Justin Fèvre, *Vie et travaux de J.-P. Tardivel, fondateur du journal "La Vérité," à Québec* (Paris: Arthur Savaète 1906) 78
43 *La Vérité*, 11 Feb. 1893. When Tardivel referred to the novels one read in newspapers, he was including most of the great nineteenth-century novels. Dickens, Dostoyevsky, Hugo, Balzac, all had their works serialized in the periodical press.
44 *Pour la patrie* 3
45 Ibid. 60
46 Savard 194
47 Ibid. 193
48 *Mélanges religieux* III 53, in Fèvre 68
49 Ibid.
50 Quoted in Savard 27
51 *La Vérité* 22 June 1884

52 Quoted in Savard 170
53 *Mélanges* III 155, in Fèvre 80
54 Savard 283
55 Several of the other names turned out in the end to have been pseudonyms used by Taxil himself.
56 In Savard 277
57 Ibid. 281-2
58 Ibid. 283-5
59 Ibid. 293
60 In Weber, 156-7
61 In Savard 301-2
62 *La Vérité* 4 Apr. 1885
63 Ibid. 15 Jan. 1888
64 In Fèvre 86
65 *La Vérité* 11 Aug. 1881
66 *La Langue française au Canada* 63, in Fèvre 101
67 *La Vérité* 5 Nov. 1887
68 Ibid. 8 July 1882
69 Ibid. 21 Jan. 1882
70 Ibid. 7 July 1883
71 Ibid. 23 May 1885
72 Ibid. 15 Jan. 1888
73 Ibid. 12 June 1886
74 Ibid. 28 July 1883
75 Ibid. 4 Apr. 1885. Also 23 May 1885
76 Ibid. 8 Aug. 1885. Also 7 Nov. 1885
77 Ibid. 21 Nov. 1885
78 Ibid. 20 Feb. 1886
79 Ibid. 24 Apr. 1886
80 Ibid. 3 July 1886
81 Ibid. 15 May 1886
82 Ibid. 12 June 1886
83 Ibid. Also 15 May 1886
84 Ibid. 12 June 1886
85 Ibid. 8 Oct. 1887
86 *Pour la patrie* 71
87 *La Vérité* 23 Oct. 1886. Also 2 Oct., 12 June 1886
88 *Pour la patrie* 138
89 Ibid. 4-5

90 *La Vérité* 19 Nov. 1887
91 Ibid. 12 Oct. 1901
92 Eg, *L'Union nationale* (Montreal) 3 Sept. and 7 Nov. 1864
93 Eg, *Le Courrier du Canada* 24 Mar. 1875
94 *La Revue canadienne* XVIII (1882) 252. Also XXVIII (1892) 473
95 Eg, *Notre Avenir politique*, a collective work of prognosis by various French-Canadian intellectuals, under the auspices of the nationalist *Action Française* (Montreal 1923)
96 The most important analyst of Tardivel's work, Pierre Savard, has written that in that work 'we find the essence of the ideology according to which French Canada lived for a hundred years.' In Pierre Savard, *Jules-Paul Tardivel* (Montreal: Fides 1969) 9
97 Mathieu Girard, 'La Pensée politique de Jules-Paul Tardivel,' in the *Revue d'histoire de l'Amérique française* XXI 3 (Dec. 1967) 397-8
98 *La Vérité* 28 July 1883
99 Ibid. 8 Apr. 1882
100 Eg, J.W. Dafoe, *Laurier: A Study in Canadian Politics* (Toronto: McClelland & Stewart 1963) 3-5. This is also a main theme of Jean-Paul Bernard, *Les Rouges: Libéralisme, nationalisme et anticléricalisme au milieu du XIXe siècle* (Montreal: Presses de l'université du Québec 1971).

For my country

JULES-PAUL TARDIVEL

Rejoice not over me, O mine enemy; when I fall, I shall rise; when I sit in darkness, the Lord will be a light to me.
MICAH 7:8

(Biblical quotations are from the Revised Standard Version, Ecumenical Edition)

Preface

FATHER CAUSSETTE, WHO IS QUOTED by Father Fayollat in his book on the Apostolate of the Press, calls novels 'an invention of the devil.' For my part I rather think that the worthy priest is right. Novels – especially the modern novel, and the French novel most of all – seem to me to be weapons forged by Satan himself for the destruction of mankind. And yet, despite this conviction, I am writing a novel! Yes, and I do so with no scruples, because it is permitted to capture the enemy's war machines and to use them to assault his own ramparts. It is a tactic that even affords certain advantages on the battlefield.

The novel has an undeniable influence on modern society. Jules Vallès, a reliable witness, has said: 'How many young people I have seen for whom one passage, read one morning, has dominated, unmade or remade, lost or saved their lives! Take Balzac for example: how he has made judges labour and mothers weep! How many consciences he has snuffed out! And how many of us have been lost, have stumbled into the slough where we will die, with a page torn from Balzac's *Comédie humaine* in our hand? ... Love, vengeance, passion, crime: we copy them all. All. Not one of our emotions is a true one. There's always a novel to take them from.'[1]

Today, then, the novel has formidable power in the hands of a literary evil-doer. There is no doubt that if it were possible to destroy this dreadful invention outright it would have to be done for the good of mankind; for Satan's apprentices will always use it for the cause of evil far more than the friends of God will be able to make use of it for the power of good. And I believe that the same can be said of newspapers. However, we must admit that nowadays the Catholic press is a necessity, even a pious work. The fact is that to fight the good fight we must make use of all available weapons, even those that we take from the enemy's hands. Always on the condition, of course, that we can make legitimate use of them. We must be certain that we know how to handle the devices without wounding our own troops. Certain diabolic inventions exist only to do evil: the holiest and ablest man could not draw the slightest good from them. Neutral schools, for example, or secret societies, will never be accepted as a means of action by the Church. These things should be touched only in order to destroy them; they should be mentioned only to destroy them. But the novel, despite its satanic origins, does not come into this category. The proof that it can be used for good is that it has been used *ad majorem Dei gloriam.* I am not speaking of the simple, honest novel that can provide an hour of pleasant recreation without sowing deadly seeds in the soul of the reader; I speak, rather, of novels that strengthen the will, that elevate and purify the heart, that encourage love of virtue and hatred of vice, that inspire noble feelings and are, in a word, the exact opposite of the infamous novel.

For me, such a Christian *combat* novel, if I may so describe it, would be the delightful work of a priest of the Company of Jesus, entitled *The Novel of a Jesuit.* It is a real novel, with all the strength that the term implies, but nevertheless Satan has never been better beaten than in its pages. I admit that reading it dispelled any doubt that the novel, in the correct sense of the term, could be used to serve the Catholic cause. A more recent work, *Jean-Christophe,* whose author is also a priest, only confirmed my belief. Since a Jesuit and a parish priest have taken one of Satan's favourite weapons and turned it against the City of Evil, I believe that I may be permitted to undertake the same adventure. And if I fail, it will be because I lack the necessary skill, not because the undertaking is impossible.

In a conservative newspaper that supports the political status quo in Canada, the following remarks appeared in reply to *La Vérité:* 'Aspiration is a flower of hope. If the atmosphere in which it grows is not favourable, it will wither and fall; and if, on the contrary, the atmosphere is suitable, it takes on strength, is fertilized and bears fruit. But if someone takes it into his head to gather this fruit before it is ripe, all is lost. Maturity is attained only at the time that Providence has chosen, and one must have the wisdom to await that moment.'[2]

God has planted a 'flower of hope' in the heart of every patriotic French Canadian. It is the aspiration to establish, on the shores of the St Lawrence, a New France whose mission it will be to continue on this American soil the work of Christian civilization that the old

France pursued so gloriously for so many hundreds of years. This national aspiration, this flower of hope that is nurtured by an entire people, requires a favourable atmosphere in order to develop, take on strength, and bear fruit. I write this book as my own feeble contribution to providing a healthy atmosphere for this precious flower; and to destroy, if possible, some of the noxious weeds that threaten to choke it.

Maturity is only attained at the hour decided upon by divine Providence. This is certain, but man can and must work to prevent any delay. He can and must work so that maturation occurs without hindrance. Do we accuse the farmer of trying to hasten unduly the providential hour when, in springtime, he protects his plants against wind and frost and concentrates the sun's rays upon them?

Between the troubled and feverish activity of the materialist who, in his pride and presumption, counts on just his own efforts for success, and the inertia of the fatalist who, fearing effort, shrugs his shoulders and tries to convince himself that his laziness is only a sign of his trust in God – between these two opposing sins we find Christian virtue that labours as much as it prays; that plants and waters, and waits for growth as a gift from God.

No one should be surprised to see that my hero, although he takes part in political battles, is not only a believer but a practising Catholic: a Christian in his heart as much as in his mind. In his history of Canada, Abbé Ferland tells us that 'from the early days of the colony we see that everywhere religion plays a leading role.' In order to reach the level among the nations that Providence has destined for us we must return to the spirit of our ancestors and restore religion to its leading role; love of the French-Canadian homeland must be closely tied to faith in Our Lord Jesus Christ and to the zealous defence of His Church. The instrument that God will use in the final establishment of the French-Canadian nation is less likely to be a great orator, a skilful politician or a fiery agitator than a perfect Christian who will work and sacrifice himself and pray: less likely a Kossuth than a Garcia Moreno.

I shall perhaps be accused of dreaming patriotic dreams that will never be realized.

I have been inspired in these dreams – if they are only that – by reading the history of New France, the most beautiful story of modern times, because it is so filled with the apostolic breath and the spirit of chivalry. But are these only dreams? Can we not see here, rather, hopes that are justified by the past, aspirations that may be realized in a future that Providence is reserving for us, in the accomplishment of our national destiny?

Dreams or aspirations, these thoughts hover over the places where I live, on the heights that witnessed the supreme struggles of our fathers. They come out of the earth that has been watered with the blood of the two valiant races that I love (I may add) equally, for I belong to both.

My days are spent between the Plains of Abraham and the Plains of Sainte-Foye, between the battlefields where the French succumbed gloriously and those where they gloriously took their revenge. Is it surprising that in this atmosphere where heroes have breathed, such bold ideas come to me; that in remembering the battles of giants that once took place here for the possession of New France, I foresee a glorious future for this site of such memorable combats? Is it surprising that, living as I do nearer the Plains of Sainte-Foye than the Plains of Abraham, I never forget that the last victory to be won on these heights was a French victory; that even though I am half English, I strive ardently for the final triumph of the French race on this corner of the earth, in which Providence has given it a share, and which Providence alone can take away?

During my twenty years as a journalist I have rarely written anything that was not polemical. On the field where I struggle I have cultivated few flowers, aiming at clarity and conciseness rather than stylistic ornaments. Confined within the narrow limits of a small newspaper, I have grown accustomed to condensing my thoughts, to sticking to the main lines, the principal points. Do not, then, look in these pages for the exquisite touch and details that give so many novels their special charm. I do not claim to offer the public either a finely honed literary work or a carefully drawn study of manners. Rather, this is a simple outline in which, lacking graceful developments, I have attempted to suggest a few ideas that the reader must complete with his own imagination.

If any public figure – journalist, Member of Parliament or Minister – should recognize some of his favourite themes in these pages, on the lips or in the writing of unworthy characters, I hope he will believe me when I say that I dispute his doctrines, not his person.

J.-P. Tardivel
Chemin Sainte-Foye, near Quebec
Holy Thursday, 1895

1 Quoted from Father Fayollat
2 *La Minerve*, 11 September 1894

All these will I give you, if you will fall down and worship me.
MATTHEW 4:9

Prologue

'EBLIS! EBLIS! SPIRIT OF LIGHT! Eternally persecuted! Vanquished but avenging God! I, thy elect, Chosen One, I, sworn enemy of thine enemy Adonai, invoke thee. Come to mine eyes, soul of the universe! Spirit of fire, come strengthen this arm that is devoted to thy work of vengeance and destruction! Come, guide me in the struggle against the Persecutor!'

So spoke a very young man who was standing before a kind of alter on which incense was burning. An immense luminous triangle hung above the altar.

The young man's appearance matched his terrible words. His black eyes blazed, his features, though beautiful by nature, were distorted by hatred. Everything about him bore the mark of passion, vengeance, and dark energy.

Luxurious furnishings were arranged around him. Objets d'art, statues, and paintings that exuded the most dreadful kind of lewdness adorned the room, and at the end stood the satanic altar.

From outside came the noise of a large city, confused and indistinct. For even though the hour was late, Paris slept little during these troubled days that marked the end of the year 1931.

The young man had hardly finished speaking when a vague shape appeared between the altar and the triangle, surrounded by the smoke from the incense. Or rather, the smoke itself, instead of rising in irregular puffs as it had done before, took on a mysterious form.

Lucifer's desciple trembled.

'Eblis! Eblis!' he cried. 'You come!'

The shape rapidly became more distinct. Its outlines were clearly defined: it had the form that artists give to angels. The apparition was luminous, but its light was neither brilliant nor pure. It seemed, rather, troubled and obscure. The phantom's face was veiled.

'Eblis!' exclaimed the young man, ever more excited. 'Speak to thy Chosen One. Tell him whither he must go, what he must do to work for the triumph of thy cause, to avenge thee against Adonai.'

An inhuman voice, a murmur that seemed to come from afar and to speak to the mind rather than the ear, replied:

'Cross the seas, go to the shores of the St Lawrence, where thy ancestors once planted the Standard of my eternal Enemy. It is there that thy task awaits thee. The Cross still stands on that corner of the globe. You must tear it down. Count on my inspiration.'

Then the voice was silent. The apparition vanished. In its place there was only the smoke of the incense, rising in spirals towards the triangle.

For every one who does evil hates the light.
JOHN 3:20

1

'WHAT A NIGHT! It's as dark as the pit.'
'But night is exactly what we need. Follow me and don't talk.'
The two men who had exchanged these words hurried away from a handsome house on one of the main streets of Quebec City, and turned down a less frequented road towards one of the suburbs. It was easy for them to pass unseen, for the streets were deserted. The weather was fierce that night. Cold rain was falling in torrents, driven by a wind from the north-east that howled around the housetops, shaking them to their very foundations. The electric lights had all gone out; the storm that had been raging for two days had completely interrupted service.
It was the beginning of November in the year 1945.
A gust of wind, more violent than the others, beat against the city. The tormented rain became dust, and the wind, swallowed up in the chimneys, howled mournfully.
'Brrr!' the one who had spoken first shivered. 'It feels as if all the devils have been unloosed tonight. Is it very far?'
'We'll be there in a minute,' his companion replied. 'But as far as I'm concerned, I like a storm that breaks crosses and knocks down churches. It is the breath of the great Persecuted One passing among us, the God of nature! He will shake off his chains and he will triumph. He will crush his eternal Enemy. He will deliver himself from the tyranny of Adonai and he will deliver us, too. Yes, I love all that is strength, all that is rage, all that is fury, everything that disturbs and breaks and destroys.'
The man who was speaking stood still. His gaze, directed toward the sky, was as dark as the night. His fist was clenched in a threatening gesture and his blasphemous words hissed through his clenched teeth.
'You talk like a real disciple of the inner circle,' said the other, rather ironically.
'And you, you could be taken for an Adonai-worshipper in disguise!'
They continued in silence.

The two companions soon reached a lane that was even darker than the surrounding streets. They turned into it furtively, and, coming to a low dwelling with all its windows firmly closed behind strong shutters, they rapped at the door in a particular manner. There was a rapid exchange of words, then the door was partially opened and the two workers of darkness glided into the house.

Workers of the dark! For it was indeed in this gloomy house that the central committee of the League for Progress in the Province of Quebec held its meetings. And the League was none other than the Freemasons, organized to carry on political battles. Aside from the name and certain antics that had been deemed useless, it was the Carbonari again: the same organization, with the same goal and the same course of action.

For fifty years the province of Quebec had been moving rapidly along the path of *modern progress*. The great social upheavals, of which France had been the theatre at the beginning of the twentieth century, had cast upon our shores a number of our overseas cousins. Some of these immigrants were good men, come to strengthen the healthy and truly Catholic element of our population. But the France that was worldly, sceptical, scoffing, impious and atheist, the France of the boulevards, theatres, cabarets, and clubs, the France that was the avowed enemy of God and His Church, had also burst upon our shores. Theatres had been flourishing for some time in Quebec and Montreal and troops of actors toured the main cities — Trois-Rivières, Saint Hyacinthe, Joliette, Saint-Jean, Sorel, and Chicoutimi — spoiling manners and weakening characters. For more than half a century the corrupting literature that was published in Paris had been spreading over our land. It brought with it deadly fruits: many hearts had been poisoned and from them arose a pestilential breath that obscured men's minds. Faith was declining. Everyone could see it; they admit it today. There was still much good in the countryside, among the great masses of rural population; but these good men were paralyzed by the apathy and corruption of the ruling classes.

We should not be surprised to find in our land, in the middle of the twentieth century, all the misery that was known in France and other European countries in the last century.

But now let us accompany the two men we have been following into the brilliantly lit room that was the site of the noctural meetings of the anti-Christian league. On the walls were various satanic emblems. Several of the brothers were chatting in a group, and the president's chair was still empty.

When the two sectarians whose conversation we heard earlier entered the room, all those present rose and bowed. The one who had blasphemed went directly to the chair and opened the session; he was the Master. In the light that flooded the room the face of this man who had uttered such terrible words could be seen. All the passions, especially hatred and pride, were inscribed on his perfectly regular features. His soul, reflected in his blazing eyes, was black as night, violent as the storm that raged outside. He was the incarnation of storm and night. However, he was a man who knew how to contain himself, and it was to his contained rage, the rage that could be heard growling relentlessly like a subterranean fire, rarely breaking out, that he owed his control over those who surrounded him. He dominated and captivated them.

'Brothers,' the president began, 'I have summoned you this evening to confer with you on a matter of the utmost importance. You are all aware of the political events that occurred several days ago. The day before yesterday, thanks to our own efforts and our agreements with our brothers in the other provinces, the Quebec legislature made a decision in accordance with our own desires. It was the last provincial legislature to come around; as you know. Now we must concentrate all our strength and all our resources on the federal parliament. There the great and decisive battle against priestly tyranny and superstition will take place. If we are victorious it will be the end of clericalism in this land.'

'And the end of our language and our nationality too,' said the one who had accompanied the president.

'Who cares about nationality or language?' replied the Master, darting a dark and blazing look at the one who had interrupted him. 'Who cares about such sentimental issues, if by sacrificing them, we can destroy the Infamous One and uproot from the Canadian soil the cross of the priests, symbol of superstition and standard of tyranny? I have already told the person who just interrupted me that he sometimes seems to be a follower of Adonai in disguise. I repeat that now, and I warn him: he'd better watch out.'

'But Master,' said another of the sectarians, 'you must admit that our secretary, Brother Ducoudray, has performed noble services through his excellent newspaper *La Libre Pensée*. It's the best anticlerical paper in the country.'

'I know that,' the president admitted, making a great effort to contain himself. 'I probably spoke too harshly and I beg Brother Ducoudray's pardon. I admire his talent and the anticlerical zeal he displays as editor of *La Libre Pensée*. But I am still afraid for him, for I know that he was brought up in the superstition.'

'But I have long since broken away from all that,' replied Ducoudray.

'Enough!' exclaimed the Master. 'Let's not speak of it any more. I was saying that the decisive battle will be fought in Ottawa. We must choose between the status quo, legislative union, and the separation of the provinces. As you know, our goal is legislative union. Through it we will destroy the influence of the priests, wipe out superstition, and spread the true light that will deliver our people from the infamous yoke they have borne for centuries. Of course we will need great daring to succeed. And prudence too and skilful and knowledgeable tactics. Here in a word is the basis of our campaign: *legislative union under the cloak of the status quo*. We shall not arrive at union directly. The mass of the people in this province are still too fanatical, too dominated by their priests for us to make them accept legislative union if we present our project openly. We would be laying ourselves open to certain defeat.'

'Should *La Libre Pensée* change its tactics then?' asked Ducoudray, who was rather intrigued.

'Not at all,' replied the president. 'On the contrary, you must speak out more than ever in favour of legislative union. But you will be careful to say that you support it only with a view to the country's economic and material progress. Be very careful not to let slip the slightest hint of our true goal, the one we hope to attain through legislative union. While *La Libre Pensée* and its school are shouting for legislative union, I shall be carrying out some diplomacy of my own. Don't be surprised if I seem to be turning my back on the unionist movement, if I give weapons and aid to the camp of the status quo, or even become one of the leaders of the party. If I do, Ducoudray, you will attack me with that beautifully violent language you use so well. You will denounce me as a conservative, a reactionary. You can even call me clerical if you want. Your attacks will gain me the confidence of the conservatives, and that will help me to operate easily.'

'And what's to be said about Lamirande and his gang of fanatics?' Ducoudray interrupted.

'Everything you have been saying and more, if that's possible. You will say that they want *separation* only to serve their personal ambition and fanaticism; that if they succeed, their first act will be to reinstate the Inquisition, pass laws to force everybody to attend low mass six times a week and high mass and vespers on Sunday.'

'And it will be obligatory for all heads of families to subscribe to Leverdier's newspaper!'

'Excellent! Brother Ducoudray I see that you understand me perfectly and I am certain that you will carry this out faithfully. By overwhelming the clerics and the super-papists with ridicule you will convince the conservatives of the need to remain in the centre and avoid the Catholic or radical extremes. That is the state of mind I want them to be in so that they will be more inclined to accept my plans.'

For another hour the workers of darkness continued their task. Then they dispersed and left as they had come, furtively.

Pour la patrie

> Whoever forsakes his father is like a blasphemer.
> ECCLESIASTICUS 3:16

2

THAT SAME EVENING, in another part of Quebec City, a very different scene was being enacted. Despite the fierce weather several members of the St Vincent de Paul Society had come to the vestry of the basilica for the weekly meeting of the Notre-Dame Chapter. Among those present was Dr Joseph Lamirande. No storm could keep him from such a duty. He was perhaps forty years old; in his grave but gentle features there was an expression of great energy tempered by goodness. No-one could remember hearing him laugh or seeing him sad or depressed. But though he seldom laughed, his features were often illuminated by a brilliant smile as he spoke, and his voice would become infinitely tender. When he arrived at the meeting he sat down among a group of labourers in the last row and joined in their conversation.

After the prayer and the usual reading, the chairman spoke:

'Gentlemen, several people came to see me this morning to tell me about an old man – no one knows where he came from – who was found in an attic on the Rue de l'Ancien Chantier, near the Palace, where he had gone to take refuge. He is obviously sick and he appears completely destitute. He says little to those who speak to him and refuses to tell his name. He is not seeking help for himself, but some of the people in the neighbourhood thought we should know about this rather unusual case. They're afraid this strange old man will die of hunger and misery if the St Vincent de Paul Society does not take care of him immediately. I think we should arrange for a visit of enquiry tomorrow morning.'

A moment of silence. Then:

'No one is opposed? Very well, the visit of enquiry is hereby ordered. Who will undertake it? Very good: Dr Lamirande will be pleased to do so along with M. Saint-Simon who is not here but who will no doubt be happy to accompany the doctor. If anyone can help to save the body or soul of this unfortunate man it is you, Doctor.'

'I shall do all I can, Mr Chairman, first thing tomorrow morning.'

Next morning, true to his word, Lamirande, accompanied by Hercule Saint-Simon, the editor of *Le Progrès catholique*, went to the Palace.

What irony in that name! Long ago, 'at the time of the French,' the Intendant's Palace had been built in this part of the city. But the building had fallen into ruin, and the ruins themselves had disappeared. Nothing remained of the old splendour of the Palace but the name, which had been given to a section of the city, specifically to a small area between St Roch and the Lower Town. The very memory of the old Palace had been so effectively erased that many people wondered where the name had come from. By a curious twist of fate, the section called the Palace had become the very poorest part of the city. What misery, both physical and moral, was concentrated in its dilapidated buildings, all of them badly lit, unclean, and foul-smelling!

'What a sad thing poverty is!' said Saint-Simon. 'It is the cause of all the moral and physical ills of the world.'

'I dare say it is sad, because it is one of the bitter fruits of the first sin,' replied Lamirande, 'but its cause is sadder than its effects. Let us not forget, my friend, that Jesus Christ Himself was poor. He blessed poverty and made it noble, and He has given us the poor as His own representatives. If there were no physical and moral misery to relieve, where would holy charity be practised? And without charity what would become of this selfish world of ours? It would cease to be a vale of tears, agreed; but it would be instead a vast and horrible desert.'

'Perhaps you are right, in theory; but in practice I find poverty very disagreeable,' replied Saint-Simon.

'But you are not poor,' Lamirande smiled. 'You must be joking. When we speak of poverty we mean a lack of what is necessary or very useful.'

'Everything is relative,' replied his companion. 'Of course I am not poor compared with the man we are going to visit. But compared with others – Montarval for instance – I am really very poor indeed.'

'Even so, if a person can provide himself with what is necessary, and even with what is useful, he has no right to call himself poor. We are entitled, of course, to strive to improve our material position, but only on the condition that we do not make the slightest complaint against Providence if our plans do not succeed. Perhaps the wealth you desire would be a curse for you. But we may be certain, my dear friend, that God who loves us gives each of us what suits us best. He knows our true needs better than we do.'

'The *aurea mediocritas*,' sighed the journalist, 'is suitable for mediocre minds, those without ambition, those who live from day to day and do not aspire to glory or power, nor dreams of grandeur; to those who are closed inside their own little affairs and whose horizons end at the doors of their shops or the boundaries of their fields. The golden mean the poets sing about is for them. But the others, like you and me, who live an intellectual life, should be rich. The man who works with his head from morning till night, thinking for his fellow men, providing them with ideas, needs a certain material luxury in order to relax and revitalize himself. In fact, he not only needs it, he is entitled to it. It is absolutely necessary to be rich in order to do good. What can you expect a poor devil like you or me to accomplish in the modern world? If we were rich, think of the ravages we could carry out in the enemy camp!'

As he spoke Saint-Simon became more and more excited. He gesticulated wildly, and Lamirande looked at him with pity and terror.

'My poor friend,' he began, 'those ideas are totally false, and I cannot imagine where they come from. I should need more time than I have this morning to refute them in detail. Besides, you yourself must realize that they are only wretched sophisms. You must know that great deeds, even in the purely human order, have rarely been accomplished by the rich. My friend, you must pray to resist this temptation.'

Saint-Simon shrugged his shoulders and shook his head, but made no reply.

Reaching their destination, the two men entered a miserable little hovel. They climbed three flights of rickety stairs, and stopped at the door of a little attic room. The doctor knocked and a bitter voice bade them enter. When Lamirande opened the door, a heartbreaking sight met his eyes: a low, dark, empty room, dirty and cold; at one end an old man stretched out on a pallet. Lamirande's practised eyes could read the ravages of disease on the old man's face; or rather, the signs of hunger and misery. And he saw no less clearly the traces of great moral suffering. This was no ordinary pauper. His clothes, elegantly cut and still fairly clean, were in singular contrast to the dreadful appearance of the room. Lamirande approached the bed and looked closely at the old man.

'Where have I seen those features?' he asked himself.

Then, aloud:

'My dear sir, you appear to be suffering. My friend and I have come to bring you help. You need food, I am certain, and drugs and care as well. Wouldn't you like me to have you admitted to the Hôtel-Dieu? You would be infinitely more comfortable there than you are here.'

The old man's face was distorted in an expression of bitterness and pain.

'No,' he replied, 'I want to die here; somebody will bury me, even if it's just to get rid of my corpse.'

'We aren't talking about burying you, my dear sir,' said Lamirande, 'but of caring for you and curing you.'

'Why are you so interested in me?' the old man asked. 'I don't know you, you don't know me. I haven't any friends.'

'Oh, but you do have friends. It is true that we do not know each other, but we see that you are alone and sick, that you are a suffering limb of Jesus Christ. That is enough to give you the right to our friendship.'

'Who are you? Why did you come here? Why don't you leave me to die in peace?'

'My name is Lamirande, and I came here because the St Vincent de Paul Society sent me. And as for dying, are you sure that you will die in peace?'

As he uttered these last words, in a voice choked with emotion, Lamirande looked deeply into the old man's eyes. The stranger was troubled. Lamirande continued:

'Trust me. Tell me who you are, where you came from and why you are in this miserable hovel. Tell me what we can do for you.'

The old man's lips trembled and his eyes were wet.

'You are truly good, both of you,' he said. 'Forgive me for having received you so rudely just now. My heart is overflowing with bitterness. But I need nothing. Leave me, I beg you. My name is of little importance, nor my story.'

The stranger looked at Saint-Simon. Lamirande understood that the poor lonely old man did not wish to speak in the presence of two strangers, and resolved to return alone.

The two visitors exchanged a few more words with their strange protégé and then left for other places where more loquacious old men awaited them.

Finding himself alone two hours later, Lamirande went back to see the old man by himself. As he climbed the last step he could not help hearing the end of a conversation.

'All right, I'll put you in a boarding house in the country somewhere. That's all I can do.'

'And I repeat, my hard-hearted son, that I will die here, in this attic. I will not accept the crumbs you throw to me as you would throw them to a dog. You're ashamed of me. Very well! You won't have to blush at your father much longer!'

At that moment Lamirande knocked at the partly opened door.

'It's probably one of my miserable neighbours,' the old man said to his son in a low voice. 'Go and open the door. They'll think you're visiting as an act of charity to a sick stranger.'

As the door opened Lamirande found himself face to face with Aristide Montarval, a young Frenchman, rich and brilliant, who had been established in Quebec for several years. Although they were not friends, the two men knew each other well.

There was embarrassed silence for a moment as they exchanged a look that contained many explanations. Lamirande could read on the young Frenchman's face spite, fear, anger, even rage; and Montarval seemed quite disconcerted by the strength of the gaze that seemed to pierce to the depths of his soul.

It was Montarval, however, who found the boldness to break the silence.

'What are you doing here?' he asked in a haughty, provocative tone.

'I have come to comfort your father, since you have abandoned him to the care of strangers,' Lamirande replied calmly.

'Ah! So you've been listening at keyholes, you hypocrite!' Montarval exclaimed, beside himself with rage.

Lamirande did not deign to reply. Pushing him aside with a gesture, he entered the room and went to the old man, who had been deeply moved by this scene.

'Sir, as I came up the stairs, I involuntarily discovered your secret. Allow me to take you to my home.'

The old man burst into tears.

'How good you are!' he exclaimed. 'But I cannot accept your offer. I want to die here, unknown, so that my son will not be ashamed of me. For he is my only son and I love him, in spite of the pain he has caused me.'

As he spoke, the old man sat up on his pallet. Lamirande was aware of the striking resemblance between father and son; two faces that were sombre, one because of sorrow, the other because of passions. The father inspired sympathy, the son an invincible repugnance.

Lamirande sat down beside the old man and gently put his arm around him for support.

'Speak, sir; pour out your heart. That will relieve you.'

'Oh, my son!' the old man went on, as though speaking to himself. 'I do not curse him, because if he is evil today it is my fault. I brought him up with no discipline; I allowed him all his whims, and his destructive inclinations grew with him. That seemed to me to be required by a father's love, but today I see my folly. He ruined me, and then he left France, many years ago. I didn't even know where he was because he never wrote to me, but then one day I learned accidentally, when I was reading a Canadian newspaper, that he had established himself in Quebec and that he had become a rich man. I still loved him, and I resolved to come and find him, for I was so lonely! Ah, if only I had stayed there in my solitude. I was poor, and the thought of my absent son made me so sad! But at least my heart was not broken then as it is now. I had saved just enough to pay for my passage to Quebec, and when I arrived I went immediately to my son.'

The old man's voice was choked in sobs. In a few minutes he went on.

'The wretched man! He refused to recognize me, his own father! He called me an imposter, ejected me from his own house and told me, with threats, never to darken his door again. You can imagine the rest. Finally I took refuge here to die.'

Lamirande, unbearably moved by the story, let the old man weep silently for a few minutes, still holding him. Then he asked him gently,

'But if your son refused to recognize you, why did he come here to look for you?'

'I had hoped that it was a sign of repentance, but alas, what he said makes me think that he acted only through fear of scandal. He was afraid my story would leak out. He wanted to send me to a hospital or a nursing home in the country. He would be humiliated to have his old father in his own house. And I cannot accept the crust of bread he throws me. I wanted his heart, but he refused me that. He only wants me to die unknown, to spare him shame.'

A new outburst of sobs prevented him from going on.

While the old man was pouring out his sorrow, the son, his back to the bed, had lit a cigar and was looking out the window, tapping his fingers against the grimy panes. Taking advantage of the interruption in his father's confidences, he turned around abruptly. There was an infernal gleam in his eyes, but he held back his anger and appeared to speak calmly.

'Those are a lot of useless words. I cannot and will not be burdened by this old man. What would I do with him in my bachelor's quarters? I make him a reasonable offer and he refuses it. What am I supposed to do?'

And the hard-hearted son went towards the door. Lamirande, still supporting the old man, who was on the verge of fainting, cried out:

'But what you have just said is appalling! Is that how a son should treat his father?'

'I can do without your sermon,' Montarval replied.

'My sermons, yes, but you cannot refuse to obey God's commandment that orders us to honour our parents.'

'Another sermon!' Montarval sneered. 'Do you expect me to be bothered with the commandments of your God?'

'But you poor insensate fool, do you want to be damned?'

'Call it what you like, but I don't want anything to do with your Heaven, where one must wallow eternally in ignoble slavery at the feet of the tyrant Jehovah. I want to be free in this world and in the next. Do you understand?'

Lamirande shuddered. He had often read of such horrors in books that dealt with neo-manicheanism, but this was the first time he had heard with his own ears such an infernal cry, seen with his own eyes the fires of the abyss shedding their dark light on a human face.

'Lord Jesus!' he murmured. 'I beg your pardon for this blasphemy.' Then, turning towards the blasphemer,

'Let's drop this subject, so I won't have to hear any more of these abominations. But if you do not fear the judgement of God, do you not at least dread human justice? I could denounce you publicly, if not in the courts.'

'But you won't. I would deny it and where is your proof?'

With his left hand Lamirande indicated the old man whom he was still supporting with his other arm.

'He won't say anything,' said Montarval. 'I know him.'

'But my word will be sufficient,' said Lamirande. 'No honest man would hesitate between my affirmation and your denial.'

'The old man would substantiate my denial if it were necessary to save my honour. And your affirmation will be worthless against two denials.'

'I shall wait until your father is dead before I denounce you.'

Montarval was dismayed, for he was well aware that others would put more faith in Lamirande's word than in his own.

The old man looked pleadingly at his protector.

'Have pity sir, do not denounce him! Do not bring dishonour on him!'

'But he deserves it!'

'Oh, but I beg you, I beg you, do not denounce him!'

'Come, my dear sir,' replied Lamirande. 'Come to my house. You are exhausted by fatigue and emotion, and you need to rest. We can return to this painful subject later. Come!'

'Do you really insist on taking me to your house?' the old man asked.

'Indeed, I do insist, more than I can tell you.'

'Very well then, I shall go, but on one condition: that you promise never to denounce my son.'

Lamirande hesitated. To make such a promise would mean implicating himself in an unpunished crime. But if he persisted in opposing the heartless son it would mean condemning the father to a miserable death in his attic room. Then he thought of the man's poor abandoned soul, sicker perhaps than his body.

He hesitated no longer.

'Very well, I give you my promise.'

Then he turned to the son.

'Miserable wretch! Men will remain ignorant of your crime and of your shame. But the curse of God awaits you. Go!'

'I am grateful for your kind permission and your good wishes,' said Montarval with his customary aplomb and audacity.

Then, without uttering a single word to his father, without even looking at him, he left the room, humming an air from some opera.

'He has gone! My son has gone!' murmured the unhappy father.

'Allow me to replace him,' said Lamirande. 'Come, we shall stay here no longer.'

The stranger let himself be led like a child. A carriage was waiting for Lamirande, and a few minutes later protector and protégé arrived at the door of a modest house in the Upper Town.

'Here we are,' said Lamirande, offering his arm to the old man, whose gait was weak and unsteady. 'Let us go inside.'

'What will your wife say when she sees you bringing a dying stranger into your house?'

'She will welcome you.'

At that moment Madame Lamirande came to meet them. If the old man had had any doubts about his reception, the sight of her madonna-like face must have reassured him.

'My wife,' said Lamirande, 'here is a stranger who has fallen into misfortune. Divine Providence has entrusted him to our care and we shall welcome him for the love of Jesus Christ. For reasons I respect, he does not wish his identity to be known, so we must be content simply to take care of him.'

'Sir,' said the young woman, as she pressed the old man's hand affectionately, a celestial light glowing in her eyes, 'you are a thousand times welcome. We shall make every effort to help you forget your grief, which I can see is very great.'

The poor, forsaken old man tried to thank his benefactors, but he could only stammer a few unintelligible words. His strength had left him all at once, and he would have fallen to the floor if Lamirande had not supported him.

They carried him to a bed where he lay motionless and apparently lifeless. Madame Lamirande thought that he had died.

'No,' said her husband, 'he is not dead yet. He will regain consciousness but then he will leave us soon. He has only a few hours left. Tell the maid to go quickly to Father Grandmont and ask him to come without delay.'

Then the young doctor hastened to give the sick man all the attention required by his pitiful state. Soon he saw with satisfaction that the old man was gradually coming back to life. Finally he opened his eyes and looked around him with consternation.

'What is it? Where am I? Oh — I remember everything now. My protector! You are so good! Thank you! Thank you a thousand times! But I shall not burden you much longer. I feel that I am about to die.'

'Yes, my friend,' said the doctor quietly, 'you are going to die. You must think of God and of His judgement, but of His mercy as well.'

'Ah!' the old man sighed. 'It has been a long time, a very long time since I began to neglect my religious duties. My heart was so hardened — I fell victim to indifference. Your charity has melted the ice in my soul. I want to confess. Will you send for a priest? I think I have little time to lose.'

'A venerable Jesuit Father whom I have sent for will be here in a few minutes. In fact he is coming in now. Trust him, and have no fear, for he is the personification of goodness. His passion is the salvation of souls and the return of sinners to God.'

As he uttered these words the door opened, and Father Grandmont entered the room. His saintly face, deeply furrowed, was framed by snow-white hair; it was a face of supernatural beauty, for one could read in it a vast love for God and for his fellow creatures.

'May the peace of the Lord be with you, my children,' he said as he approached. 'Our friend needs me more than he does you, my dear doctor. Will you leave us?'

Lamirande and his wife left the room. The two old men remained alone for a long time. When Father Grandmont came to find Lamirande, he was beaming with celestial joy, for he had reconciled a soul with God.

'Oh, my dear friend!' he exclaimed. 'How good is the Lord! That is a sentence we often repeat without attaching much significance to it, but it is so true! God's mercy! Who could ever measure its extent? For it is not only infinite, boundless, ready to forgive any sin; it is also aggressive, pursuing us to our last breath. Until then we have only to cast ourselves into that vast sea of love, and wait there for the everlasting port. Oh, why are there so many sinners who do not take advantage of that time of mercy we call life? Why reject God's mercy to confront His justice – which is no less infinite? Go, my friend, prepare the room. I will administer extreme unction and give him the holy viaticum.'

A few minutes later Lamirande, his wife, his little daughter Marie, and the one servant of their modest household were kneeling piously around the bed of the dying man as Father Grandmont administered the Last Sacraments.

The old man fell quickly into a prolonged swoon. Then, suddenly regaining consciousness, he squeezed Lamirande's hand convulsively and sighed,

'Thank you! Thank you! Jesus! Mary! Joseph! My son!'

They were his last words.

*A modest wife adds charm to charm,
and no balance can weigh the value of a chaste soul.*
ECCLESIASTICUS 26:15

3

LET US LOOK BACK AT THE PAST.

Fifteen years before the events we have just described Joseph Lamirande was twenty-five years old and had just begun the practise medicine. He had chosen this profession only because it enabled him to help his fellow men. His father had left him a modest income that freed him from the need to earn his daily bread. He knew, though, that such freedom is not given to certain people so that they may spend their days in idleness and indolence. On the contrary, the greater a man's freedom from material concerns, the greater should be his devotion to the welfare of his fellow men. The man who must labour hard and incessantly to provide the necessary things in life may be excused if he thinks first of himself and then of others. But it is the duty of the Christian whom God has exempted from the care of providing for his own existence to exert himself on behalf of others. Thus it was to be useful to his fellow citizens that Lamirande had embraced the medical profession. It was soon well known that those who could afford his services need not apply to him: his only patients were the poor, and he cared for them as assiduously as any doctor whose practice is restricted to the rich and who has the legitimate ambition of creating a lucrative clientele.

Young Dr Lamirande had long been a friend of the Leverdier family. When the father had died, leaving his widow and orphans in difficult circumstances, Lamirande had helped the mother with her children's education. The eldest, Paul, who was only a few years younger than his protector, and gifted with brilliant talent, had devoted himself while still quite young to journalism. Lamirande followed his career with interest, guiding him with good advice and foreseeing with satisfaction the day when his young friend would be directing a newspaper and able to give free vent to his ardent patriotism. The two men loved each other like brothers.

While the father was still alive the Leverdier family had adopted Marguerite Planier, an orphan who was a little older than Paul. Gentle, affectionate, devoted, intelligent — the qualities of her heart and mind were even more remarkable than the charm of her face, which was, however, singularly beautiful.

In his immortal poem the singer of the Acadians describes his heroine, Evangeline, in this remarkable line, one of the most beautiful in the English language:

'When she had passed it seemed like the ceasing of exquisite music.'

It was an exquisite music that Lamirande wanted to enjoy for his whole life.

One June evening he was walking with his friend Leverdier along the heights of Sainte-Foye, under the handsome trees that form a border along each side of the road, their branches blending and joining to make a long green archway.

'My friend,' said the young doctor, 'what would you say if a new tie were added to those that already unite us?'

'I should say that it was a new source of happiness for me,' Leverdier replied enthusiastically. 'But what is this new tie? I think I can guess, and I don't need to be a wizard to do so. You are very discreet but believe me, the beating of your heart is quite visible. You love my adopted sister, she loves you and you are going to marry; for nothing and no one is opposed, and no one will spoil your happiness. It is certainly not like in the novels, where the hero and heroine come together only after tearing out their hair and trying to rid the earth of their useless presence. That will do nothing to reduce your happiness, though. But to be serious – truly, I am delighted.'

'But I still haven't told you what I wanted to talk about,' said Lamirande, smiling quietly. 'The premises I have suggested do not necessarily support your conclusions. Perhaps I was considering proposing that we start a newspaper.'

'But I still insist I am right,' replied the young man impetuously.

'Very well!' Lamirande admitted. 'You are not mistaken, my dear friend. I cannot tell you how happy I am that you agree with my proposal. I was afraid.'

'Of what? You are too sincere to say that you did not believe yourself worthy of becoming a member of our family. So what were you afraid of?'

'You're so good at guessing, you should be able to imagine.'

'No, I swear, I have no idea.'

'I was afraid that you might be a rival!'
'A rival?'
'What else? You know that Marguerite is no more your sister than she is mine. And I don't see how anyone can know her as you do without loving her as I love her.'

'If that's all you're afraid of I can reassure you. I love my sister Marguerite just as I love my little sister Hélène. There is no difference. Far from causing me the slightest sorrow, the idea that she should become your wife fills me with joy. And besides, you know that my young brothers will need me for a long time. And I will not even be able to think of marriage for another ten years.'

The two friends walked for a long time under the trees, speaking of the great happiness that had entered the life of one of them and that the other shared like a brother. The sun sank behind the violet Laurentians; shadows, coolness, and the silence of evening spread over the sleeping countryside; and still the two happy men talked. At this moment their hearts were as calm as nature. It seemed to them that the great elms now gently caressed by the breeze would never shed their ornamental foliage, never be bent and twisted by the storms of autumn; and that their souls could never be troubled by bitterness or sorrow.

Finally they headed back to the city. When they came to the chapel of Notre Dame du Chemin, whose door was still open, Lamirande, pushed by a sudden thought, suggested to his companion,

'We are happy, but we must not forget those who are not. Perhaps one of those we love has been overcome by pain. Let us go and say a "Hail Mary" for those of our friends who are suffering.'

Although the two friends were unaware of it, their brief but fervent prayer was offered in behalf of Paul's only sister.

Hélène Leverdier was sixteen years old. She was a charming, merry, playful girl with big, laughing, grey eyes that had never shed a tear since her father's death. She was the life of the house, but no one knew what innocent daydreams passed through her young head. And no one could guess; she herself would have found it hard to define them. Lamirande thought of her as a child, and treated her as though she were a true sister of the woman he wanted to marry. Could she see that Lamirande and Marguerite were in love? Was she herself in love with this grave young man who was almost ten years older than she? Probably she would have been unable to answer these questions herself. She was aware of only one thing, that she was completely happy when Lamirande was near her and, although she was not unhappy during his absence, she always looked forward to his arrival.

At dusk on that same June evening Marguerite confided her happiness to Hélène. A heartbreaking sob and an expression of unspeakable pain made Marguerite understand what Hélène herself barely suspected.

'My poor sister!' exclaimed the older girl, opening her arms to the child.

Hélène wept as her sister embraced her. Finally she was able to murmur, 'You surprised me. It was a secret I was hardly aware of myself. It must never be mentioned again, not even between us. Forget what you have seen, or if you cannot forget think of it only when you are praying for me. My heart is broken, but with the grace of God it will never have reason to feel guilty. Pray for me, dear Marguerite, that I may never envy you your happiness.'

'Poor sister! My poor sister!'

Marguerite was happy as Lamirande's wife, but the memory of that summer evening, of the pale and anguished face half glimpsed in the uncertain light of dusk, followed her everywhere and tempered her happiness with a salutary bitterness.

As for Hélène, she had struggled and prayed, and at length she had won that victory which God always accords to those who struggle and pray: a victory that does not suppress suffering but makes it bearable by sanctifying it. Except for Marguerite, no one suspected the wound and then the scar that she bore in her heart. The fun-loving young girl had suddenly become grave but not melancholy; that was all that outsiders could observe. Her large eyes no longer laughed, but they had become infinitely deep and gentle.

The angels that God sent to Lamirande stopped on earth only long enough to take flight toward Heaven; all except little Marie. Despite the natural sorrow caused by the loss of his children, the young doctor sometimes worried at the intensity of his domestic happiness. 'If I do a little good for my fellow man,' he used to say to himself, 'am I not thereby amply rewarded in this life? And if one must suffer in order to be worthy of Heaven, my God, what will happen to me?' He did not lack trials, however; but he humbly believed that Heaven had sent them to him on account of his weakness.

Several years before the period when our story begins, he had, through pure devotion, entered political life, the better to serve his Church and his country. It never occurred to him that he might thereby attain certain honours, although he could legitimately have aspired to the highest positions, for he was gifted with superior intelligence, extraordinary eloquence, a pleasing appearance, and a sympathetic character. But he had noticed that those who seek the heavy burdens of state do not always use them for the benefit of the country; and fearing that he would be like so many others, he was satisfied with the simple title of federal Member of Parliament.

With Lamirande's help, his friend Paul Leverdier had finally succeeded in founding a newspaper that was completely free of party affiliation: it was called *La Nouvelle-France*.

And now let us return to the year 1945.

Pour la patrie   31

> I hate, I despise your feasts, and
> I take no delight in your solemn assemblies.
> AMOS 5:21

4

IN OTTAWA, the capital of the Confederation, there was great political activity. The House of Commons had been summoned for a special session. (The Senate had long since been abolished.) Members, journalists, public works' contractors, and those seeking ministerial favours arrived from all parts; they overflowed the hotels, invaded public offices, the halls of Parliament, the clubs and salons. It was a whirl of more or less shady affairs and more or less illicit pleasures.

The days were devoted to politicking, intrigues, plots, dubious speculations, the buying and selling of votes and consciences, in small secret meetings. The nights were spent at dinners and balls.

A month had passed since Lamirande and Montarval had met in the hovel on the Rue de l'Ancien Chantier.

The ground was covered with snow, a sparkling mantle that concealed mud, dried grass, and dead leaves. The ground that had recently been desolate, black, and soiled was now made beautiful and pure. It glittered and sent back to Heaven a reflection of the lights that it received. Beautiful snow! it is an image of divine mercy that sheds an immaculate garment over the ugliness of the soul that transgresses but is repentant. This is not baptismal innocence, nor springtime with its tender flowers, its gentle warbling of birds, its thousand murmuring streams, balmy breezes, rustling leaves, its exquisite perfume, and music as sweet as a childhood prayer. No, nothing is comparable to the beauty of spring nor to the innocence of a regenerated soul untarnished by the breath of sin. But when summer's heat has burned the earth, when autumn's rains and storms have covered it with mud and strewn it with fallen leaves, then the snow falls, soft, white, and pure, and the earth becomes beautiful once again in the eyes of man. Thus, when passions have ravaged the soul, when crimes of vice have disfigured it, the grace of God descends on it and covers it with a mantle, the mantle of forgiveness that makes the angels rejoice. The soiled earth receives its mantle unsolicited, but the guilty soul must seek it from Him who never scorns a heart that is humble and contrite.

Lamirande and Leverdier were reflecting on such matters as they walked in glorious moonlight towards the sumptuous residence of Sir Henry Marwood, prime minister of the Confederation. Sir Henry lived in a fashionable part of Ottawa that had the prosaic name Sandy Hill. That evening he was giving a dazzling reception followed by a political dinner party. Lamirande and Leverdier had been invited, for reasons that were unclear to them, and they had accepted rather reluctantly.

'What are we going to do at this silly affair?' asked Leverdier, suddenly breaking the silence. 'We'll be meeting a bunch of Freemasons and political jokers and people who meddle in all kinds of unsavoury affairs. Not one of our friends will be there, and it will be a dreadful bore. You know, if we were to stay away...'

'No,' replied his companion,' let us make this sacrifice. I assure you that I am not going because I want to. It seems to me that these dinners where one spends hours at table, where food is prepared with effeminate refinement and eaten simply for the sake of eating, are inspired far more by the demon of gluttony and intemperance than by the angel of hospitality. But it is not in itself a bad thing to attend these political dinners, and we should see what goes on at this get-together. Before we get there we'll say a *Sub tuum* to obtain the protection of Her who procured the miracle at the wedding feast at Cana.'

'The idea is even better when you consider that we're going to have to put up with such boredom as well as the ordinary dangers of a banquet.'

'It is a necessary chore, my dear friend. During the present crisis it is essential for us to know what all these illustrious scoundrels think and say and intend to do. We have to know, so that we can fight them more effectively.'

'My dear Lamirande, I am beginning to think that your preventive against the excesses of the table is the only worthwhile remedy against the political evil that is gnawing at us. I fully believe that your speeches and my articles are magnificent, but one must admit that they have not had a dazzling success. If we put away our speeches and our articles and bring out our rosaries perhaps our fortunes will change!'

'Yes, let us bring out our rosaries, pray more, but at the same time continue our struggle, fight to the end even against all human hope.

When we have done as well as possible the small amount that is all we can do, prayed with all our strength, written with all our strength and talked with all our strength, the good Lord will not ask for more and He will do the rest.'

'Those are words of gold, my dear friend,' replied the journalist. 'As God is my witness, I do not want to give up the fight. I only wanted to say that our prayers are more likely to be successful than our work. And besides, will real success, the return of the world to Christianity, ever come? I don't think it will. I think that the superb edifice we call modern civilization, which is not based on Him who is the sole foundation, is doomed to collapse in a barbarism worse than that which destroyed the proud Roman empire. I fight because I must, not because I have any hope of seeing the slightest success in this world. The great success will come in the Valley of Jehoshaphat.'

'Of course,' replied Lamirande, 'one must not work only for success in this world. One must accept in advance all the failures it may please God to send us. But we are permitted to carry out our struggles in the hope of success even here on earth; we are permitted to hope that God may deign to make fruitful our efforts and answer our prayers, not for our personal enjoyment but to save our country from universal ruin. Everything is being swallowed up in Masonic barbarism, worse than that of Attila and Genseric, it is true; but who can say that God does not want to spare this little corner of the earth that is so dear to us, this French Canada with its beautiful history, so that it may mark the beginning of a new civilization? I cannot help but hope that this will be so.'

'But would success not spoil the slight merit that we might have?' asked Leverdier.

'No. Even the most dazzling success will spoil nothing, if we are submissive to the will of God. But success is dangerous, I admit that. Do you know, my dear Leverdier, that it is far more difficult and, I suspect, more deserving to accept happiness in a Christian manner than it is to accept adversity?'

'I don't understand. "Explain," as they say in Parliament.'

'Very well. By confronting us with the absurdity of life in this world, misfortune leads us naturally to God, unless we are completely perverse. Happiness, on the other hand, makes us forget our ultimate goal. Tertullian says that in prosperity the soul directs its gaze to the Capitol; but in adversity it looks to Heaven, where it knows the true God resides. The happy people in this world who remain united to God are rare, I suppose, but there must be a special reward for them in Heaven, for they undergo a particularly difficult trial. To be rich without being attached to wealth requires an effort that is in itself deserving. But to be surrounded by friends and relatives who love you and whom you love, to know the pure joys of family without tasting any bitterness, to enjoy good health, see one's projects succeed, to be happy, in a word, here in earth, and still yearn for the celestial homeland as a Christian must do, is that not the ideal, the masterpiece of grace?'

Lamirande's effusion was followed by several moments of silence. The two friends walked slowly, leaning on one another. Their thoughts rose higher and higher toward Heaven in a marvellous outpouring of love and holy enthusiasm.

There are times when the presence of our soul seems to be felt within us in a physical and material manner. It is there, as tangible as our fleshly hearts. It seeks to escape from its prison, climbing, climbing incessantly, swelling our breasts to the point of causing real pain, a pain that is, however, exquisite. We think that something in us is going to break, that a part of our being is about to leave us, to launch itself into space. It is a mysterious and intoxicating struggle of the immortal soul against the body that holds it captive and enchained, a struggle that everyone experiences sometimes. It is a struggle that occurs independently of our own will. Who has not been thus overwhelmed, either in a moment of fervour or while listening to beautiful music, especially the songs of the Church, or in the great presence of nature, the beauties of the firmament or some sublime act of Christian devotion? It is our soul that, hearing the voice of the Creator, is lifting itself instinctively toward Him!

Both Lamirande and Leverdier were experiencing these profound emotions as they walked along in silence.

'Here we are,' said Leverdier at last. 'This is the moment to take refuge on safe ground.' And the two friends together recited, in an undertone, the *Sub tuum*.

'We're in no hurry,' said Lamirande. 'Let us say the *Salve regina* to ask for the conversion of a friend who is very dear to me.'

Then they rang the doorbell of an ostentatious house from whose large windows broad beams of light were cast onto the snow.

'Whose conversion are you seeking?' asked Leverdier as they waited for the door to be opened.

'George Vaughan, one of the MPs from Toronto. We shall probably meet him here this evening. He has a soul that is naturally upright and beautiful, but unfortunately he is not of the faith.'

'But at least he believes in God?'

'No; he seems to believe in nothing at all beyond or above this life.'

'Then he must be a monster!'

'No, only an unfortunate man. As I said, his soul has natural beauty. Let us pray that God may give him the inestimable gift of faith.'

At that moment the door opened. A lackey helped them take off their overcoats, and another led them to the salon where the leading lights of the Canadian political scene were already assembled. The immense room was bathed in the soft and penetrating light of an electrical apparatus that was concealed in the panelling; an intoxicating odour filled the atmosphere, while an invisible orchestra produced a harmony that seemed to come from far away. Groups of men were having animated discussions about the recent political events.

Sir Henry Marwood approached the new arrivals and welcomed them graciously. He overwhelmed Lamirande particularly with his flattering words.

'What does the old fox want of me?' Lamirande wondered. 'Nothing good, that's certain. We'd better be on our guard.'

Sir Henry Marwood had a face that was remarkable as much for its ugliness and the irregularity of its features as for its extraordinarily crafty and intelligent appearance. His small eyes, which appeared even smaller because of his prodigously large nose, sparkled with feeling. But they could not meet Lamirande's calm and luminous gaze.

'My dear Lamirande,' said Sir Henry effusively, 'how happy I am to see you here with your friend Leverdier. When I saw that you were a little late, I was afraid I was to be deprived of the pleasure of your company this evening. I don't deny that our opinions differ on a number of questions, but I admire talent and convictions wherever I find them. Both of you think forcefully and you express your thoughts with energy and originality. That is enough to make me admire you.'

'Talent is admirable, it is true, when it is used for good,' replied Lamirande, 'but must one admire it when it is devoted to evil?'

'Talent and energy, my dear sir, are always worthy of admiration, because they are gifts of the Supreme Being, a fragment of the universal soul.'

'It seems to me that one must consider two things when considering human intelligence: the work of God, which is always a thing of beauty, and the work of man, that is to say the use to which man puts his faculties. Unfortunately, the latter work is often evil and ugly.'

'Here you are launching into high philosophy. You soar, but my poor old wings do not allow me to follow you. I am content with admiring your flight.'

'All these compliments must be concealing some trap,' Lamirande thought. Then, aloud, 'I'm afraid you will not admire me so much in a few days after you have heard me speak about your project.'

'But you know nothing about my project! You may even like it, although you are usually rather difficult to please.'

'It's true that I do not know the details, but I know you, Sir Henry, and your project must bear some resemblance to its originator. Now, as you are well aware, your ideas and aspirations are not at all like my own.'

'Of course, of course. But say what you like about my project — you cannot prevent me from admiring your own great talent. Anyway, I'll have something to talk to you about in a while that has nothing to do with politics.'

Just then the Baron de Portal entered the room. Sir Henry called to him.

'Monsieur le Baron, may I introduce two of our most distinguished French-Canadian politicians? M. Lamirande is a Member of the House, and I assure you that he would bring honour to any Parliament, even that of France. His friend M. Leverdier is a journalist who would be noticed even in Paris. The Baron has only just arrived in Canada. He is on a fact-finding mission and he is particularly interested in learning about our political affairs. M. Leverdier, I believe you are eminently suited to advise M. le Baron.'

Leverdier realized that Sir Henry wanted to be alone with Lamirande. He accepted the invitation and began to talk with the Baron.

'Certainly, if M. le Baron wishes, I should be pleased to initiate you into our political affairs. You will find them more interesting than attractive, I suspect.'

And the journalist smiled rather maliciously at Sir Henry.

'What a rogue!' the Prime Minister exclaimed, with a gesture that was half friendly and half threatening. 'He certainly won't sing my praises to you, but no matter! He, too, is a very gifted man, and I admire such gifts, even when they are used against me.'

And taking Lamirande by the arm, he left the room.

The Baron and Leverdier went and sat on a sofa. Their conversation will be instructive as to the Canadian political situation in the year of grace 1945.

'I am very interested in your country,' the Baron began, 'but I must confess that I find your political affairs rather puzzling. What is your status at present? I know vaguely that Canada was once a British colony but is not now. Can you explain how that came about?'

'Gladly. You know as well as I, of course, that once-proud England has fallen to the rank of a third-rate power. She has lost India, or virtually so. Before long Russia will take over what is left of her eastern empire. Germany is snatching up the African colonies, piece by piece. Australia has shaken off the imperial yoke and Ireland has just regained her full independence. There are new agitations in Scotland and in England itself the secret societies she nurtured and encouraged have weakened the country and thrown it into chaos. She still possessed Canada until one fine day the United States, whose president wanted to expand American influence as far as possible, took advantage of a diplomatic crisis in which England was apparently in the wrong, and decided to present the breaking of this last colonial bond as an ultimatum. We strongly suspect that Canadian and American Freemasons are at the bottom of it, but be that as it may, England was completely powerless and so she ceded to the ultimatum. Barely three months ago she gave official notice to Canada that on the first of May the Governor-General will be recalled and he will not be replaced.'

'In other words you are now free,' said the Baron.

'Yes,' Leverdier replied, 'here we are, free. But what are we going to do with our freedom? It is a rather embarrassing gift. It is certain that the cabinet in Washington had some ulterior motive when they sponsored our independence. They fully intended to give us the honour of annexing us by force under some pretext or other, but Providence lent a hand and suddenly our friendly neighbour was at war with Spain over the island of Cuba and storm clouds are hovering on the Mexican horizon. To say nothing of the growing number of strikes that are breaking out and taking on the proportions of a chronic civil war. It is unthinkable for them now to consider annexing Canada, so we are seeking to establish a country that will be completely autonomous.'

'That should be relatively simple.'

'Unfortunately it's not. We have three possibilities: the status quo, legislative union, and separation. I shall explain each one briefly. If we adopted what is called the status quo, the transition would be quite smooth. We should keep our federal constitution, our central government, and our provincial administrations. Instead of being appointed in England, the Governor-General would be elected by us; that would be the only difference. The Conservative party, which is currently in power in Ottawa, favours the status quo. The party is made up of moderates, meaning first of all those people in place, along with their friends and relatives, as well as the people who would like to be there, along with *their* friends and relatives; then the contractors and public suppliers and everyone who has anything to do with them; finally, the people who lack the energy and independence to want anything but what the newspapers or political leaders tell them.'

'The party that favours the status quo must have an enormous number of members. I wonder who is left for the other two parties.'

'In every province there are people who support legislative union. They are mainly radicals, well-known Freemasons, and the avowed enemies of the Church and the French-Canadian element. The group is very active in the province of Quebec, under the leadership of a journalist named Ducoudray, who puts out *La Libre Pensée*, a Montreal newspaper. It goes without saying that the unionists conceal their game as well as they can. They ask for legislative union, ostensibly to make the administration of public affairs more economical, but it is a well-known fact that their true goal is the abolition of the Catholic religion. They are ready to sacrifice the French element, which is the chief support of the Church in this country, in order to attain their goal.'

'That party has little to recommend it to honest men. I am curious to hear what you have to say about the third!'

'The third group are the separatists. Their leader is M. Lamirande, whom you have just met and I myself am also a member. We believe that the time is ripe to establish French Canada as a separate and independent state. Our geographical position, our natural resources, and the homogeneity of our population enable us to aspire to be ranked among the nations of the earth. It is possible that Confederation offers certain material advantages, but from the religious and national point of view it is filled with dangers for us, for our enemies will certainly manage to wear it away until it is a legislative union in everything but name. Moreover, the chief material advantages that are derived from Confederation could be obtained equally well through a simple postal and customs union. Militant Catholics in the province of Quebec who have not been blinded by party loyalties support our project. The clergy too, are generally in favour, although they don't dare say so out loud because for a long time now our priests have not had the right to leave the sacristy. The idea of peaceful separation has made some headway in the other provinces. There is a fairly large group that is opposed to legislative union and prefers separation to the radicals' project. This group is made up of English Catholics and a few Protestants who are not fanatics. Their rallying cry is "No Ireland, no Poland in America!" They do not want French Canada to be forced into a union that would only be a long, cruel martyrdom. Their parliamentary leader is Lawrence Houghton, who is a Protestant but a man of integrity and honour, filled with respect for the Church and sympathy for the French element. So there you have it, M. le Baron: a brief look at the political situation in Canada at the present time. I hope I have made myself clear.'

'Your account has been most interesting, my dear sir; and I thank you for it. I am a separatist too, I assure you, and I cannot conceive of a French Catholic being anything else without betraying his religion and his nationality. But tell me, is Parliament meeting in Ottawa right now to resolve this question?'

'Yes, M. le Baron. The federal government, under the wily and skilful leadership of our host, has managed to get all the provincial legislatures to pass "resolutions" that authorize the parliament in Ottawa to make the final decision on our political and national future. We have fought this project in the Quebec legislature, as we want the provinces to have at least the right of veto. But our efforts were in vain, as party loyalties, intrigues, and corruption got the better of us. So we are here in Ottawa now to make one final, supreme effort, but without any great hope of success.'

'How do you think it will end?'

'Under the pretext of improving the present constitution, Sir Henry will present a new bill in a few days. I have every reason to believe that it will provide for a true legislative union disguised under the name of "confederation." They will claim that the broad goals of the *status quo* will be retained but in fact both the Church and French Canada will be strangled. I can tell you confidentially that Sir Henry is a high-ranking Freemason and therefore profoundly hostile to the Church. If he does not openly propose legislative union it is simply because he is afraid of defeat.'

'You suspect him of playing a double game?'

'I do, and I assure you I do not speak rashly. He must have had some ulterior motive for inviting Lamirande and me here this evening.'

'As long as he has not compromised you! Look at him deep in conversation with your friend.'

'Don't worry about Lamirande. He's as solid as a rock, and he's intelligent enough not to let himself be taken in, even by Sir Henry. We accepted his personal invitation tonight to get a better idea of the traps he is setting and the intrigues he wants to bring to a head.'

While Leverdier and the Baron were talking, Sir Henry had taken Lamirande aside, still holding his arm affectionately.

'My dear Lamirande,' said the old diplomat in his most wheedling voice, 'I've wanted to talk frankly with you for a long time. We have often been opponents, but I have always been very interested in you. I consider you to be a true representative of your race, and whatever I think of your race, I desire nothing but good for it. I want to pay honour to it through you.'

'You are far too flattering,' Lamirande replied coldly, already aware where Sir Henry wanted to lead him.

'He thinks he can buy me,' Lamirande was thinking. 'Alas, he has seen so many of our people give in to him for a few pieces of gold or some paltry honours.'

At first he was inclined to refuse indignantly the offer that Sir Henry had not yet clearly formulated, but he thought better of it. Better not to rush into anything, he thought to himself; I shall be able to judge how evil are his plans for us by the efforts he makes to get rid of me.

Lamirande remained silent and Sir Henry continued: 'I know your ambition is not personal, that you desire nothing for yourself and that your sole passion is to serve your country and your compatriots. Your unselfishness is admirable; you are a Member of Parliament not through taste but through duty, are you not? And if you were offered another position where you could be of even greater service to your people you would accept it, would you not?'

'It is true,' Lamirande replied, 'that I am not in Parliament through taste, but I know of no other position where I could be of real use to my compatriots at this time.'

'Well, I can think of one, and I'm offering it to you. It's the position of Canadian Consul-general at Paris or at Washington, whichever you prefer.'

If the old scoundrel is offering me such a prize it must be very important to get rid of me, thought Lamirande. His plan must be truly diabolical. After a moment's silence he looked hard at Sir Henry, forcing him to drop his eyes.

'Your offer is, of course, a splendid one; too fine, in fact. It is even suspect. I beg you to believe me when I say that for the moment my job is here, and here I will stay.'

'But you are not thinking! Consider the good you could do in Paris, establishing intimate relations between France and Canada; or in Washington, working for the advancement of your compatriots who are still in the United States!'

'Perhaps I could do some good there, but it is my duty to stay here and prevent you from doing any harm. Besides, why do you offer me this position just now? Why have you not waited until our national future is decided? Do you really think, Sir Henry, that I cannot read to the very depths of your soul?'

Lamirande's voice trembled with emotion. Sir Henry could not look at the young man directly. The old schemer, who had already concluded a hundred similar deals, felt that he was being dominated, crushed. However, he changed his tone and made one final attempt, a bold one.

'Very well!' he said, in a voice that had suddenly become hard and abrupt. 'Let's put our cards on the table. I know very well that my bill will not please you. You will fight it but you know as well as I that nothing you can do will prevent the Commons from passing it. Given that, why refuse a position where you could be useful to your friends and your race? Are you going to deprive them of real advantages through sheer stubbornness, for the simple pleasure of opposing me? Is that fair? Is it patriotic?'

'But if my opposition does not frighten you, why do you go to such lengths to silence me? And if you are acting out of sympathy for our race, why do you demand that I buy this position at the price of a wicked betrayal? Sir Henry, I am a guest in your house, and I shall not say what you deserve to hear. But you understand, I am sure, that after what has happened I cannot remain under your roof or sit at your table. I have the honour of bidding you good night.'

Then he walked away with dignity, leaving the prime minister dumbfounded. In all his long years of experience, Sir Henry had never seen anything like it.

'After all, I do admire him,' he murmured, and he meant what he said.

Lamirande went toward the salon where Leverdier was still talking with the Baron de Portal.

'I do apologize for interrupting you, but I must leave and I am sure you will want to leave with me.'

Leverdier realized what had happened and, apologizing to the Baron, he went to join his friend.

'I assume he tried to buy you off and you left him in the lurch. Well done! But is it really necessary for us to leave right away? I'd like to find out a little about what is going on.'

'I know enough already! Let's go. I'll tell you all about it in a while. Let's get out of here; this is no place for Christians. The air is thick with demons – you can almost see them. Come on!'

Leverdier hesitated no longer. As they went toward the door of the salon, the two friends met a young English Canadian with a pleasant, open face.

'My dear Vaughan!' Lamirande exclaimed. 'I'm so happy to see you. May I introduce my friend Leverdier, my right-hand man? Or rather, I should say that I am his right-hand man, for he is a journalist, who makes and unmakes politicians. Come on, put on your coat and walk with us to Rideau Street. Then you can come back in time for dinner.'

'Then you're not dining here?' asked Vaughan, surprised. 'What's going on?'

'Come with us and we'll talk about it in the moonlight.'

As they walked past Parliament Hill, Lamirande told his friends what had gone on between the prime minister and himself. Then he spoke to Vaughan.

'What do you think of your respected leader's behaviour?'

'First of all,' replied the young English Canadian, 'he is not my leader. I have political ideas that guide me, but no politician tells me what to do. Besides, you know how I hate those wretched underhanded dealings that go by the name of "diplomacy." That kind of practice is shameful and unworthy of human nature.'

'However, my poor friend, human nature becomes the slave of those dealings as soon as religion ceases to uphold and fortify it.'

'I don't want to praise myself but I can say that only the respect I have for my human dignity is enough to protect me against these contemptible actions.'

'Your life isn't over. Wait for the future before you make your final pronouncements. Perhaps you have not yet encountered any serious temptation. As far as I am concerned, I am convinced that sooner or later you will throw yourself either into the arms of the Church or into some horrible abyss. For without divine grace man cannot be sustained merely by the awareness of his dignity, nor can he be strengthened against downfalls that may lead to the end of his career. But let's talk politics. You say you have no leader; you repudiate Sir Henry and his conduct, but you still share his ideas and support his projects, freely and honestly. Now Sir Henry only manages to have his projects accepted because of the wretched underhanded dealings you condemn so heatedly. Does that not make you a little suspicious of the merit of those ideas and projects? Is it not reasonable to say that that which is truly good does not need such ignoble means to succeed?'

'I condemn the means and I would never want to use them myself. But I recognize that it is difficult to have any success in the world of politics without having some recourse to them, because of the corruption that is rampant everywhere.'

'And what about the famous human dignity?'

'If everyone were aware of that dignity, that would be enough, but everyone is *not* aware of it.'

'Why does everyone not respect this human dignity, since it is a purely human feeling? Why are all men not honest?'

'If I only knew! Why is every man not endowed with physical beauty? Why are there cripples and hunchbacks and deaf-mutes and men who are blind or one-eyed?'

'On the other hand, there is too much order and harmony in the visible world for a reasonable man to be able to speak of "chance." Admit, then, the existence of a Divine Creator; a future life in which everyone will be rewarded according to his deeds; original sin which has seriously weakened and tainted human nature; a Saviour who has redeemed fallen man and given him the means to regain his celestial heritage. Admit these truths and you will be able to resolve all the redoubtable problems that humanity offers us.'

'I am quite willing to admit that your system is entirely logical; everything in it holds together. In fact, if there is something true in any religion, it is in the Catholic faith. But we can talk of that later. Now, goodbye. I must return to the party.'

The three companions parted. Vaughan went back to Sir Henry's party while Lamirande and Leverdier returned to their hotel.

'You were quite right,' said Leverdier. 'He is not a monster, but a very unhappy man. If only we could teach men to believe as we teach them to read!'

'Faith is a gift that God gives freely to whomever He chooses. We should thank Him for having deigned to give us this inestimable gift while so many others who could make better use of it have not received it. Let us pray particularly for those who do not have faith. They are like the paralytics described in the Bible who were unable to make their way to the Saviour to be cured. They needed the help of charitable neighbours. The other sick people, representing sinners who have faith, could go unassisted to the feet of Christ. However terrible their infirmities, however dreadful their sores, they were less pitiable than the paralytics, because they could place themselves unaided before the human God and cry, "Jesus, son of David, have pity on us!" Let us imitate those charitable souls of Judea who carried the cripples to the edge of the road where Jesus was to pass. Let us, through our prayers and good deeds, carry those spiritual cripples who do not have faith before the Divine Master so that He may heal them.'

While the two Catholics were having this conversation on the way back to their hotel, Vaughan was going slowly in the opposite direction. He was thoughtful. Lamirande's words had upset him in a curious way. He felt oppressed by a vague and indefinable malaise, like a foreboding of some misfortune. Confused yearnings that he could not analyse disturbed his soul.

George Vaughan had met Lamirande several years before during a trip to Quebec. A feeling of sympathy was established between them from the first words they exchanged. Both were loyal, frank, and open; both felt the attraction of statesmanship and an invincible repulsion for the contraband kind of politics that is based on corruption and modelled on intrigue. But the similarity between them ended there: the young English Canadian was as much a sceptic as the French Canadian was a believer.

When they met in Ottawa later the sympathy of their first meeting changed to true friendship. Vaughan scarcely questioned the source of his singular affection for Lamirande or, rather, he attributed it to a great similarity of tastes and character. Lamirande, more perceptive, was convinced that there was no natural explanation for the mysterious current that he felt between the stranger and himself from their first meeting. A firm believer in the supernatural, he told himself that their friendship was the work of Vaughan's guardian angel, that the celestial spirit had chosen this means to bring about the salvation of the soul entrusted to its care.

Vaughan, as we have said, was a sceptic. He had been inculcated with the poison of incredulity in his childhood, in the public schools of his province. As a young man he had spent several years in London and Paris, and the life that he led there, although it was not debauched, was not designed to make him a believer. But although he was sceptical, he was not a militant atheist. He did not deny the existence of God the Creator. He even thought that there must be some universal principle. If pressed, he could pass for a deist. When anyone spoke to him of the supernatural world, he invariably replied, 'I deny nothing and I affirm nothing.'

However, after becoming associated with Lamirande, he had studied the Catholic religion, and at the time when we meet him, he knew it better than many Catholics. He often repeated, as we heard him say this evening, that if there were any truth in the supernatural, it was in the doctrines of the Church. But if he had the *knowledge* that man can acquire through his own forces, he did not have the faith that only God communicates to the soul, through His grace. His conversations with Lamirande about religion always disturbed him; nevertheless, he would not have given them up for the greatest fortune in the world. Even though he was a non-believer, his friend's faith fascinated him. And this evening he was more tormented than usual.

'Ah!' he sighed as he returned to Sir Henry's house. 'If only I could believe like Lamirande.' It was the first time that his heart, filled until now with only vague emotions, had expressed so clear a wish.

The guests were at the dining table and Vaughan was soon pulled along by the whirlwind of conversation, forgetting his earlier troubles. He became once more affable, correct, witty, and sceptical – a man of the world.

Vaughan found himself seated next to Aristide Montarval, the MP for Quebec City. A by-election had been held at the beginning of September, following the inexplicable resignation of the sitting MP. Montarval, who had previously had little to do with politics and had passed for an advanced radical, had suddenly entered the race as a Conservative against another Conservative of long standing. To everyone's surprise, Sir Henry had accepted him, a new convert, as a ministerial candidate, in preference to his rival. The title of ministerial candidate, together with the support of the radicals who were not too unhappy to see him run as a conservative, had brought him a resounding victory that was the talk of the political world. The election, which still held some mystery, was one of the subjects of conversation at Sir Henry's table. Montarval was very rich and already distinguished as a speaker. Everyone said that he was a fine acquisition for the Conservative party, for it was well known that although the new MP had not previously participated directly in political affairs, he had always professed and helped to spread advanced ideas. Sir Vincent Jolibois, the main representative of the French element in the cabinet, had even timidly expressed some concern at recognizing the ministerial and conservative orthodoxy of this candidate. He spoke freely about it to his colleagues and to his leader, Sir Henry Marwood. The latter reassured him, saying that

Montarval was remarkably talented and that talent always deserved to be admired. Sir Vincent gave in to this reasoning without reply. Besides, as he remarked to a friend who had also expressed some fears about the neo-Conservative candidate, discipline must be maintained inside party ranks, and when the leader is satisfied, other members must be too. Just as it is not necessary to be more Catholic than the Pope, it is not required that an MP be more conservative than the leader of his party.

And so the radical Montarval became a Conservative. *La Nouvelle France* had hazarded a simple observation on the ease with which the Conservative party absorbed and assimilated the most indigestible elements and there was a general hue and cry against Leverdier in the other newspapers. For two weeks the press of both languages called him crass, boorish, hypocritical, jealous, ambitious, and so on. Even *La Libre Pensée*, which had run down Montarval for turning reactionary, played its part in the cacophony of imprecations.

Vaughan started a conversation with his neighbour and as one is glad to speak about what one loves, he wanted to ask the new MP about their absent colleague Lamirande. At the mention of his name Montarval's eyes were filled with such an expression of hatred that Vaughan felt chilled by it.

'Our new colleague,' he told himself, 'is most certainly not a sympathetic man. What a difference there is between him and Lamirande! Lamirande attracts, this one repels – they're like the two poles of a magnet. Is it animal magnetism or could it be something else?'

The banquet went on until late at night and ended without incident.

> Love not sleep, lest you come to poverty.
> PROVERBS 20:13

5

BACK AT THEIR MODEST APARTMENT on Wellington Street, Lamirande and Leverdier began to discuss the political situation seriously.

'It's very grave,' said Lamirande. 'I'm certain that Sir Henry is planning some stab in the back that will be even more perfidious than usual. But what can we do?'

Leverdier replied, 'I shall write an article immediately. It should stir up some reaction in the ministerial camp.'

'Very good; and while you're doing that I'll put together some letters to let our friends know what is going on.'

The two friends set to work in good spirits. Here is Leverdier's article, which he entitled 'Sleep in Peace!':

Next week Sir Henry Marwood will submit to the Commons his proposal for a final solution to Canada's political fate.

For us, French Canadians, our national future – all that is most sacred and dear to us – is at stake: our language, our religion, our institutions, our laws, our autonomy.

Will we still exist as a people tomorrow? That is the vital question now facing us.

The ministerial and so-called conservative press is flooding the country with its soporific optimism. Sleep, it tells the inhabitants of the province of Quebec; sleep in peace, sleep soundly, for Sir Henry is prime minister and Sir Vincent is his very humble servant.

What is there to worry about? Sir Henry is a Freemason, true, but he respects our Church, he adores our language and speaks it fluently, he admires our institutions. He used to be an outspoken advocate of legislative union, but today he would shed his blood for the status quo. Provincial autonomy has no more loyal friend than this converted centralist. We can sleep in peace while this born guardian of our rights keeps watch.

The other day *Le Mercure*, the leading Quebec ministerial organ, wrote that "troubled minds are trying to upset our populace by creating prejudice against our own public men, against the conservative leaders who have the God-given mission of leading our country along the paths of moral and material progress."

Wicked and troubled minds, it would be better if you slept! What right do you have to remind us ceaselessly that the prime minister is a Freemason? that his colleague Sir Vincent once voted for obligatory neutral schools? that M. Vilbreque, another of Sir Henry's colleagues, in an excess of Anglomania, deplored the expense required by the use of the French language? that M. Dutendre, a third French colleague, announced that the provincial governments are, after all, nothing but municipal councils on a larger scale? Those are *prejudices* that you stir up most unworthily against the fine men who distribute *patronage* and *grants* in a completely orthodox manner. Sir Vincent himself said only last summer, in his major policy speech, that a country where *patronage* is distributed in a judicious and equitable manner is a country that is well governed, a country that is happy.

Why do you doubt, you with troubled minds?

It is a matter of elaborating a constitutional project to safeguard the rights of the Church, parents' rights concerning the education of their children, the right of the French element and provincial autonomy. So let us put our complete trust in this project of the Freemasons, in those who support the role of the State in education, in the enemies of our language and our provincial institutions. Those are the wishes of the party, and only troubled minds choose logic over party discipline.

It is a crime to doubt the effectiveness of well-distributed *patronage;* and to rise up against party discipline in favour of logic is an act of folly.

So, inhabitants of the province of Quebec, sleep in peace, for Sir Henry and his brilliant colleagues are keeping watch over you.

Leverdier gave Lamirande his article to read.

'It's nothing out of the ordinary,' said the journalist, 'but it will make the pro-government papers howl a little and they might compromise themselves as a result. What else can we do for the moment? You and I know very well that some dark plot is hatching here, but we don't know how to share our convictions with the public. If you were to tell of your conversation with Sir Henry, he would deny it categorically. The old scoundrel wouldn't shrink from a lie. Besides, our own people are so infatuated with him that they would consider his attempt at corruption as a very gracious act. "Look!" they would say. "The excellent Sir Henry only wanted to honour our race, and that mule-headed Lamirande has grossly insulted him! We must be very sick!" '

'You're right. The future is very bleak,' Lamirande replied. 'But we must not lose hope, even when everything seems so desperate. Let us not forget that Lazarus had been buried and was already beginning to decompose when the Lord raised him from the dead!'

Who forsake the paths of uprightness
to walk in the ways of darkness.
PROVERBS 2:13

6

TWO DAYS AFTER Sir Henry's reception and banquet the newspapers in the capital announced that the prime minister was so indisposed that he could not attend the sessions in the House or receive visitors. The truth was that he had left Ottawa the morning after the dinner and gone secretly and strictly incognito to Kingston.

Around nine o'clock in the evening he left his hotel and went to an isolated house outside the city limits. He knocked at the door in a special way; someone inside asked some questions which he answered, the door was opened and Sir Henry found himself in the meeting place of the Supreme Council of the League for Progress. This council was composed of two delegates from each Central Council. The president was the same man we have already seen presiding over the Quebec Provincial Council. One of the representatives from Montreal was Ducoudray, editor of *La Libre Pensée*, who appeared earlier in Quebec City.

Soon after Sir Henry arrived, the session opened with a horrible prayer to Satan that the president recited as he turned to face an immense triangle at the back of the room. Before this triangle, the emblem of Lucifer, with its apex pointing down, there was incense burning on an altar.

'Brothers,' said the president, 'we are all here. I congratulate you for arriving so promptly at this session of the Supreme Council. Thanks to the zeal with which you carry out your work, we are able to face the future with confidence. At our last meeting I had the honour to tell you officially that our efforts had been thoroughly successful; that with the intelligent co-operation of our brothers in the United States and England, the colonial bond had been broken. This was a step in the right direction, but it was only the first step. As you know, our goal was to have Canada enter immediately into the American union. Unfortunately, the grave events of which you are aware have forced us to postpone this project indefinitely. It has been necessary to adopt another political goal. The executive committee has calculated that given the impossibility of incorporating Canada into the United States, legislative union of all the provinces offered us the best way of uprooting from the Canadian soil the infamous superstition that is preventing our people from proceeding along the path of true progress. The Supreme Council ratified that decision at its last meeting. Then the executive committee exerted the influence that our order has over the provincial legislatures to persuade all of them to give the federal parliament the final ruling on the question of our political future. Today I have the honour to announce officially that this part of our program has been carried out. On my instructions, Brother Marwood immediately summoned the federal parliament. Now we must determine what it is most appropriate for us to do in Ottawa. What is your opinion? I give the floor to those brothers who have some observation to make, some project to submit to the Supreme Council.'

There was a moment's silence.

'Our Brother President,' said one of the members, 'must have a proposal to submit to us; we should like to hear what he has to say.'

'As a matter of fact, I do have a project to submit to the Council; but before I do I'd like to hear what my brothers have to say about the situation.'

'We could deliberate more easily,' said the same member, 'if Brother President would be good enough to tell us his project first. It is rare that the Council has to modify the plans of its leader.'

'Very well,' replied the president, 'this is how I see the situation. We will never have legislative union accepted by proposing it openly in Parliament. The French Canadians, the Catholics from outside Quebec, and Houghton and his group would never allow it. What we must do, then, is present the government project so cleverly that legislative union will be effectively established but the name and appearance of Confederation maintained. Today we must be content to sow the seeds of union; later our work will develop gradually until it is widely and completely accepted. We must be certain that each guarantee that is given to the provinces contains one equivocal word or phrase that we will be able to interpret in favour of the central power when the time is right. This is a constitutional project I have prepared with the help of the executive committee; I submit it now to the Supreme Council for its consideration. Brother Secretary, will you be good enough to read it?'

The secretary, who was none other than Ducoudray, read the document, which was a veritable masterpiece of diabolical cleverness. In every article some trap had been concealed with superhuman craftiness; every clause was cleverly equivocal. All the brothers were filled with admiration. The project was accepted with virtually no discussion.

'It is therefore decreed,' said the president, 'by the Supreme Council of the League for Progress, that the constitutional project we have just adopted must be presented to Parliament without delay. The secretary will keep the original in the files of the Supreme Council, and he will submit an authentic copy to Brother Marwood. Moreover, it is required that Brother Marwood have the federal parliament vote on the project, which cannot be modified without the consent of the Executive Committee. Is this the pleasure of the Supreme Council?'

All indicated their assent, and the secretary recorded the inscriptions required by the League.

'And what are we to do,' asked Brother Marwood, 'if Parliament refuses to vote on this project? I fear that despite the great skill with which it was prepared, Lamirande and Houghton will see the true significance of this new constitution.'

'We have been exceedingly cautious,' replied the president. 'Now we must be bold and hardy if we hope to succeed. If the Commons balks, you will dissolve the House. An appeal to the voters will be favourable to us because we will take steps to ensure it. Party loyalty and corruption have always been strong forces in politics. Count on it, Brother Marwood, count on our admirable organization which covers the entire country and particularly on the help of our God, the God of Liberty, Progress, and Vengeance. But are you quite sure that this man Lamirande cannot be bribed?'

'Bribe Lamirande? As you know, Brother President, I've done my best; and the brothers know that I don't exactly lack talent when it's a question of getting rid of a troublesome adversary. However, I have not been able to break down his defences and I know human nature well enough to know that it's useless to try again with him.'

Then Brother Marwood told the Supreme Council what had gone on between himself and Lamirande the evening of the banquet.

The president leaned towards Ducoudray and whispered, 'Remember all the details Marwood has just given us; take notes. They will be very useful some day.'

'I don't see how we can use this incident against Lamirande,' replied Ducoudray. 'It's more in his favour, in fact.'

'Later on you'll see how we can use it.'

The Supreme Council soon dispersed. The president and Brother Marwood went back to Ottawa together, while Ducoudray took the files with him to Montreal.

> To set the mind on the flesh is death.
> ROMANS 8:6

7

LEVERDIER WAS NOT MISTAKEN; his article stirred up a storm. *Le Mercure*, the leading ministerial newspaper, opened fire with a pompous article from which a few excerpts follow:

We have arrived at a decisive moment in our history; it is a solemn time, for a nation is about to be born. We are about to pass from our former colonial status that of a free and completely independent people. Thus the time is solemn, as we said, and we must express ourselves in a language that is worthy of the events we are about to witness.

We were most distressed to read a few days ago, in an obscure Quebec City newspaper, an article that was entirely out of place in both style and substance. The style was light, trivial, bantering, and ironic. This is no way to discuss the serious questions of the day. The substance of the article was even worse: appeals to national and religious prejudice, a lack of Christian charity, a notable lack of respect for established authority and for our political leaders. All these lapses were present in the same article.

The author was so indelicate as to note that our Prime Minister is a Freemason. We, of course, condemn Freemasonry because our Church condemns it. But we must remember that the Protestant churches do not condemn it, and that Sir Henry is a Protestant. We must remember that not only do the Protestant churches not condemn Freemasonry, but that several of the most outstanding Protestant ministers belong to this society. This proves that the Protestant religion does not look unfavourably on Freemasonry and that Freemasonry is not, as certain highly-placed individuals claim, hostile to all religions, even to Christianity itself.

Despite these undeniable truths, the article makes it a crime for Sir Henry to be a Freemason. It sows doubt and dismay among our people; it makes the people suspicious of our heads of state; it undermines authority and stirs up the fires of national and religious prejudice. Such behaviour is revolutionary and anti-social. We live in a country with a varied population, and let us never forget that; we are the minority in this country and let us not forget that either. Let us live peacefully with the Protestants, the English, and the Freemasons. This is our duty, for Providence has placed us here in the midst of these diverse elements. Let us respect their opinions if we want them to respect ours. Let us extend a fraternal hand to them. Let us not become embittered if we do not want them to form a coalition to wipe us out. Let us trust our leaders' wisdom and patriotism and loyalty, and be assured that our privileges will be respected. Let us not lift a sacrilegious hand against Confederation but be content with perfecting it, under the guidance of the leaders who have been given the mission of directing our country. Those who ask for legislative union are no more revolutionary than those dangerous utopians who wish to disunite the provinces. We represent the happy medium; let us not destroy that.

All of the small ministerial papers began immediately to sound the same note, with variations that consisted mainly of violent personal attacks against Lamirande and Leverdier, who were accused of jealousy, ambition, and hatred. Several of the writers of these attacks, men who were grossly overpaid to sing the praises of the ministers, were indignant at the thought that the scandalous crusade against civil authority undertaken by *La Nouvelle-France* and its partisans had been inspired by the love of lucre. And their outbursts invariably ended with a fervent appeal to Christian charity.

La Libre Pensée, organ of those radicals who strongly favoured legislative union, also made raging attacks against the separatists. Idiots, church-mice, hypocrites, imbeciles, sanctimonious frauds, Jesuits in short skirts, cockroaches, backwards candle-snuffers, medievally-minded enemies of progress, fanatical inquisitors, Torquemadas with bound feet, encrusted descendants of Peter the Hermit, Tartuffes: this was the canvas on which the newspaper and its satellites embroidered. All cried out in the name of the economy for legislative union. We have too much government, they repeated endlessly. No more provinces, no more provincial legislatures, no more petty racial and religious prejudice. Let us destroy all that and construct one single government – strong, broad, concerned with the economy and a single nationality.

In Quebec City at that time a newspaper called *Le Progrès catholique* was published, edited by Hercule Saint-Simon, whom the reader met in the company of Lamirande when the two made a visit of enquiry for the St Vincent de Paul Society.

A man of real talent but not particularly agreeable, Saint-Simon appeared somehow false, rather cold, making those who came into contact with him feel somewhat uneasy. Gifted with a certain energetic, even violent allure, he appeared (to those who see only the surface of things) to be a man of character. Before the beginning of our story he had thrown himself enthusiastically into the separatist movement, hard on the heels of Lamirande and Leverdier. But even though he proclaimed their leadership and waved their flag, he did not always follow their advice or adopt their firm but moderate language and their wise behaviour. For the past month, particularly, he seemed to have become a professional window-breaker.

Of course it is sometimes necessary to break windows, real ones as well as figurative ones. A man is closed into a room with no air to breathe at all. The door is locked, barricaded; all the exits are hermetically sealed. The man is stifling; he has already lost consciousness. What are you to do? You break a window; he breathes the air and is saved. In the moral world there are analogous situations where it is necessary to smash some windows. It is the only way to circulate a little pure air in the prison whose victims, closed in by routine and prejudice, have been asphyxiated. But Saint-Simon rarely did anything *but* smash windows. He did it everywhere, at any time and for no apparent reason. The sound of broken windows had attracted everyone's attention to him but it had not won people's hearts.

As editor of *Le Progrès catholique,* then, Saint-Simon replied to the article in *La Nouvelle France* with a violent outburst. He called his article, 'Do We Want War?' In it he not only demanded that Quebec leave Confederation, but he urged French Canadians to organize themselves into an army, to obtain weapons, and go to Ottawa to watch the deliberations in Parliament. He loosed an unbelievable attack against all Protestants, stating that they had always come together against the Catholics to massacre them. And he ended his hysterical outburst with the unequivocal claim that on the day when Quebec became free of the federal yoke, the English who were still in the province had better watch out.

When Leverdier read the article he had a moment of holy rage. He rushed out of the parliamentary reading room, crossed the corridor, and had a page summon Lamirande from the Commons.

'Have you read Saint-Simon's latest nonsense?' he exclaimed.

'Yes,' Lamirande replied quietly, 'I saw it and it's worse than nonsense, it's criminal.'

'Is he out of his mind?'

'No, my friend, he isn't. He's something even worse.'

'I can't think of anything worse than a madman who gets mixed up with writing,' replied Leverdier hotly.

'A traitor is worse than a madman,' said Lamirande.

'Great God!' cried the journalist. 'Do you suspect him of betraying us? You go farther than I do; I only accuse him of an unbelievable lack of tact and judgement.'

'Yes, I do go farther than you. And I do not speak rashly when I say that Saint-Simon is openly betraying us.'

'But what basis do you have for believing that this man who claims, after all, to support the same causes we do, is openly betraying us?'

'You must know that one can betray a cause while claiming to defend it. It's one of the most popular tactics these days — a kind of refined treason.'

'Yes, but do you have any proof against him? What basis do you have for your suspicions?'

'It's not a case of suspicion, it's a moral certitude, a profound conviction.'

'But tell me what it's based on, this moral certitude you feel. You're not in the habit of passing judgement lightly and without proof. I agree that the article is dreadful, despicable. When I read it I shuddered with indignation, and if the wretch had been here I don't know what I would have done to him. But can't we, after all, simply add this article to the long list of human foolishness?'

'It's true the list is long, but human perversity is great too. Only God can see their limits. If I had only Saint-Simon's article to guide me, I should probably judge the incident as you have done. But I also know that the wretched man has been assailed by the demons of wealth, and I have reason to fear that he has succumbed to temptation. I learned this very morning that for some time now Saint-Simon has been very friendly with Montarval.'

'I knew that too.'

'I didn't until now. But I did know that Montarval is the most despicable man I have ever seen. A monster. The thought of him makes me shudder. I can't tell you more, as I've promised not to reveal certain details. Perhaps it's a promise that can be broken, but for the moment I'll just say that anyone who frequents Montarval must be some kind of monster too. Events will prove me right only too soon.'

Although he was intrigued, Leverdier did not ask more questions. He knew his friend too well to doubt his judgement. After a moment's silence the journalist asked,

'But what are we to do about the article?'

'I have done everything in my power to repair the evil. When the session opened, I disavowed both the article and its author. I said that this article was a piece of insanity, not an expression of our feelings, that we are moved not by hatred of the other peoples, who inhabit this country but by love of our own race, our nationality, our religion, language, and traditions; that we think it better to safeguard these sacred things by withdrawing from Confederation now that the opportunity presents itself; but that we threaten no one. I think you would be wise to repeat the same things in your newspaper. For the moment there is nothing else to do. Things will happen quickly enough. Let's wait and see.'

> He who loves gold will not be justified,
> and he who pursues money will be led astray by it.
> ECCLESIASTICUS 31:5
> 8

HERCULE SAINT-SIMON had gone into journalism without moral preparation, without having sufficiently purified his intentions. He wanted to do good through his newspaper, but he also wanted to become prosperous, even wealthy. His daily bread, the minimum necessary for a man of his social position, was not enough; he wanted the good things in life, and as true Catholic journalism is richer in disappointments than in financial success, he became increasingly bitter and irritable. Discovering that he did not have the qualities of self-sacrifice necessary to continue his work, which was thankless from the most earthly point of view, he should have given it up and sought elsewhere, through legitimate means, the earthly goods he so coveted. But he liked journalism for the prestige and influence the profession confers on those who practise it with skill. The sound of polemics intoxicated him and the arguments around his name flattered his pride. His first dream was to continue as an honest journalist, even a Catholic one, but to grow rich in the process as well.

He began by publicizing, for a consideration, certain commercial and industrial enterprises. As they were honourable, he could, if pressed, maintain that he was being paid for legitimate work; but his imagined needs increased and this kind of work began to seem too restricted, so he enlarged his scope. When the promoters of big business did not come to him he approached them, and gave them to understand that the surest way not to make an enemy of him was to pay him handsomely for his co-operation. Then, still slipping down the slope, he put his pen to the service of undertakings that were dubious, shady or, finally, downright rotten.

However, he still did not grow rich quickly enough. Trying to keep on being a Catholic journalist seemed to hamper him now. In the troubled times when our story begins he was trying to think of a way to make his fortune at a single stroke; but to attain this goal he would have to abandon his fellow citizens in their patriotic struggles, give in to the enemies of his race, favour their shady manoeuvres and, in a word, betray the sacred cause of country and religion. The wretched man clung to one idea which came back to him endlessly: I will not go the limit, and when I am rich and completely independent I'll be able, quickly and easily, to repair the wrongs I have done.

He was at that point when we heard him utter the sophisms about the power of gold and the need to be rich in order to do good in the world of politics. Was he already lost at the time of his conversation with Lamirande? For a very long time he had been sorely tempted by the demon that caused one of the Twelve to fall. However, as no one is ever tested beyond the limit of his endurance, he could have resisted this formidable assault if he had only followed the sound advice of his true friend: a short and fervent prayer, one single cry of distress to the Heart of Jesus, and he would have been saved.

When the disciples were about to be engulfed in the waves, it was a prayer of only six words that took them out of danger: 'Save us, Lord; we are perishing.'

But a gesture of pride stifled the cry that was already on his lips. It was a last grace, and he refused it.

When he left Lamirande, he was entirely under the Tempter's sway. A curious rage against all his old friends, particularly the closest one of all, had taken hold of his soul. He now loathed Lamirande as much as he had once admired and esteemed him. Previously, despite weakness and adversity he had tried to copy the young politician's virtues – his unselfishness and his strength of character. But these salutary aspirations had suddenly changed and become a cruel and atrocious jealousy. He was too lazy to raise himself to the heights his old friend had attained, and so he tried to drag him along into the gutter where he himself was about to plunge. Realizing that he was powerless to bring this Christian soul down to his own level, he was determined to do him as much harm as possible.

He was in this state of mind when he met Montarval at the club that it was one of his bad habits to frequent, under the pretext of gathering news and ideas.

'Well, Saint-Simon,' Montarval began, 'how are you getting along with your high-standard journalism? Marvellously well, I expect, because they say that when one works for your God everything else follows: fancy clothes, expensive furniture, pure-blooded horses. Is that really true?'

Rather than make a proud reply to this blasphemous joking, the unfortunate man blushed and stammered,

'You shouldn't interpret the Bible so literally – there are many allusions and allegories in it. All I can say is that the kind of journalism I have been practising does not, unfortunately, make a fortune for me. It's a pity, because I do love the profession.'

'Perhaps there is some way to make the profession more lucrative,' Montarval replied, darting a piercing glance at Saint-Simon.

The journalist, disturbed, lowered his eyes and murmured 'perhaps' in a voice that could barely be heard. But it was enough for Montarval to be assured of the value of his man.

'Come over to my house,' he said. 'We can talk more comfortably there.'

Saint-Simon followed him and a few minutes later they were climbing the steps to the young Frenchman's sumptuous dwelling. It was a princely mansion overlooking Frontenac Terrace and the St Lawrence. Montarval had a magnificent view from his windows: on the right, Saint-Romuald and the countryside to the south, bounded in the distance by a fringe of blue mountains; opposite, Notre-Dame and Saint-Joseph-de-Lévis, and on the left, the Ile d'Orléans and the pleasant hill of Beaupré backed against the Laurentians. The house was furnished in oriental luxury: everything in it breathed softness and sensual delight. For Saint-Simon it was a dream come true.

Montarval took him to a vast room that was half salon, half office. A valet, answering his call, brought wine and cigarettes.

'Now,' he said, 'we can talk without fear of being disturbed. So you tell me that high-principled journalism doesn't pay well. A wise man once said that virtue without money is a useless piece of furniture.'

'As a matter of fact,' Saint-Simon replied, 'the press in this country is paralyzed by a lack of resources. And all our public figures are paralyzed too. In a country with a constitution like ours you need a fortune if you want to pursue a career in journalism or politics. You're a rich man: why don't you go into politics yourself? You'd soon make your mark.'

'I've thought about it; as a matter of fact I'm considering it even now,' replied Montarval. 'It would probably be easy for me to get elected. But an MP has to be very sure of the support of one of the newspapers if he wants to get ahead in a hurry. You may say it would be easy enough for me to start one, but I must admit that I don't care much for business. If I went into journalism I'd be afraid of losing my shirt. But I would be prepared to pay a flat fee to guarantee the support of a newspaper, without having to risk my entire fortune.'

Montarval paused to let his words sink in. He offered Saint-Simon a glass of wine, which was seized nervously and drained in one gulp. Montarval, slowly spinning his Tokay, went on:

'Couldn't we come to some kind of understanding? You're a journalist, you know your trade, but you lack money. I have the money but not the experience. We both have something to offer, but if we want our respective talents to produce something useful we'll have to put them together. What do you think?'

'It seems like an excellent idea. Will you be kind enough to tell me the details of your plan?'

'Oh, it's very simple. I'll give you, let's say, twenty thousand dollars; or rather, to make it more orderly, I'll lend you the money, but with the formal understanding that I won't ask to be repaid as long as your newspaper satisfies me.'

'But what line would the newspaper have to take to satisfy you? Would its tone have to be completely changed?'

'Not at all. I would rarely ask for changes, because if I run it will be as a Conservative.'

'Conservative!' Saint-Simon exclaimed, astonished. 'But I had always thought that even though you weren't active politically your ideas were a bit...'

'Advanced? Youthful folly! If you really want to accomplish something you have to pull in your horns and become a conservative, like it or not. If I want to have a newspaper at my disposal, it is simply to have my speeches printed and perhaps read something complimentary about myself from time to time — without overdoing it, of course.'

'If those are your conditions,' said Saint-Simon, who had become rather pale, 'I see no reason to disagree with your proposal.'

'Very well, let's conclude our agreement right now. I shall give you a cheque for the amount we mentioned and you'll give me your note.'

Half an hour later Saint-Simon left Montarval's house. He had sold himself, become a slave. He understood perfectly what he had done and was profoundly disgusted with himself. But the demon of money never left his side, and it made him say such things as, 'After all, you aren't being asked to make such a great sacrifice. A few bits of publicity here and there, that's all. Most of the other papers do the same thing.'

'But what will you do if you're asked to commit some wicked deed?' his guardian angel asked.

'You'll pay back the money and that will be that,' the demon murmured.

'And what if you've spent the money? Will you be able to pay it back then?'

'Put the money in the bank and just use the interest. That way you'll always be able to honour the note if someone asks you to do something that goes against your conscience.'

This last argument from the demon outweighed the angel's warnings, and Saint-Simon deposited the price of his freedom in the bank. And the demon, who was a clever little fellow, left him in peace for a few days. When the edge had been taken off the first horror that had invaded the journalist's soul, the evil spirit took over once again.

'You should improve your office and your house so that you can entertain more stylishly. And your table, your cellar, even your clothes leave something to be desired.'

'What about the note?' the angel asked in a very low voice. 'How will you pay it back if you're asked to do something dishonourable?'

'Oh, it would be easy to borrow the money if the public sees that your business looks prosperous. Money attracts money. Besides,' the evil spirit added boldly, 'you can trust in Providence.'

'You must trust in Providence, but not tempt it,' replied the angel.

But as he had done the first time, Saint-Simon listened to the Tempter, and giving into his natural inclinations, in a few days he had spent several thousand dollars.

Montarval, who was having his victim's every movement watched, judged that the moment was ripe to take the next step. When he met Saint-Simon at the club again he said,

'I'm not completely happy with the tone of your paper, and as you undoubtedly don't want to change it because of your inflexible principles, perhaps it would be better to cancel our agreement before it's too late.'

The journalist reacted to these words as though he had been slapped. What would he not have given to be able to throw the cursed gold in the face of the man who had corrupted him! For a moment he thought of breaking away from Montarval, borrowing the money, and paying his debt. Or if he could not do that, to let his seducer take his presses and equipment. He felt a violent longing for freedom and a profound disgust for the ignoble slavery into which he saw himself descending. But it was a purely human impulse and consequently without real force. The difficulties of his position, the sacrifices he would have to make, both of which the demon had caused to grow immoderately, terrified him.

'Come now,' he told himself, 'no foolishness. Let's at least see what he wants of me.' Then, aloud, 'In what way does the paper not please you, M. Montarval?'

'As you know,' he replied, 'I have become a conservative. As a result, I support the status quo. And I am equally opposed to both legislative union and separation. Yours is a separatist paper and you know as well as I that that will have to stop.'

'Could I simply avoid the question for a while?'

'That's not good enough. I need positive actions, not negative ones. I really think we should cancel our agreement. It's quite simple – just give me back my cheque and I'll return your note. We can still be friends.'

'But you're asking me to oppose the separatist movement that I've always supported so enthusiastically! That is what sailors call tacking – it's a manoeuvre that is easy enough to carry out in a boat, but in journalism, while it's done often enough, it is always very unpleasant.'

'Precisely,' said Montarval, 'and it is because I can tell that your principles will be an obstacle to this operation that I suggest we break our agreement immediately. When can you pay me back? Or perhaps you could simply return the cheque if you still have it. I don't want to press you – this is Wednesday. Shall we say next Saturday morning?'

Saint-Simon had another movement of revolt, but weaker than the first. The demon whispered in his ear,

'After all, it's a purely political question. Many good Catholics are opposed to separatism and in favour of the status quo. It will be easy to find some specious reasons to explain the change in your point of view.'

'Wretched man,' said the angel, 'do you not see that you are sliding rapidly into the abyss? Do you not see that what might be an honest opinion for others would be the fruit of corruption and betrayal for you? It is because such methods are used to preserve the status quo that this solution must contain some hidden trap. Besides, you know the man who is tempting you. You know he is a despicable person.'

Montarval stared fixedly at his victim. It seemed that he was following the vicissitudes of the battle that was being fought in the weakened soul of the pale, defeated-looking journalist.

'Very well,' he said, rising as though to leave. 'It is agreed that you will repay me the $20,000 before noon on Saturday. I am always at home in the morning.'

'Wait!' cried the unfortunate journalist. 'I've thought it over and I will make the changes you want. One can certainly change one's opinion on this question. I shall gradually come out in favour of the status quo.'

A diabolical smile twisted the lips of his tempter, but Saint-Simon could see nothing as his eyes were lowered.

'I don't ask you to do that much,' said Montarval. 'I want you to fight the separatists, but I don't want you to give your support to the status quo; not for the moment, at any rate. And to make your task easier, I want you to argue against separatism not by criticising it but by exaggerating its features, turning it into a bogey for the English and compromising it in the eyes of the French Canadians. You understand what I'm saying, don't you?'

'Perfectly.'

'Very well! I hope that from now on your paper will carry some very strong articles in favour of separation. If the idea doesn't suit you, you know the alternative. Good luck!'

And on that note they parted.

From then on Saint-Simon gave up the struggle. He surrendered to his infamous role with a zeal that equalled Montarval's admiration for him. He went from exaggeration to exaggeration, from excess to excess, until he finally wrote the article that Lamirande publicly disavowed before Parliament.

Lamirande's action brought a storm of abuse from the fallen journalist, who called his old friend faint-hearted, cowardly, a bleeding heart, a traitor to his race. He went so far in his cynicism as to say that Lamirande had sold himself heart and soul to the English.

He who is mighty in speech is known from afar.
ECCLESIASTICUS 21:7

9

THE BOMB HAD BURST. Sir Henry had presented his constitutional bills and debate had begun.

The prime minister opened fire with a speech that was short, syrupy, and full of cunning. In it he attempted to conceal the poisonous aspects of his work beneath flowers of rhetoric. He even offered very flattering compliments to the French Canadians, heaping praise on them and recalling the outstanding events in their history. He ended his harangue by expressing the hope that when all the trouble was over his bill would be passed. Peace, prosperity, and the country's future greatness demanded it.

The prime minister had barely uttered his last word when Lamirande was on his feet, his Christian and patriotic indignation terrible to behold. For two and a half hours he spoke, thundered, raged. Under the power of his logic all the perfidy of this constitution that had been drawn up in the political backrooms was brought to light. He exposed all the traps and ruses that a devilishly clever hand had concealed in every article of the project. He demonstrated that under the proposed regime provincial authority would be only a hollow phrase; that the legislatures, stripped of their autonomy, would be at the mercy of the central government; that the provincial courts would lose all their prestige; that the Treasury Department in Ottawa would absorb all the sources of revenue; that the state would take over education under the pretext of encouraging it; that French could be abolished as an official language, even in the province of Quebec, if a majority in the Commons so desired; in a word, that the country was being led directly but hypocritically to legislative union.

As he tore aside veils and uncovered all the government's ruses, both the MPs and the public who were overflowing the galleries were affected by a growing sense of discomfort. When he had finished speaking, the faces of the ministers and their chief supporters were filled with consternation. There was total silence, followed by a dull murmuring. The members formed groups, worried and distressed. No one rose to speak.

Finally Sir Henry Marwood, very disturbed and barely able to contain himself, advised the Speaker that it was six o'clock. The House rose amidst great confusion. Most of the French MPs, and Lawrence Houghton and his friends surrounded Lamirande, congratulating him warmly.

Sir Henry glanced at the tumultuous scene and his political experience told him that Lamirande had won, that his bill would surely be rejected. He hurried out of the Chamber and met Montarval in the corridor.

'We're lost,' said the prime minister in a low voice. 'The bill will never be passed. Lamirande killed it with his first shot; we forced the issue too much. What do we do now?'

'Quite simple,' replied Montarval. 'You shall dissolve the House this evening. Go to Rideau Hall right now and advise the Governor-General. He must be here at eight o'clock to notify the Members.'

'But that would be a *coup d'état!*'

'Probably, but now is the time to act boldly. This is the only resource we have left, and we have to make good use of it. Besides, you have a ready-made pretext for both the government and the public: you have encountered unexpected opposition and you want to consult the electorate.'

'And if they go against us?'

'We have to take measures to be sure that does not happen. We have to spread money with both hands; empty the treasury if necessary; stir up fanaticism in the English provinces and count on corruption and party loyalty in Quebec. Be bold, I tell you!'

'But I'm going to have a ministerial crisis on my hands! After Lamirande's speech all the French ministers will resign.'

'Let them. I'll replace one of them, and you can find two ambitious imbeciles for the other portfolios. Besides, things will calm down, because we're going to quiet people's emotions with gold. Don't lose your composure, and get moving!'

The prime minister followed his advice and at eight o'clock that night the House was dissolved.

For I am ... a man who is weak.
WISDOM 9:5

10

SIR VINCENT JOLIBOIS, a colleague of Sir Henry, turned in his portfolio in a gesture of pure indignation. It was the first time he had acted forcefully in more than a quarter of a century of political life. It was also the last. He was not used to thinking for himself, acting independently, forming manly resolutions and sticking to them; the feeble character that nature had bestowed on him had gradually become completely atrophied.

When he left the emotional session in which Lamirande had unmasked the prime minister's perfidy, Sir Vincent, totally distressed by his fiery words, had gone to Sir Henry and asked him to accept his resignation. If he had met some slight resistance he might have reconsidered, but the old chieftain acted indignantly, as though he were the victim. He accepted his colleague's resignation forthwith, and at the same time gave him to believe that his conduct was totally improper. 'Should officers abandon ship when a storm is raging?' he asked. 'If you find my policy unacceptable you should have said so before, rather than wait until it had been submitted to the House.'

His reproach was justified. Sir Vincent had known of the bill but he had not realized its perfidy. He was, therefore, in a false position. He left Sir Henry with a troubled soul; he had no portfolio and he felt that he had not carried out his duties properly.

When Lamirande learned of Sir Vincent's resignation, he went immediately to look for him.

'I've learned of your resignation, Sir Vincent,' he said as he entered the ex-minister's office. 'I have come to offer you my respectful congratulations and to invite you to become the head of the separatist movement.'

'Yes, I have resigned, unfortunately. I mean, I *had* to do it because I cannot take responsibility for the government's policy in the face of the interpretation the House seemed to give it after your own speech.'

'But is that not the only interpretation possible?'

'Yes, I suppose so. But all the same it is most unfortunate. Now everyone is all worked up and the Conservative party is exposed to disaster. Don't you think, my dear Lamirande, that it would have been better not to criticize the government so forcefully? It would probably have been quite easy to come to an agreement and introduce certain amendments, certain guarantees for our province. I don't deny that you spoke very well indeed, but diplomacy never hurts, you know. This is all most unfortunate.'

'But don't you see, Sir Vincent, that a few amendments could not have safeguarded our position? The bill is fundamentally bad, rotten to the core. It's nothing but a trap. Since you resigned you must have thought that yourself.'

'Yes, I did think it was a trap. The bill is certainly a bad one, but we might still have reached an understanding. Now it's too late; the deed is done. People are all worked up, my resignation has been accepted, I am no longer a minister, I can do nothing.'

'Sir Vincent, there is a great deal that you could do, precisely because you are no longer a minister. You can lead the province of Quebec. Aside from the radicals, who are a relatively small group, all French Canada will rally around you if you resolutely wave the national flag.'

'But this nationalist movement is upsetting everybody. The Conservatives are suffering as a result of it. I myself am basically a Conservative, and I have no sympathy for anything extreme or revolutionary; I believe in moderation and conciliation. Then we must consider the English and the Protestants – we must not irritate them. Saint-Simon goes too far, yet he claims to belong to your party. Believe me, M. Lamirande, it is much wiser to accept the status quo. It's part way between legislative union and separation; everyone should be satisfied with that.'

'But can you guarantee that we will have a true status quo? Aren't you afraid that Sir Henry will get the better of us with his scheming and manage to impose a disguised form of legislative union on us if we deal with him on his own ground?'

'I don't deny that Sir Henry is very skilful, and I can't promise that I could prevent him from playing some trick on us. Perhaps if I had remained in the cabinet ... but I fear that now it will be too difficult to obtain an acceptable version of his Confederation bill. It would have required a great deal of diplomacy. We must protect our rights, and yet some sacrifices must be made. What a mess!'

'But since the *status quo* policy presents so many perils and problems, would it not be better to adopt another? You know what the separatists want — the real ones, that is, not Saint-Simon! We want a just and reasonable policy, one that is clearly defined in such a way that it could not conceal any unpleasant surprises.'

'But it is so contrary to the traditions of the Conservative party; it is truly revolutionary. What will become of the great federal Conservative party if your policy prevails?'

'Do you put party interests above those of your own country?'

'No. But is your policy a practical one? Can the province of Quebec form an independent country?'

'There is nothing to prevent it. Thanks to the fact that a large number of our people have returned from the United States, we have a homogeneous population of more than five million. Is that not enough to form an autonomous state, living its own life?'

'You want to form a French and Catholic state: a New France.'

'Exactly. Our people have aspired towards that goal as long as we have existed, and Divine Providence has led us toward it across a thousand obstacles. The predestined hour is sounding at last. It is time for us to take our place among the nations of the earth.'

'And what will you do with the Protestants and the English who live among us?'

'As you know, their number has decreased so rapidly that it is easy to foresee the day when we will all have the same language and religion. But as we await that day, we will treat the minority with the greatest generosity, just as we have always done.'

'You would like a state religion. That is hardly compatible with freedom of conscience and freedom of worship, which are at the basis of modern society.'

'But not a very solid basis, you must admit. Everything is crumbling away. If the state were to recognize one true religion, it would not exclude fair and civil tolerance of other forms of worship, if such tolerance were necessary to avoid a greater evil.'

'I don't want to argue these questions with you. Perhaps you are right, in theory, but I cannot put myself at the head of your movement. It is contrary to party traditions. What would I do if the bill failed? I would be compromised forever and I would be reduced to political impotence. Can you not find a middle course, something that would be acceptable to everyone?'

Lamirande realized that it would be a waste of time to argue further with this man who lacked both will and devotion, so he left and went to look for his friend Leverdier.

'You were right,' he said. 'There's nothing to be done with Sir Vincent. But we still need a leader. Have the other two French ministers resigned?'

'No, and they won't either. I've just seen the editor of *Le Mercure* coming out of a meeting with them. It's hard to believe, but they are staying in the cabinet. For patriotic reasons, of course! If they left their posts, you see, Sir Henry would replace them with English Canadians. By staying, they may be able to introduce some amendments to the bill. Brilliant, isn't it?'

'Our poor country!' sighed Lamirande. 'No men and no leaders.'

'We don't need all that many leaders. One will be enough. And while I don't want to offend your modesty, our leader is you.'

'I a leader?'

'Yes, you, beyond any doubt. You are the one who will lead us to victory if we are destined to attain it, or to defeat if that is God's will. But you are the only one who can lead our little army. It's useless to look elsewhere.'

'But the masses won't want to follow me, and we need a majority in Parliament.'

'You must do your duty. God will look after the rest.'

'You're right, my friend, we should not look for human leaders. We lack everything on that side. We have hardly any political prestige, true enough, but we shall do our duty. We shall explain to the people of our province as clearly and energetically as possible all the perils of the situation and how, with the grace of God, we can overcome them.'

O faithless and perverse generation.
LUKE 9:41

11

A FEW DAYS LATER Lamirande, Leverdier, and a small group of friends, all worthwhile men, though little known in political circles, published a manifesto. Calm in tone but firmly worded, it was distributed all across the province. This appeal produced a tremendous emotion. It looked at first as if the entire Conservative party was going to rally around Lamirande. From the beginning of the crisis the French-Catholic press had unanimously denounced Sir Henry's bill as a treacherous, infamous outrage against French Canada. Not even *Le Mercure* could ignore public opinion; it published violent denunciations of the prime minister. Meetings were held everywhere. The government's policy was vigourously condemned and the need for Quebec to withdraw from Confederation was loudly proclaimed. If the election had been held two weeks after Parliament was dissolved not one of Sir Henry's supporters would have been elected in the province.

Almost as soon as Sir Vincent had resigned, it was announced that Montarval would replace him. This choice increased the general discontent; his old dealings with the radicals were no secret, and conservatives distrusted him because of them. His lack of religion made him even more suspect in the eyes of the Catholics. *La Libre Pensée* and the other revolutionary papers tried in vain to repudiate the new minister, calling him a retrograde, a reactionary, and even a clerical, but they failed to change public opinion, which was increasingly opposed to the cabinet.

For two weeks the ministers gave no sign of life. They were not seen anywhere, did not communicate with the press, did not even let themselves be interviewed. It was a clever tactic, for by keeping quiet they avoided adding fuel to the fire they had lit. It was certianly not a straw fire; but even the hardest wood, even coal itself, is finally consumed. The strongest warrior is partially disarmed against those who do not defend themselves.

Only Saint-Simon's fury continued to mount in a crescendo. *Le Progrès* was no longer a newspaper but an erupting volcano, vomiting a continuous stream of flame, smoke, ash, boiling water, burning stones, and lava. And, most of all, mud. Saint-Simon piled mountains of it on the heads of the ministers. He used epithets that were so insulting, so outrageous that even those who were the most indignant finally said that he had gone too far. He called for a virtual war of extermination against the English Canadians and the Protestants. His articles were reprinted by the English Canadian press in the other provinces, and were considered to be a faithful echo of the feelings and aspirations of the mass of French Canadians. Lamirande and Leverdier tried with all their strength to repudiate the atrocious statements that appeared in *Le Progrès,* but their efforts were in vain, and they could not undo completely the damage that had been done. In two weeks Saint-Simon had inflicted incalculable harm upon the French-Canadian cause throughout the English-Canadian provinces.

Despite this, Quebec itself remained united. The majorities that the ministers could have secured in the other provinces would probably not be large enough to overcome the compact delegation from French Canada. It was necessary, therefore, to destroy at any cost the union that had been established among our compatriots.

Oh the cursed power of gold! 'Auri sacra fames!' the Latin poet exclaimed two thousand years ago. And human nature has not changed since then; the miserable thirst for wealth is still our most shameful infirmity. There is no doubt that lewdness, pride, and intemperance cause terrible ravages and countless victims. But is there any passion so degrading to man as cupidity? Is there any other vice that leads him into such bottomless abysses of infamy? Do not forget that it was his thirst for gold that led Judas to commit his crime. The Blessed Saviour had chosen him and raised him to the supreme dignity of an Apostle: he was destined to become one of the pillars of the Church, one of the evangelizers of the world, one of our fathers in faith. He must, then, have possessed real qualities that led the Divine Master to single him out. But he had one defect: an inordinate love of wealth. And despite the superabundant graces he must have received during the three years he spent close to Jesus, this defect led him to commit the most unbelievably monstrous crime the world has ever known: monstrous because never had we seen and never will we witness such a criminal act against such a Person; unbelievable because such a puny motive had never led to the commission of so great a crime. Judas could have had no hatred to appease, no insult to avenge, no triumph to hope for. He had given up his Master – for whom he must, however, have felt some love – for the miserable sum of thirty pieces of silver, the price of one small field!

Huysmans says that this power of money over the souls of men either is diabolical or inexplicable.

By considering the crime of Judas we can form some idea of the frightful power that gold can wield over the human heart.

Montarval and Sir Henry Marwood knew this power; it was one of the things they most relied upon.

Two weeks after the House was dissolved Lamirande and Leverdier met in the editorial offices of *La Nouvelle-France*. They had worked well, each in his own way. The journalist had written a brilliant, solid series of articles that exposed the situation with strength and dignity. Lamirande had appeared at many public meetings, electrifying his listeners with heated speeches and an enlightened, ardent patriotism.

'Have you seen *Le Mercure* for the last three days?' Leverdier asked his friend.

'I must confess that since the start of the campaign I have hardly looked at any paper except yours. What does the God of commerce – and thieves – have to say? *Le Mercure* is a curious name for a Catholic paper, isn't it!'

'The name is fore-ordained. What does the God of commerce have to say? Nothing. But he does a great deal. He's looking after what interests him: commerce, business.'

'What do you mean? I don't understand you at all. I seem to remember seeing some reprints of articles from *Le Mercure* in your own paper; they were quite well written.'

'You have, but that has all stopped. The day before yesterday there wasn't a word on the situation but there was a long article about the electric light monopoly in Montreal. Yesterday, still not a word about the crisis, but a long and learned report on grain trading in Chicago. And here is today's issue: still not a single reference to what is on everybody's mind, but they go on for columns about railways.'

'Perhaps the editors are just exhausted. Not everyone has a mind as fertile as yours.'

'If the editors have run out of things to say, at least they could take things from other papers. They could let their reporters have their say. There's no more coverage of public meetings, just a few lines at the bottom of "Recent Events." If a stranger picked up the last three issues of *Le Mercure* he'd have no idea that we are going through a crisis that is endangering our national future. My dear friend, you know human nature well enough to know it's not a simple question of intellectual exhaustion. It's their hearts that are worn out.'

'I must say, it does't look good.'

'Not good at all. And here's a note I've just received from a friend in Montreal. He says, "You have probably noticed *Le Mercure*'s silence over the last three days, and you probably suspect the reason: the people who run the paper are frozen. The editor went to Ottawa a few days ago and I know that he had long talks with various ministers. Since his return the paper has adopted the interesting stand you have been seeing and I have it on reliable authority that the paper is doing a great deal of government printing; their presses are running day and night." That's what my Montreal correspondent has to say. As you see, the God of commerce is looking after things nicely.'

'In other words those wretched fellows have sold themselves body and soul to the government.'

'They call that "getting explanations".'

'My God!' Lamirande exclaimed. 'Then You will never have pity on us. Alas! all we deserve is Your hardships because we know of no greater sacrifices to make for You. We don't even know how to devote ourselves to defending our own interests when they can't be translated into figures. And it's all the result of the practical education we've had inflicted on us for the past twenty-five years. Words like honour, national dignity, patriotism and devotion have become meaningless for many people.'

'But there is still much good to be found among our rural people,' said Leverdier. 'You must realize it more than ever now.'

'That's so, there still is some good there, and faith still exists. But there is apathy too, even in the present effervescence. You have the feeling that it would take very little to compromise everything, stop this patriotic fervour and hand us over to our enemies, quite powerless. The masses are indignant with the government, but they don't see what we do — I mean you and I and a few others. They don't see that government policy is inspired by the Freemasons. We need something very dazzling to open their eyes. We'd have to catch the Masons red-handed to show how they are plotting our ruin. You and I know that infernal sect is at the bottom of this crisis, but how can we prove it? How can we convince the people? We need *undeniable facts* if we want to stir up the people. *Inductive proof* isn't enough. What I wouldn't give to tear aside the veil that conceals the lodges' perfidy from our compatriots!'

'I've often thought of that,' replied the journalist. 'If I were rich I would gladly spend my entire fortune to make a golden key that would open all the lodges in the country.

'I don't really trust in gold as a power for good. It is all-powerful where evil is concerned, but Our Lord and the Apostles didn't make great use of it for founding the Church and converting the world. It was through devotion and sacrifice that they changed the face of the earth. If we have no more success, my dear friend, we must realize that it is because we do not know how to sacrifice ourselves.'

'But without singing our own praises,' said Leverdier, 'it seems to me that we can claim to have worked with true devotion and unselfishness for the cause that we defend. Neither you nor I nor the others I could name have any motive of personal advancement.'

'Of course we are not selfish, but we must not confuse that with the spirit of sacrifice. A man is unselfish when he lends his own money without asking for interest; but is he making a true sacrifice? I'm afraid that if we look at ourselves closely, we will see that our spirit of sacrifice is no more than a very ordinary virtue. Let's suppose that during our conversation an angel from God suddenly came to tell us that our cause would triumph if we consented to give up our lives or our honour or even our health; if we would consent to be blind or mute for the rest of our lives. What would our answer be?'

'I know that you would consent to any sacrifice.'

'Alas, I am not nearly as certain as you!'

On the fourth day *Le Mercure* broke its silence and devoted one article to the burning question of the day. Black treason leaped from the opening lines. Here is the article:

'For more than two weeks the winds of revolution have been blowing through our province. We admit that we allowed ourselves to drift along with the current, with the general panic. Although we did not go as far as some of our colleagues, we have written things that we now regret. After three days of silence and reflection we see that it is our duty to retrace our steps and we do so now, courageously. Retracing one's steps is not an activity that is flattering to a journalist's self-respect, but it is sometimes a duty, a duty that is as imperative as it is disagreeable. When one whose mission it is to guide public opinion realizes that he is giving the wrong directions it would be a crime if he were to persevere, through pride, along the ill-starred path he has set out upon. We shall not commit such a crime. We shall do our duty, no matter how painful it may be.

'What will be the outcome of this feverish activity in which our province has been plunged for the past two weeks? What will be the outcome of the campaign in which we have been so thoughtlessly engaged? It will come to nothing or it will bring about civil war. It is because this answer has struck our minds as powerfully as sunlight strikes the eyes that we have decided to shout to our compatriots, "Stop while there is still time!"

'The violent language of some of the agitators among us has been very irritating to the English provinces.

'We cannot hope that the politics of separatism will receive the slightest support from them. In the new House there will not be ten MPs from the other provinces who will consent to our leaving Confederation. Even if our own 65 MPs were unanimous in calling for it, they would not be able to obtain it through constitutional means.

'Therefore, as we said earlier, the ill-considered campaign in which we are engaged will inevitably come to nothing or it will lead to civil war. Civil war is unthinkable. Why, then, should we give ourselves so much trouble when we know that it will lead to nothing?

'It is true that the government's plan is unacceptable in its present form. Several details will have to be modified. The province should demand guarantees, but at the same time, if we want to be of real use to our country, if we want to be practical patriots, not visionaries and utopians, we must accept the government bill in principle and give up any ideas of separation. Whatever we do, we cannot simply put aside the federal union of the provinces. Hence, the only sensible policy is to work to make that union as acceptable as possible.

This clever and treacherous article, probably written by Montarval himself, caused a great stir all across the province. It set the tone for nearly all the newspapers that had previously supported the government, and were now re-entering the ranks one after the other, repeating the sophisms of *Le Mercure* with a few changes and amplifications. Only *La Nouvelle-France* and *Le Drapeau National*, in Montreal and Quebec City, now supported separation. Saint-Simon's *Le Progrès catholique* continued to compromise the cause of which it claimed to be the only true supporter. The radical papers still openly demanded legislative union, but their voices were weak. The government's perfidious policy of legislative union skillfully disguised under the name and appearance of Confederation presented the real danger to the national cause.

The ministerial journalists had re-entered the ranks along with a large number of chiefs, sub-chiefs, captains, and lieutenants. It was difficult to hold public meetings that were hostile to government policy. Speakers failed to show up, some claiming that they were sick or too busy, others declaring cynically that they had changed their minds, that *Le Mercure's* ideas seemed sound to them. Of all those who were used to speaking out, Lamirande and Leverdier were virtually the only ones to continue the struggle. But even they could not be everywhere at once and a number of assemblies called by the national committee had to be cancelled while others took place but worked to the advantage of the fickle. The French ministers began to appear in some parts of the province; they were hissed, but two weeks earlier they would have been stoned.

However, despite the sudden change on the part of the journalists, political speakers, and campaign organizers, the government still did not dare to risk the supreme battle. Their writs, which were awaited from day to day, did not arrive. Whole layers of the population were still indignant at the ministers and strongly attached to

Lamirande, who inspired great confidence wherever he went. The ground was not ready to assure the ministers of victory. As long as Lamirande was active the government could not be sure of triumph. He was an obstacle who had to be struck down. But how?

Their wine is the poison of serpents
and the cruel venom of asps.
DEUTERONOMY 32:33

12

MODERN SCIENCE HAS PUT MURDEROUS WEAPONS into the hands of wicked men. At the end of the nineteenth century violent explosives capable of splitting mountains were much in vogue among evil-doers. Fifty years ago bombs exploded frequently. But bombs were brutal and inconvenient. If they spread terror and death they were also fatal to those who used them, because those men inevitably fell into the hands of the law or of outraged mobs. In the middle of the twentieth century bombs had gone out of style. There had been much progress in the art of killing. Of course subtle poisons had always existed, ptomaines that caused death without leaving a trace; and many crimes could be attributed to these mysterious toxins. In the past, however, only a small number of people had access to these redoubtable substances. Today, science is democratic; according to modern ideas people need chemistry more than theology; public laboratories are more useful than churches. To know God, His laws and His greatness, the marvels of the spiritual world, man's supernatural destiny, and the actions necessary to attain it — such simple yet sublime knowledge is out of date and no longer necessary to mankind. But chemistry is a science that everyone needs to know! What is the result? With the progress and popularization of chemistry, bombs have been replaced, to the assassin's advantage, by microbe cultures that can destroy their victims with the symptoms of cholera, typhus, smallpox, or consumption. By crossing different strains of bacilli we have even invented new diseases. A few drops poured into a drink may cause the most natural kind of death. Learned scientists may be amazed to see the number of sporadic cases of violent illnesses that had previously occurred only in epidemics. They may wonder where the infections originate, even suspect that a crime has been committed. But they cannot supply the slightest indication to help the law root out the cause. Someone whose disappearance was useful to someone else is suddenly stricken with a contagious disease that does not exist anywhere in the area. Doctors may well have suspicions, but to worried magistrates they can say only, 'He died of natural causes.'

At the back of a vast and richly furnished room, half salon and half office, it was decided one night that the troublemaker Lamirande was to die of the new fever that was puzzling doctors on both sides of the Atlantic. The Executive Committee was not present; the Master had made the decision alone. One of his creatures was given the task of carrying out the execution at the first favourable moment.

'I have to go to Ottawa tomorrow,' Lamirande told his wife one evening. 'There was a message from Houghton about some important business.'

'Shall I go with you? Something tells me you will be exposed to great danger on this trip.'

'Did you have a bad dream?' Lamirande asked with a smile.

'No, and I don't believe in dreams anyway. But I do believe in presentiments, or in those strange warnings the angels send us. Will you let me come with you?'

'But my dear Marguerite, if there is some misfortune in the air would it not be better for you to stay here so that if something does happen to me you will be left to bring up our child?'

'But something irresistible tells me that it is my duty to go with you, that I can somehow protect you against some danger. I beg you, do not refuse me; let me go with you.'

'Since you insist, my dear wife, you may come with me. Anyway, a short trip will do you good and help you get rid of these gloomy ideas. As far as I am concerned, although I am a strong believer in the angels and their warnings, I believe no less strongly in the natural influence of the body over the soul. A slight indisposition is enough to make us see everything in the darkest light. Yes, we shall go to Ottawa together.'

There was not the slightest incident during the trip.

Marguerite's vague foreboding was dissipated like a cloud. Returning to Quebec, Lamirande and his wife, along with the other travellers, were having a meal at the station in Trois-Rivières, as the train had been delayed because of the snow. They had just sat down when a young boy, unknown to them and poorly dressed, who had been standing near the dining room door, uttered a horrible cry and fell down as though struck by lightning. Everyone got up instinctively, except for one man sitting near Lamirande who stayed in his chair. No one noticed him. No one saw him quickly pass his hand over the cup of tea that had just been set down at Lamirande's place. Lamirande himself had gone to the young boy, whose body was contorted with convulsions. Marguerite, the other passengers, and the staff followed him. No one paid any attention to the man who stayed alone at his table.

'He's coming to already,' Lamirande said a moment later. 'I've never seen an epileptic attack that looked so serious disappear so quickly. It's really amazing.'

Everyone returned to his table.

'Look, they made a mistake,' said Marguerite; 'they brought coffee for me and tea for you. Let's exchange cups.'

Lamirande gave Marguerite his cup and took hers. It was the only incident of the whole trip.

Once again, the richly furnished room, half salon, half office. It is night. The Master is speaking:

'One bit of negligence, one bit of awkwardness on the part of the waiter, and he escaped death. But at what a price! Perhaps it is better like this: Eblis must have inspired the error himself. He will see his wife die, and all his art will be powerless to save her. The pain and fever that were destined for him would have been sheer pleasure compared to the moral tortures he will have to endure. And added to that will be his despair at being unable to leave his wife to take part in the battle. Yes, it is definitely better like this. Great Eblis knows better than his servants! But this evil man must still be beaten. It is probably better that he will not die, since Eblis has spared him. If he were dead, his memory could be harmful. People might even be suspicious about how he died. But his influence must be destroyed forever and his compatriots must cease to trust him. That will be a hundred times more effective than his death.'

Thus the Master spoke to himself in the silence of the night.

Calumnia conturbat sapientem, et perdet robur cordis illius.
(Calumny confounds the wise man, and shakes even a heart of oak.)
ECCLESIASTICUS 7:7

13

OH THE POWER OF SLANDER! As the Latin poet said, the just man could be crushed but not frightened by the ruins of the universe. But a perfidious word, a simple gesture, even silence can, by damaging a man's reputation, fill his soul with unspeakable agonies.

Two days after the Master's monologue, *La Libre Pensée* published these remarks:

> As our readers know, we have no sympathy for the policies of the government and its leader, Sir Henry Marwood. But he is at least a gentleman who deserves our respect. If we dispute his bills it is because of our convictions, but we know someone else who fights them only out of spite. M. Lamirande, that great friend of the clergy, could give us some very specific information on this subject. If he does not wish to do so, we shall be obliged to pass on the information ourselves.

Lamirande did not deign to reply to this vague insinuation. He did not even know what the sectarian journalist was alluding to, his own motives were so pure. Leverdier suspected what was coming.

'My poor friend, they are going to accuse you of wanting to sell out to Sir Henry,' he said.

'But that's impossible! Besides, even though their political dealings are so underhanded, Sir Henry is a gentleman, and he would deny it if anyone accused me of such things in so many words.'

'These people are capable of doing anything to ruin you.'

'I think you are something of a pessimist.'

Leverdier was not a pessimist, however. Two or three days later, *La Libre Pensée* made a formal accusation. It declared, with a wealth of details as to the day, time, and place where the conversation had taken place, that during a reception given by Sir Henry, Lamirande had told the prime minister that he would support the government bill, but only in return for the promise of a position at the consulate in Paris or Washington. All this by a servant of Sir Henry's named Duthier. The conversation had taken place near a window where Duthier had come to rest for a moment. Hidden by the curtains he had heard everything without being seen. At first he had kept quiet, but as he saw the unjust war that Lamirande was waging against his beloved employer, Duthier decided it was his duty to speak out.

Duthier was an unknown, recently arrived in the country. No one knew where he had come from. At first very few people gave any credence to his story, a very unlikely one given Lamirande's character and the state of his fortune. Lamirande himself, of course, issued a formal denial of the atrocious accusation and privately invited Sir Henry to put an end to the slander. Just as he was awaiting a reply, he was astonished to read in an Ottawa newspaper the following account of an inverview the prime minister had given to a reporter:

As M. Lamirande has denied the accusation brought against him by Sir Henry's servant Duthier, *The Sun* sent a reporter to speak to the prime minister and try to learn exactly what he had to say on the subject. Here is their conversation:

'Q. Sir Henry, you have no doubt read the accusation made by one of your servants against M. Lamirande and the latter's formal denial. In the interest of truth I have come to ask you, with all respect, to tell the public what this is about.

'A. I profoundly regret this incident. M. Lamirande is a very gifted young man who is quite wrongly waging war against me, but all the same I admire him greatly.

'Q. Did he, in fact, say to you what Duthier claims he said?

'A. Oh, these servants! Duthier was very wrong to make that statement and I regret the incident very much. I dismissed the man from my service immediately. When a servant accidentally overhears something it is his duty to be quiet. Acts of indiscretion like Duthier's are quite intolerable!

'Q. Am I to conclude that Duthier is guilty only of an indiscretion?

'A. You are becoming indiscreet yourself!

'Q. Then there was a conversation between yourself and M. Lamirande about a position at the consulate in Paris or Washington?

'A. M. Lamirande himself does not deny that such a conversation took place.

'Q. You do not wish to tell me the nature of this conversation?

'A. Do you think that I am about to commit an indiscretion as my servant did? I repeat, I deeply deplore this incident, and I am determined not to aggravate matters by becoming involved in any way.

You may consider the interview closed, because no matter how clever you are, you will not make me reveal what M. Lamirande and I might have discussed in a conversation that was strictly confidential. It is useless to insist further.

'With that our representative left Sir Henry.'

Lamirande was overwhelmed by Sir Henry's betrayal. He understood that there was some sort of conspiracy against him on the part of the prime minister and his servant, and that it would be useless to appeal to Sir Henry for justice. In *La Nouvelle-France* he gave an exact account of what had happened. Leverdier and Vaughan supported his statement, declaring that Lamirande had confided in them immediately after he had talked with Sir Henry. The latter was interviewed again, and again he denied everything, without saying anything precise.

In the province of Quebec opinion was divided. All sincere men, especially those who knew Lamirande personally, were convinced that he was the victim of a dreadful slander and this only increased the sympathy, esteem, and affection that they already felt for him. However, those who for one reason or another wanted to follow in the minister's wake used this as a pretext to declare themselves openly against the separatist leader. Although not one in a hundred truly believed the accusation, there is nothing more intransigent or fierce than the man who for reasons of self-interest pretends to believe a slander. And those who claimed to believe Duthier's story and Sir Henry's wily reticence supported their cause ardently. This affected not only Lamirande but the principles that he defended as well. It was a veritable rout for the nationalist cause. The ministers saw that it was the *psychological* moment. They sent out the writs and set the election for the earliest possible date, towards the end of January 1946.

All thy waves and thy billows have gone over me.
PSALMS 42:7

14

LAMIRANDE, WHO WAS UNSELFISHNESS PERSONIFIED, had been atrociously slandered and accused of venality; he who had nothing but noble sentiments, who rejected government policy to obey inspirations of the most sublime patriotism, was accused of fighting the government only out of spite. All this had overwhelmed Lamirande, submerged him in profound disgust. With the grace of God, obtained through prayer and frequent communion, he was able to put out of his soul all hatred, desire for revenge, and other evil passions. But he could not escape an unspeakable sorrow that enveloped and penetrated him like a cold heavy cloud.

To crown his misfortune Marguerite had fallen gravely ill, a victim of the mysterious fever that had appeared at various points on the globe in the past several years. Learned scientists had succeeded in giving it a Greek name and describing minutely the shape and habits of the germ that caused it, but they had not yet discovered how to destroy this little life that caused only death. Lamirande, like the medical colleagues he consulted, was reduced to impotence in the face of this infinitely small creature. No one could even imagine where Madame Lamirande had contracted the disease, as hers was the only case that had been reported in all of Canada.

Lamirande spent all his time with his wife, whose condition continued to deteriorate. He could play only a small part therefore, in the great struggle. Leverdier was everywhere at once; he was a candidate in one of the ridings near Quebec and was taking part in other campaigns, attempting to stir up the ardour of the patriots. He ran off articles for his newspaper right in the middle of electoral meetings while fifty people talked deafeningly at once around him, interrupting him at every moment. He wrote one sentence, answered a question, and then would have to stop in the middle of the next phrase to settle an argument or give instructions.

All this time Lamirande was condemned to an inactivity that was torture for him. Despite the anguish that tore his heart as he watched his beloved Marguerite move closer to the grave, he did not allow his pain to absorb or overwhelm him. His patriotism prevailed even over his conjugal love. He could not bring himself to leave his wife for long, but he was directing the work of the central committee, helping to edit *La Nouvelle-France,* and speaking at various meetings in and around Quebec. He had little to do in his own campaign, for his supporters had known and loved him for many years, and they remained faithful to him. It was his one consolation in the midst of the trials, the disappointments, and all the poignant concerns that overwhelmed him.

Therefore let anyone who thinks
that he stands take heed lest he fall.
I CORINTHIANS 10:12

15

SAINT-SIMON WAS RUNNING IN THE RIDING OF QUEBEC, against both the government candidate and one of Lamirande's followers. Saint-Simon presented himself as far more separatist than Lamirande and his friends, whom he accused of betraying the nationalist cause.

One day he called a meeting of the electors in Jeune-Lorette and challenged Lamirande to debate with him there. Lamirande accepted, although he found such meetings, where the discussion was rarely dignified, thoroughly repellent. But if he refused to face his accusers, he would be compromising the changes of his group's candidate, which were already very weak.

For several days the weather had been superb. The sun was blazing in an azure sky, there was not a breath of wind and only the thermometer, which registered twenty below zero, gave any sign that it was winter. On the morning of the meeting there was a change in the atmosphere: the temperature had risen ten degrees but the cold seemed more intense as the dampness entered into one's very bones. A red sun had risen in a pallid sky and a bank of grey clouds could be seen in the south-west, while from the opposite direction, the redoubtable north-east, the wind had risen very weakly at first, barely perceptible, but ceaselessly augmenting as the clouds grew denser and more widespread. Soon it began to snow — a fine, powdery, but penetrating snow. It was a powerful crescendo: wind and snow became more furious by the minute. The trees, their branches frozen stiff, made sinister cracking noises, and twisted and bent under the powerful gusts of wind.

Despite the blizzard, the meeting was held. In the morning the roads were still passable, and those who were going to Lorette from Quebec had the wind at their backs. Lamirande, absorbed in his own troubles, paid no attention to the roaring in the air.

The meeting was as he had expected, loathsome and unpleasant. Saint-Simon made all the same accusations against Lamirande that had been running in the newspapers for some time. He said that he was ambitious, interested only in assuring himself of a brilliant position, and going against the government out of spite because he had been unable to obtain one. Montarval's miserable slave proceeded to embroider upon this theme for three-quarters of an hour. Lamirande replied with all the dignity and aloofness he could command. A few sensible and reasonable members of the audience were sympathetic to him, but many more shouted insults.

Lamirande had never felt so profoundly disgusted as he did when the meeting was over; and he had never experienced any emotion that was so close to hatred.

When the meeting ended and he had to think about the trip home, Lamirande noticed for the first time that the storm had become extraordinarily violent. The cold had not decreased and to return to Quebec it was necessary to face the terrible, stifling northeast wind and the biting snow. Lamirande did not hesitate for a moment. He had been away since morning and the thought of his dying wife tortured him and would have made him face far greater dangers. Besides, his horse was vigorous and his driver careful and sober. Under these conditions the return to Quebec would be very difficult, but it was not a mad undertaking.

However, the people of Lorette had a sense of foreboding when they saw Saint-Simon leave a few minutes before Lamirande. His horse was exhausted and ill-suited to travel in such a wind; people noticed that both Saint-Simon and his driver had consumed large quantities of brandy under the pretext of warding off the cold.

The blizzard was increasing in force. The fine-powdered snow had become truly terrifying. It was impossible to see ten feet ahead or behind, and in the fields on both sides of the road there was nothing but a vast white whirlwind that moved with dizzying speed.

Lamirande's driver had turned to the left to escape the wind. Suddenly there was a brief lull, and during this respite Lamirande saw, on his right, something that made his blood run cold: a horse and sleigh half-buried in a snowbank. He recognized Saint-Simon's horse, and he saw the situation in a flash: Saint-Simon and his driver had lost their way and were probably already numbed by the cold. They would be condemned to certain death unless someone came to their rescue.

Lamirande's driver, still facing the left, had seen nothing. Horrible thoughts ran through Lamirande's mind, burning lines like fire. He saw as in an instantaneous tableau all the harm this wicked man had done to the national cause, all his slanders, his abominable accusations, his gross injustices. He saw all that and told himself, 'It is God's justice that has struck him; may God's will be done!'

Yes! this horrible thought entered Lamirande's mind and had almost penetrated to the superior part of his soul. He was about to give in to temptation and commit a crime that only the eye of God could see.

Two or three days later, when the storm had abated, the bodies of Saint-Simon and his companion would be discovered, and who could suspect the Lamirande had seen the beginning of the tragedy and allowed it to run its course? He was, then, leaning over the edge of the abyss that is never far from us and into which we would fall at any moment if Divine Grace did not hold us back; the abyss of sin.

Lamirande got hold of himself and uttered a cry of horror and fright at the thought of the unspeakable sin he had been about to commit. In fact the struggle lasted only a moment, the time it took to advance a few feet. He stopped the driver and told him what he had just seen. Luckily there was a house nearby where they went to get help. Then, moving carefully so that they would not lose their way as well, they went toward the spot where Lamirande had seen the victims of the storm. Eventually they found them. They had lost the rug they had used to cover themselves in the sleigh and had nothing to shelter them from the cold. Completely disoriented, exhausted by their desperate efforts to disengage their horse and make themselves heard, they were already halfway into the fatal sleep that is the forerunner of death.

With great difficulty they were moved to the house. Lamirande gave them the first aid their condition required and then continued home, thanking God for saving him from the abyss.

Because thy steadfast love is better than life.
PSALMS 63:3

16

THE ELECTION WAS HELD, and turned out a disaster for the national cause. The government triumphed all along the line, especially in the province of Quebec. Houghton was more successful in Ontario, where his group elected more MPs than there had been before dissolution. It was French Canada, deceived and misled, that gave the strongest majority to the very government that was contemplating the ruin of the Church and of the French-Canadian nation. Lamirande was elected, along with Leverdier and a small number of their supporters, but the mass of the French delegation was composed of pro-government MPs. Saint-Simon was among the winners, thanks to money from Montarval, who had secretly supported this apparently ultra-separatist candidate.

For Lamirande, patriotic hopes and domestic happiness were crumbled at the same time. His wife was dying; the cruel disease had done its work. Gentle and resigned, she was leaving her life as she had lived it, as a perfect Christian. That is not to say that she was indifferent: she was still young and she clung naturally to life. She fought against death as it advanced. Loved and loving, she was terrified at the thought of being separated from her husband and child. But she repeated the words of the Saviour on the Mount of Olives: 'My Father, if it be possible, let this cup pass from me; nevertheless, not as I will, but as thou wilt.'

Lamirande could not accept the bitter cup. He left his wife's chamber and went into the next room where he threw himself on his knees before a statue of his patron saint. There he poured out his soul in a supreme prayer, a heart-rending supplication: 'Holy St Joseph,' he repeated ceaselessly, 'you can obtain my wife's life from Him whose foster father you were. Obtain this grace for me, I beseech you. God has permitted the destruction of my political dreams, of the great projects I had formed for my country. But He cannot want to crush me completely. St. Joseph, save my wife!'

He prayed thus for half an hour, his eyes fixed on the statue. Suddenly he thought he was having a hallucination. 'My sorrow is

disturbing my mind,' he said to himself. For the statue had come to life. It was no longer cold white marble, but a living man that stood before him. The lily he held in his hand was a real flower. And St Joseph spoke:
'Joseph, if you insist on the temporal grace you ask for, it will certainly be granted. Your wife will live. But if, on the contrary, you leave everything to the will of God, the sacrifice of your domestic happiness will be repaid by the triumph of your homeland. Your prayer will be granted. And so that you will know that you are not imagining all this, take this.'

St Joseph removed a leaf from the lily he was holding and put it into Lamirande's trembling hand.

Then the man was replaced once again by the marble statue, the lily became stone as before, but with one leaf missing.

Dumbfounded, Lamirande ran into his wife's room.

'Who was talking to you just now?' Marguerite asked. 'It was a strange voice, almost celestial. What is it?'

Lamirande flung himself to his knees beside the bed and taking her tenderly in his arms he told his wife all that had happened.

'It was no dream,' he said; 'here is the leaf that St Joseph gave me.'

'Marguerite!' he went on. 'You will live. For you do want to live, don't you?'

'I would like to live, Joseph, for God alone knows how happy I have been with you. But if it be the will of Heaven that I die ...'

'It is not God's will that you die, because he sent a miracle to tell me that you will live.'

'But if I live our country will die.'

'St Joseph didn't say that.'

'He promised that our country would triumph only on the condition that you sacrifice your personal happiness.'

'I could never ask that you die, my wife, my life.'

'But can you not ask that God's will be done?'

Lamirande was silent.

Marguerite made one final effort, gathering all her strength and the last remnants of her vitality. She went on:

'Yes, my husband, let us make this sacrifice for the love of our country. You have worked for it for a long time, but all your efforts and those of your friends have been in vain. And now, at the moment when all appears to be lost, God is promising to save everything if the two of us will sacrifice a few years of happiness. It is a hard thing to ask, but we must do it. It is not only a question of our country's prosperity and material greatness but of the salvation of many souls over the centuries. Because if the secret societies continue to flourish it will be the ruin of our religion. That thought has sustained you in the painful struggles of these last weeks, and it sustains me now. Think what good can be accomplished in return for a few years of a miserable life! It is not often that a woman can save her country by dying!'

Marguerite still had to struggle with her husband, for death seemed more awesome to him who would be left than to her who was going away. To lose his wife, see his beloved become 'that which has no name in any tongue,' take her to her grave, entrust her to worms and corruption, when he could have kept her with him for a long time yet – it was a dreadful choice. The thought of it caused him mortal agony.

Finally, divine grace and Marguerite's prayers won out over what was repugnant to human nature. Lamirande and his wife prayed in all sincerity: 'Lord Jesus, may it be done according to Thy will and not our own. Or rather, may our will conform with Thine.'

The cruel disease pursued its course.

The next evening Lamirande saw that the end was near and called for Father Grandmont. Leverdier and his sister Hélène had been with the dying woman since morning. Marguerite received the last sacraments in full consciousness and with angelic fervour. She said her simple and touching farewells to her husband and daughter, to her adoptive sister and brother and to Father Grandmont. Then she sank rapidly and seemed to see and hear no more. Lamirande thought that she would come out of the coma only when she awakened in eternity, but suddenly she gestured to him that she wanted to tell him something. He leaned tenderly towards her and she said, very softly, 'Hélène has always loved you. Don't forget me, but make her happy. Farewell! We shall meet in Heaven!'

Then, commending her soul to God, she peacefully uttered her last sigh.

That night Hélène wept and prayed for a long time by Marguerite's body.

Her soul was invaded by frightening, tumultuous thoughts. Desires she had repelled and that she thought could have been extinguished forever were suddenly reawakened, disturbing her. She wished she were experiencing nothing but pain, but another feeling that she dared not name was mingled with her sorrow, absorbing it. She wept, but her tears that should have been bitter and burning, were gentle. She intended to ask Heaven for nothing but the repose of Marguerite's soul and courage for Joseph, but it was for herself that she prayed. 'Lord,' she said, 'You have given me the grace to conquer my emotions for fifteen years; sustain me now at this supreme moment. I can think of him now without committing a crime, without any injustice towards the woman I loved like a sister and who is now at Your side. If it is possible for me finally to be happy after so many years of suffering, give me this grace, O my God. And if it is not to be, help me to bear my suffering and to bless You always.'

My days are past, my plans are broken off,
the desires of my heart.
JOB 17:11

17

AS LONG AS HE COULD STILL SEE HIS WIFE'S FEATURES, transfigured in death, Lamirande felt calm and strong. During the service in the church he shed abundant tears, but the sublime requiem mass raised his soul above earthly bitterness and introduced it to the joys and the repose of eternity. It was only when he returned from the cemetery to the empty house, now forever desolate, where he had known such great happiness, that he was overcome for a moment by a completely human sorrow. He thought he had glimpsed Heaven, that his soul had in some way entered there, following Marguerite, but now it closed and shut him out. He saw nothing but a vale of tears and the road that was left for him to travel seemed interminable.

The sisters from the convent of Beauvoir had come for his daughter Marie, thinking they did the right thing, but they had taken from the house the last ray of light that had illuminated it so graciously in the past.

Despite Leverdier's efforts, Lamirande was overcome by despair. He almost regretted his sacrifice, telling himself, 'I was presumptuous; it was pride that made me want to commit an uncalled for act of heroism for which I lacked the necessary grace. Only the saints have the right to undertake sublime actions; they alone have the vocation to leave the terrain of ordinary virtues and give themselves over to superhuman renunciations. As for me, I should have humbly chosen the less perfect but more certain way that was offered to me; I should have asked for my wife's life because God had deigned to grant my prayer.'

Then doubt invaded him. Instead of a miracle, perhaps the apparition of St Joseph was only a diabolical trick. It could not be simply a hallucination because he still had material proof of the objective reality of the vision: the leaf of the lily, that fitted perfectly the flower held by the statue. But perhaps the Tempter had wanted to set a trap for him by proposing a sacrifice that he had accepted, through pride rather than for the love of God, so that he could say, 'Look how strong I am; I can renounce what is dearest to me in the world.'

Then he suffered another kind of doubt. It was no longer the demons who had deceived and tempted him. He was quite convinced that it had been a celestial apparition; but because of his resistance and his unwillingness to accept the sacrifice, its merit was lost to him. The death of his wife would be of no use to the country. In human terms, all was lost. God would no doubt have worked some miracle to save everything because He had given His promise, but it was on the condition that he accept his trial courageously. 'And I accepted it badly,' Lamirande told himself; 'I carried out my sacrifice badly. So God broke his promise. My wife is dead and my country is going to die too!'

These bitter thoughts cast him deep into despair. He could not bring himself to open his heart to Leverdier, to tell him of the miracle. He thought his friend would blame him as he blamed himself, that he would share his doubts. Because he wanted to spare himself any new suffering he said nothing.

His dark sorrow, with no weeping, no outpouring of his heart, troubled Leverdier.

'My friend,' he said, 'you must make an effort to shake off this black sorrow that does not come from Heaven. Come with me, I shall take you to Manrèse. You will spend a day or two there with Father Grandmont.'

'You are right,' Lamirande agreed. 'I'll go there.'

And the two friends set off once again along the Chemin Sainte-Foye where fifteen years earlier Lamirande had spoken to his friend for the first time of his great joy. It had been spring then: the birds were singing the praises of the Lord, the countryside was beautiful and the Heavens were smiling. Now it was bleak winter: there was no verdure, no bird song, only bare and mournful trees beneath a cold grey sky.

Leverdier took his friend to the door of the retreat.

'Good-bye,' he said. 'May St Ignatius console you and communicate his courage to you.'

'Thank you, my friend, thank you.'

Lamirande went up to Father Grandmont's room, following a path he already knew very well. The venerable priest opened his arms, and Lamirande threw himself upon him like a child, telling Christ's minister all that had happened – all his temptations, all his failings.

They spent part of the night together before the Holy Sacrament in the small interior chapel, sunk deep in meditation on the nothingness of life.

The priest celebrated mass early in the morning. Lamirande served and received the celestial bread that expelled all doubts from his soul as the sun dissipates the night fog. Calm and trust in God returned to him, but Lamirande was still diffident.

'Father,' he said, 'I am too weak to continue the work that I have undertaken. You tell me that my sacrifice, ill-performed though it was, will be accepted and that in return God will send some unexpected aid to our country. I believe that. But my task is done now. I can retire somewhere where I will be expected to practise only the normal virtues and where I will be less exposed to sin.'

'Not yet, my child, not yet,' said the good priest with a smile. 'Your task is not accomplished; far from it. You must stay in politics and wait patiently for God to answer your sacrifice as He has promised and as He will most certainly do. These human weaknesses that you deplore, with a little exaggeration, are a great grace. They keep you humble, and without humility it is impossible to please God. Think of St Paul, who was enraptured at the Third Heaven and who told us, 'And to keep me from being too elated by the abundance of revelations, a thorn was given me in the flesh, a messenger of Satan, to harass me.' I should worry about you, my child, if you were exempt from all weakness, if you were not afraid of falling at every moment. You would be an easy prey to the demon of pride.'

'But Father, I am not just afraid of falling, I am falling.'

'And if you are falling, get up! If you had to take a road that was pitted with holes and strewn with stones in order to get home, the fear, the certainty even, that you would fall several times and scrape your hands and knees would not deter you from your journey. It is painful and humiliating to fall, but that does not prevent you from reaching your goal, as long as you get up again.'

'But you need grace in order to get up.'

'Of course, and it is always given to those who sincerely ask for it. If many people remain lying on the ground, it is because they prefer lying down to standing upright. Perhaps they ask God for the grace to raise themselves up, but they don't really want it. They like the mud or the dust or the flowering lawn where they have fallen, and secretly that is where they want to stay rather than continue their painful journey. Even though they go through the motions of asking God for the grace to raise themselves up they would be sorry if He raised them up by force. But God sees the secret and He does not raise them up.'

'Very well, Father, I shall stay at my post as long as you tell me that my task in the world of politics is not yet accomplished.'

'Very good! And I shall tell you when you can go away. It will not be very soon, I shouldn't think because there is still a great deal to do. Perhaps God will even ask for some new sacrifice before everything is finished.'

'With His grace I shall carry it out.'

> So then He has mercy upon whomever He wills.
> ROMANS 9:18

18

FEBRUARY 15, 1946 WAS THE DATE SET for the re-opening of Parliament.

The same day, around five o'clock in the evening, a secret meeting was held in the editorial offices of *La Libre Pensée* in Montreal. Montarval was there, along with Ducoudray, the paper's editor, and various other well-known radicals from the metropolis. It is hardly necessary to say that Sir Henry's cabinet colleague had not entered the offices of the impious publication through the regular door but through a secret passage that connected with a wig-maker's shop owned by one of the followers of the sect.

'All right!' Montarval exclaimed. 'We are winning. The government has an overwhelming majority. We shall present the same bills with a few meaningless and superficial changes to make the Quebec MPs think they have won some concessions. Basically though, it will be exactly as it was. I have even found a way to improve it somewhat, something I didn't think was possible. It will be passed and in ten years we shall have everything in our hands.'

'Yes,' said Ducoudray, 'everything has gone according to your plans and your wishes. God knows...'

'That expression again!'

'Sorry, it was a slip of the tongue.'

'I know your early education was filled with Christian superstitions; just see that they don't play some trick on you. What were you going to say?'

'I was going to say that the election must have been terribly expensive. I hope you and Sir Henry have arranged things so that it's not too obvious in the public accounts. A financial scandal at the start of the new régime would be a great nuisance.'

'Don't let it worry you. I defy Lamirande, Houghton, and their handful of fanatics to find the slightest irregularity in the public accounts.'

'Speaking of Lamirande,' Said Ducoudray, 'I realize that he is an enemy who has to be eliminated, but was it really necessary to invent that story about him?'

'We must leave no stone unturned. Are you by any change suffering from what the priests call pangs of conscience?'

'No, nothing like that; my conscience wore out all its teeth a long time ago. But I still find such tactics rather disgusting unless they're absolutely necessary.'

He got up and began pacing back and forth, a gloomy expression on his face.

'It's just a bad case of spleen,' said one of the others, 'probably from indigestion. Take one of Dr Cohen's pills after every meal for three days — that's all you need.'

Ducoudray did not reply. He continued to pace up and down, troubled and disturbed.

Montarval fixed his sinister gaze on him for several seconds, a malignant light glowing in his eyes. Then he got up and silently went to the secret passageway. As he went through the wig-maker's shop he whispered a few words into the shopkeeper's ear. The latter nodded his assent, growing pale as he did so.

The others left soon after Montarval, and Ducoudray was alone. When the last one had left, he locked the door and collapsed into an armchair.

'What's wrong with me?' he asked. 'Is it just indigestion or is it really my conscience? I thought I'd stifled that years ago but still I sometimes hear a weak little voice that comes from I don't know where telling me that I'm a miserable wretch. Could it be the voice of what Christians call my conscience? Could it be my mother's voice? I dreamed about her again last night — could it be her soul coming to speak to me? Is there such a thing as a soul? I felt like a little child kneeling in front of my mother who was showing me how to pray. I think I could even repeat the words she was making me say: "Hail Mary, full of grace." No, I can't go on.'

He spent a long time absorbed in bitter thoughts, then got up abruptly. 'I must shake off this torpor,' he told himself, 'get rid of these ideas. It's too late for me to change directions. I've sunk too far into evil. There's that word again: evil! What does it mean, evil? What is good? I need something to take my mind off all this. I know: tonight the famous Father Grandmont is starting what they call a retreat in Longueuil. I've heard the old guy has some pretty funny things to say. I think I'll go — it could distract me and give me something to write about tomorrow. Jokes about the Jesuits are always good for a laugh.'

When he left, he went past the wig-maker's shop, not noticing a man who left at almost the same moment — a man wearing dark glasses and with his coat collar turned — a man who feared the cold, no doubt. He followed Ducoudray, who went into a restaurant, ordered a meal, and then continued along towards Longueuil. He did not look behind him, and even if he had he might have noticed nothing out of the ordinary, only a man walking a few steps behind him, his face sheltered from the wind and his eyes protected from the dazzling snow and electric lights.

When he reached Notre-Dame Street, Ducoudray took a sleigh and ordered the driver to cross over to Longueuil.

It was a fine cold night, one of those nights that are almost as clear as daytime that occur so frequently during the Canadian winter. The moon, so brilliant that it hid the stars, shed beams of silver light on the bridge of ice that covered the giant river. The snow reflected the moonlight and added to it a special glow so brilliant you could read by it, but also bright enough to be tiring to weak eyes. Ducoudray's eyes were strong though, and he enjoyed the splendid illumination. A few hundred yards behind him there was a sleigh with a man who apparently could not endure such dazzling light.

The river was bathed in total silence, broken only by the jingling of the horses' bells. Ducoudray, though, heard neither bells of his own horse nor those of the horse behind him. He was a hundred leagues away from Montreal and thirty years away from the year of grace 1946. He was in a little village far down the river, below Quebec, where he had spent his childhood, and he was only seven years old. He was kneeling by his mother, saying his evening prayers with her. From the humble attic where he was praying one could see the broad sweep of the St Lawrence, seven leagues across, and the blue mountains to the north. He saw again this grandiose and peaceful landscape, now illuminated by the pale rays of the moon, now bathed in the fire of the setting sun. He breathed again the strong salt air and played among the seaweed uncovered by the tide. Then, as the tide came in again it covered first the rocks, then came all the way up to the road, setting afloat the old rowboat.

All this distant past came back to him as he sped along towards Longueuil. He was haunted by the memory of his mother, who had died when he was eight years old – the mother he had loved so much, who had watched over his cradle and taught him to stammer out the names of Jesus, Mary, and Joseph. Alas, he had not uttered these names for twenty years, except in blasphemy. He had never felt so tortured and tormented as he did that evening. The life he led, his life of hate and passion, sensual delight and fierce struggles against his childhood beliefs, had never inspired such profound feelings of disgust and terror as he was experiencing at that moment. He thought he had erased the last vestiges of faith by trampling beneath his feet all the laws of God and by sinking deeper and deeper into the mire of impiety. For years, in fact, he had enjoyed the frightening tranquillity that replaces the grace of remorse. However, his tranquillity had disappeared some days earlier, and as soon as he was not actively employed, his thoughts turned back thirty years and took him to the village where he had been born, to the church where he had been baptized and received his first communion, to the modest room where he said his evening prayers under his mother's watchful eye.

An entire regiment could have followed him across the ice-bridge that evening and he would have been completely unaware of it.

The bells of the beautiful Longueuil church calling the faithful to the retreat roused him from his reveries. When he reached the village he jumped out of the carriage, told the driver to wait for him and went into the church. 'I hope that Jesuit will give me a nice rococo piece out of the middle ages,' he said to himself. He went to the seat which the beadle, realizing that he was a stranger, had offered to him. Another stranger came in shortly after; the beadle wanted to seat him next to Ducoudray, but he preferred to be in the shadow of one of the pillars, claiming that the light tired his eyes. But in spite of his poor vision he never took his eyes off Ducoudray.

The sermon was simple and eloquent. When Father Grandmont spoke, he spoke from his heart: he loved God, he loved human souls and these two loves gave his words a warmth and strength that had little need of rhetorical ornaments to win over the hearts of his listeners. Another time Ducoudray would probably have noticed several expressions that were rather naïve, and would have twisted them, the better to mock them. This evening, though, he listened more seriously; he was grave and collected, and the priest's words, rather than amusing him, impressed him painfully.

As is the custom for followers of St Ignatius, the priest spoke of the two standards: the standard of Jesus Christ and that of Satan. Man must stand beneath one of the two, and it is impossible to be neutral, a simple spectator. One must choose one side or the other, march towards Heaven under the banner of Jesus Christ or towards Hell under Lucifer's flag. There are but two cities, the city of good and the city of evil. The first contains all those who possess the sanctifying grace; the second, all those who lack it. There is no intermediate state. One must be the friend of God or his enemy. No one can be indifferent to Him, just as He is indifferent to none of us. There are only two roads, the one broad and easy, descending gently through fields of flowers, containing no obstacles or contradictions, where one walks without fatigue, surrounded by things to delight all the senses; the other road is narrow, rough, and difficult and one advances along it only with difficulty and pain, falling often on the rough ground. It is useless to seek a third route through life, for there is none. There are only two eternities for man, one of happiness which lies at the end of the narrow route, the other one of misery at the end of the broad and easy way.

Father Grandmont developed these powerful and salutary thoughts for more than half an hour, and Ducoudray listened to him more and more seriously, his head drooping against his chest. From the dark corner where he was watching, the bespectacled stranger kept track of his slightest movement.

Father Grandmont seemed to have finished his sermon. He was even preparing to descend from the pulpit when he suddenly turned around to face the worshippers, his face illuminated by a sudden inspiration.

'My brothers,' he exclaimed, 'if there is one among you who suffers beneath the burden of a mountain of crimes, one whose soul is covered by a veritable leprosy of sin, someone who for years and years has outraged God and His laws, the Church and its laws, human nature and its laws, someone who in the mire where he is wallowing has been seized by a terror bordering on despair, I say let him not despair! Let him look to the Divine One on the Crucifix! Let him remember that a single drop of the blood of God can erase all the iniquities of the world. Let him despise his sins, but let him not despair. Sincere repentance can make him as pleasing to God as he was on the day of his baptism or his first communion. If he thinks his crimes demand some great expiation, let him offer generously the sacrifice of his life, if it is necessary to repair the evil he has done. And let him be assured that thus, through the infinite goodness of Jesus Christ, he can become a great saint instead of the great sinner that he was. My brothers, during the blessing of the Holy Sacrament, pray fervently that if there is such a person among you he may receive from the Blessed Host, through the intercession of Mary, Refuge of sinners, the grace to shake off the yoke of Satan.'

Then he left the pulpit. The blessing of the Host began and everyone knelt. Ducoudray too, for the first time in twenty years, fell to his knees.

Who could describe the fierce struggle that took place in his heart, so long the slave of the demon? A few days earlier he had received a first grace, the grace of disgust. His life no longer gave him any satisfaction, but he did not yet feel repentance; it was not a supernatural movement. The priest's words, especially his last ones, he felt were destined for him alone, and they had caused new thoughts and unknown feelings to be born in his heart. The disgust he had experienced for some time changed now, became spiritual. It was no longer vaguely troubling, an indefinable malaise, but a veritable horror, mixed with the love of God, Whom he had so greatly offended. 'Oh!' he exclaimed to himself, 'if only I could make good all the evil I have done, shed the burden that is crushing me, and escape from Satan's claws to throw myself into the arms of Jesus, how happy I would be!'

How many poor souls have spoken thus! How many miserable sinners wish to leave the frightful state where they find themselves but are unable to say, 'I want.' False shame holds them back, a mute demon possesses them. They need only take one step, say one word; but they do not. The grace of God is an unfathomable mystery. It is always sufficient to save a soul, yet it does not always do so; and at times it is poured into the soul so abundantly that (while it does not destroy free will) it seems to tear the man away from evil despite himself!

Would Ducoudray stop at the fatal 'I wish' or would he utter the sublime 'I want' and drop the chains of his spiritual slavery?

Like all sinners who would like to be converted, he experienced the temptation of false shame, a feeling that is both childish and difficult to overcome. But Ducoudray was also aware of a much less vague fear. He knew without a doubt that he could do nothing by halves; that in order to return to Jesus Christ he would have to leave the horrible sect he belonged to and whose secrets he shared. And not only would he have to leave it – that would be relatively easy – he would have to denounce it. In order to make good the wrong that he had done, he would have to divulge all the shadowy machinations in which he had participated. To do so, he knew, could be fatal. On the one hand he could have a few more years of a miserable existence, then an eternity of misery; or he could choose the blow of a dagger, then boundless joy. It was thus that he saw in a clear new light the situation that was presented to his spirit. In theory it was an easy choice: Hell or Heaven, with a few years of life, more or less, in between. Who would hesitate? And yet, which of us would not hesitate? What am I saying! Who among us, unless he is given a special gift of grace, would not choose Hell and a few years of life? Human nature is so weak, and Ducoudray was experiencing this desperate weakness. It terrified and immobilized him. He saw with alarm that he was about to choose Hell because of his love for a little bit of that life that inspired in him only misery and disgust. He felt powerless to make the slightest effort by himself to leave the abyss. And from the depths of the abyss he cried, in a burst of true humility, 'My God, have pity on me! Holy Virgin, help me!'

Then from the Divine Host came a burst of that grace that gives to the weakest the strength to face death.

A sword, a sword is drawn for the slaughter.
EZEKIEL 21:28

19

THE BLESSING OF THE HOLY SACRAMENT WAS FINISHED. Slowly the crowd departed. The sextons extinguished the candles, first on the altar, then in the choir, finally in the nave; only two or three still burned, shedding an uncertain light in the vast edifice. As he was closing the doors the beadle noticed that there were still two men in the church: one was kneeling, his head in his hands, his chest heaving with sobs; the other stood near a pillar, staring at the first. The beadle touched the kneeling man. 'We're closing,' he said. Ducoudray started like a man who has been suddenly awakened. He rose immediately.

'I must see Father Grandmont,' he said. 'I must see him right away.'

As he spoke he caught sight, for the first time, of the man who was half-hidden hebind the pillar. He shuddered and his whole body felt cold.

'Already!' he thought. 'My God, I am ready; give me just three hours.'

'You can see the Father in the presbytery,' the beadle told him, 'unless he's still in the vestry. Go through the sanctuary.'

Then he approached the other stranger who seemed more hesitant.

'Do you want to see Father too?'

'Yes ... no ... I mean, I would like to follow my friend. He is going to the presbytery, I imagine?'

'Yes. If you hurry you can catch up with him.'

The stranger took a few steps in the direction of the choir, then came back to the door.

'I'll go and wait for my friend outside, in front of the presbytery,' he explained.

'That's a strange one,' the beadle muttered as he bolted the main door. 'He doesn't seem to know what he wants.'

On the contrary, he knew very well, but he had been temporarily dazzled and forgot what he was doing. Was it the effect of the heat in the church or was it something else? He did not stop to wonder but muttered imprecations against himself for his moment of indecision.

'That was awkward!' he said to himself. 'I probably could have caught up with him before he went into the presbytery, even when he was at the door, alone. Now I'll have to wait here, because he must not be allowed to return to Montreal.'

At that moment Ducoudray was entering the presbytery, astonished that the man in dark glasses had not followed him.

'Thank God!' he murmured, 'I ask You for just three hours. Grant me that, not for myself but for the cause of Your holy Church.'

A servant took him to Father Grandmont's room where he was greeted most affably and invited to sit down.

'Father,' Ducoudray began, 'you do not know me.'

'No, I do not have the honour,' the priest replied.

'It is no honour to know me,' said the journalist, 'because I am a most miserable man. I want to be converted though, or rather to confess. For by the grace of God I was converted just now in the church, while you were preaching. At the end of your sermon Heaven inspired you to say some things that many people must have found rather strange. I understood them, though, because I feel that they were addressed to me. I am the sinner you were speaking about. Will you hear my confession? *Can* you hear it? For I am no ordinary sinner: I am a monster.'

'My God, how good You are, how infinite is Your mercy!' the priest exclaimed.

And taking Ducoudray's hands, he drew the man to him affectionately.

'My brother,' he said, 'how happy I am! How the angels must be rejoicing! Come! I have all the powers needed to absolve you, no matter how grave your case may be.'

Then he took the penitent to the small confessional that stood in one corner of the room, and the unfortunate man threw himself to his knees and laid his unbearable burden at the feet of Christ's minister. When he got up again he was beaming. The old priest held him close for a long time, murmuring, 'What joy! My God, what joy!'

'Father,' said Ducoudray, 'you know what I still have to do. I possess all the secrets of that horrible sect, all their files. I must tell the Archbishop of Montreal everything I know before tomorrow morning, even tonight if I can; for I know that I am already condemned to die. The leader of the sect suspected me and he had one of his henchmen follow me. He saw me in church and must have noticed how moved I was. Now he is waiting outside, and I know he will strike at the first favourable moment. I am not afraid of death. On the contrary, I am happy to offer my life to God in expiation for my crimes. But I do not want them to murder me before I have had time to unveil the abominations of satanism. That is why I ask you to help me disguise myself, not because I am afraid of death.'

Half an hour later two priests left the presbytery. One was an old man, the other at the height of his strength. The young ecclesiastic was visibly embarrassed in his soutane, but the man in dark glasses did not have the slightest doubt. He simply murmured, 'Two petticoats! The young one looks very ill at ease.'

The two priests took a cab that the servant had gone to summon five minutes earlier.

Half an hour later the look-out man began to worry, and was wondering whether he should ring the bell, when the servant came out again. He seemed to be looking for someone. The man in dark glasses watched him, saw him speak to the coachman who had brought Ducoudray from town and give him some money. Then the coachman went away.

'This must be some practical joke!' he said.

He went up to the young servant and asked, 'Can you tell me if the young gentleman who went into the presbytery around nine o'clock has left yet?'

'I don't know,' the other man replied. 'I haven't seen him since I let him in.'

'But didn't you just pay his coachman and send him away?'

'Quite possibly. The curé told me to go and find the coachman who had brought a man from Montreal, a man with a big blonde moustache, to pay him for his trip and tell him the gentleman didn't need him any more.'

'Is he sleeping at the presbytery, do you think?'

'I have no idea sir, and I find your curiosity rather excessive.'

And he started to go back into the presbytery.

'Yes,' said the stranger, 'I am rather curious, but I have one more question to ask: do you know the two priests who just went out?'

'I know one of them: he is the priest who is preaching the Retreat, but I don't know the other one; I didn't even see him come in.'

'Ah! so you didn't see him go in! Now I understand everything,' he went on, talking to himself. 'How stupid I am! That's twice I've missed him.'

The poor servant, bewildered and suspecting that he might have said too much, hurried back into the presbytery.

The stranger moved quickly. There was a store near the church that was still open. He went in and asked where to find the telephone-telegraph office. It was in the neighbourhood and he set off at a run. There was only one man in the office. The stranger made a barely perceptible signal, to which the employee replied by a seemingly accidental gesture. Then the stranger sat down in front of the double instrument. First he used the telephone, putting himself into direct communication with a certain number in Montreal. Someone answered.

'Is this number eleven?' he asked

This number had nothing to do with the telephone numbers.

As the reply was satisfactory he continued:

'Pay attention to the telegraph I'm going to write. Are you ready? All right, here it is.'

He put down the telephone, picked up the telegrapher's pen and wrote the following message, which was reproduced simultaneously in Montreal, letter for letter and in the same handwriting as that of the person holding the electric pencil in Longueuil.

'In the name of the Grand Master, number seven in Longueuil to number eleven. Number two is betraying us. I have positive proof. The Grand Master, suspecting him, ordered me to follow him and to suppress him if I discovered that he was betraying us. That he is doing so is certain. He has just escaped me, disguised as a priest. Go immediately to his house. He will go there first, I am certain, to collect the files. In the name of the Grand Master and by virtue of the order that he gave me I command you to suppress number two. Act quickly; it may be too late already.'

Then, carefully putting his copy of the atrocious note into his pocket, the man in dark glasses paid what he owed to the office and left immediately for Montreal.

The next morning two women on their way to five o'clock mass at the Gésu church saw a man lying in a pool of blood on the sidewalk of

St Catherine Street near a garage door. Horrified, they screamed until they attracted the attention of some other people on their way to church or work. A group quickly formed. Four men lifted the inert bleeding body that was lifeless but still warm and carried it to the nearby police station. The chief, seeing the man's face, exclaimed, 'It's Ducoudray, editor of *La Libre Pensée!*'

I hasten and do not delay to keep thy commandments.
PSALMS 119:60

20

THE TRAGIC NEWS SPREAD LIKE WILDFIRE. By eight o'clock all Montreal knew that the now sadly famous journalist had been murdered. The papers printed special editorials that the newsboys sold by the hundreds, their faces shining, their voices shrill. Murder! What a bargain! On street corners, in electric cars, at the entrances to hotels and railway stations, they shouted with all their might: 'Terrible murder in Montreal! M. Ducoudray, editor of *La Libre Pensée*, was stabbed to death in Saint Catherine Street, just two steps away from the police station.' They used the same tone of voice in which they would have announced the result of a race or an election.

The coroner soon chose his jury and began his enquiry at the police station where the body had been taken. At first there was very little information. At the newspaper offices they knew that M. Ducoudray had gone out the previous evening around six o'clock without saying where he was going and that he had not returned. It was all they could find out. No one in the police station near which the murder had been committed had heard anything. No one in the house where he had a four-room apartment had seen him since morning. If he had come in, no one had seen him and he had certainly not gone to bed. One of the maids had passed the room he used as an office around ten o'clock and heard someone walking around inside. She was surprised, next morning, to find that the bed had not been slept in.

The doctor who examined the body declared that death was due to a single stab wound in the back which had cut through the aorta. The dagger, a formidable weapon, was found next to the body. The murderer, who must have been hidden in the doorway, apparently had a strong arm and a sure hand, as well as some knowledge of anatomy. The crime was not motivated by robbery, for a large sum of money and a valuable watch were found on the body.

That was all that could be learned, and the coroner was about to adjourn the enquiry when, to everyone's great surprise, the Archbishop of Montreal and Father Grandmont arrived at the police station.

The two venerable ecclesiastics were both nervous and distraught. They asked to see the body and were taken to a small cell where the murdered journalist had been placed on a cot. They fell to their knees and uttered a brief fervent prayer.

'Dear martyr!' said the bishop as he got up. 'You were so right to tell me that in twenty-four hours I would have indisputable proof of the truth of your revelations. Here it is, as horrifying as it is convincing!'

The coroner thought he had heard incorrectly.

'Your Grace,' he said, 'the dead man is Ducoudray, editor of the anticlerical newspaper *La Libre Pensée.*'

'I know, my friend,' replied the prelate, 'and when you have heard Father Grandmont's testimony and my own, you will understand what I just said.'

Father Grandmont testified first. In a few words he told what we already know of Ducoudray's last minutes on earth. Then he went on:

'So that M. Ducoudray could leave the presbytery without being observed by the man who had followed him from Montreal to Longueuil, I had the curé give him a soutane and a Roman hat. He shaved off his moustache and put his own clothes into a small suitcase that I lent him. Then I begged him to let me go to Montreal with him. When we left the presbytery, I saw a man who seemed to be waiting for someone. He was wearing dark glasses and the lower part of his face was hidden by a scarf or his turned-up coat collar. It would be impossible to recognize him. He apparently suspected nothing when he saw us, as he did not follow us. M. Ducoudray assured me that he knew perfectly well who the man was. "He is an executioner, one of the people who carry out death sentences for the horrible sect I still belonged to scarcely an hour ago." "But they have not had time to hold a meeting to sentence you to death," I replied. "In these urgent cases the Leader's order is sufficient," he explained. "The leader receives his information from clairvoyant spirits that are far superior to even the most intelligent human beings. He obviously suspected me, so he had this man follow me, with orders to suppress me – that's the word they use – if he found my behaviour suspicious. The emotion that I could not hide – that I did not even think of hiding in the church – followed by my visit to the presbytery, was more than enough to make them want to kill me. What amazes me is that he didn't try to murder me while I was going from the church to the presbytery. He must have been prevented by some divine intervention. As you know, I am the secretary of the society; in that capacity I have all the files and I know all their secrets. That is why they will move Heaven and earth to suppress me before I have time to reveal anything!"

'That is a faithful resumé of what M. Ducoudray told me,' said Father Grandmont, 'both in the presbytery and while we were going as quickly as we could from Longueuil to Hochelaga. When I pressed him to name the man who was following him he did not want to do so. "I forgive him in advance," he said, "with all my heart; I need God's forgiveness so badly."

'I left him in front of his house,' Father Grandmont went on, 'after arranging to meet him around one o'clock in the morning at the Gésu. He wanted to hear mass and take communion to prepare for his death. It was then about half past ten. I went on to the college and explained the situation to my superior in as few words as possible and obtained his permission to wait for my dear penitent in the church. He arrived shortly after the time we had agreed on. He told me he had managed to give the files to the archbishop; that two executioners had followed him from his house to the archbishop's palace; that three times he had thought all was lost but that he had been saved by a visible celestial protection; that he had noticed three hired assassins following him to the church but that he had experienced the same supernatural protection. "Now," he said, "let them do their work; I am ready to die and want to die to expiate my crimes." He heard mass and received Holy Communion with a fervour that was truly angelic. After our prayer of thanksgiving I begged him to spend the night with me at the college or at least to allow the Brother who had served the mass to go home with him. He refused, gently but with a firmness that admitted no reply. "It would only be a few hours' respite," he said. "Nothing in the world, no human power can save me from the death that awaits me. Even if I stayed in the college they would find a way to enter it within forty-eight hours. Right now I am sustained by the Bread of Life and I do not fear death. Would I be as well prepared later? I shall leave now, then, knowing full well that I shall never return to my house, for I am quite certain that the celestial protection that was given me because of what I had to do will be withdrawn from me. So be it!

Farewell, Father! And I thank you a thousand times for having opened the gate of Heaven to me." And so he left, despite our pleas. There is no need for me to tell you that the Brother and I wanted to follow him and that we decided not to only when we realized that M. Ducoudray would be very pained by it.'

Father Grandmont's cheeks were bathed in tears.

The archbishop presented his testimony next.

'Between ten and eleven o'clock I was getting ready for bed when somebody rang the doorbell. The servant opened the door and came to tell me that a priest wanted to see me about something very urgent. I had him shown into my room. He was carrying a suitcase and a rather large package and he told me immediately that he was not a priest, gave me his real name, and told me in a few words what Father Grandmont has just recounted. Then he gave me the documents which he said were the files of the secret society and gave me a detailed account of the organization – I do not believe it is necessary to go into detail just now, but I must admit that even though I listened very attentively and with the greatest interest, I wondered whether it were all a great hoax. He seemed to be reading my mind, for he said, "Your Grace, in twenty-four hours you will have proof that this is no hoax." Our conversation lasted nearly two hours. Before he left he asked permission to remove his priest's clothing. "I don't have to disguise myself now," he explained. He had already told me that he had disguised himself to avoid recognition, but he had said nothing about the killers who were following him. I sent him into my bedroom and shortly after he came out, dressed in lay clothes. He gave me the soutane and the hat he had been wearing and asked me to have them returned to the curé in Longueuil. Then he left, after asking for my blessing. I saw him to the door myself, then spent the rest of the night examining the documents he had left with me. When I learned this morning of his tragic fate, I understood that he was no trickster but someone who had been touched by a miracle – a great sinner who had suddenly become a great saint, through the extraordinary action of divine grace.'

As soon as the contents of the two testimonies were known, the city and the entire country were thrown into a state of excitement that was impossible to describe. The inquest was adjourned to allow the police to conduct enquiries. It was useless. They found the coachman who had driven the man in dark glasses to Longueuil and picked him up two or three hours later at the Dalhousie station, but he said the man was a stranger whom he had not seen before or since.

They interrogated the Longueuil storekeeper whom the 'executioner' had asked for information. All he knew was that around ten o'clock on the night before the murder a stranger in dark glasses, his face concealed behind his coat collar, had asked him where to find the telegraph office.

The caretaker of the telegraph office was interrogated more severely because his rather odd behaviour made the police suspect that he knew more than the others about the identity of the man in dark glasses. But all he would say was that the stranger had telephoned and written to someone in Montreal; that he had not noticed what number he had called, only that he had heard the man ask if it was number eleven who had answered. This number eleven shed no light on the mystery for at that time, in February 1946, it was the telephone-telegraph number of the Hôtel-Dieu hospital.

After several days of enquiry the jury returned the following verdict:

'We find that Charles Ducoudray died of a stab wound inflicted by an unknown person. It is our opinion that the assassin is a member of a secret society to which Ducoudray belonged and whose secrets the latter had revealed to religious authorities, and that he was murdered as punishment for this revelation.'

For it is better for me to die than to live.
TOBIT 3:6

21

TEN DAYS AFTER DUCOUDRAY'S DEATH people were talking of nothing but the extraordinary testimonies given by the Archbishop of Montreal and Father Grandmont at the coroner's inquest. In Ottawa the Commons sat for barely half an hour a day, the MPs were so distressed and preoccupied. The government bill had not even been given first reading. For reasons that can easily be guessed, Sir Henry and Montarval wanted to push it through as quickly as possible but the other ministers and many back-benchers, not knowing what the two leaders were so afraid of, thought differently. 'Give people time to calm down,' they advised. 'Ducoudray's murder probably has no political significance, but it has caused a great deal of malaise among the MPs from Quebec. If we began the debate under such conditions we would be exposing ourselves to dangerous complications.' Sir Henry, a skilful old parliamentarian, could not deny the strength of this argument, but as a member of the sect he was fully aware of the danger to which he and his accomplices would be exposed if they delayed. As far as his party was concerned, he could act only as an experienced politician, so that at each session when the single important bill was called to be included on the order of the day, the old chief called out 'Stand!'

'However,' Sir Henry said to Montarval as they were having a secret meeting one afternoon, 'we have to finish it off. Whether the House is disturbed or not, we will begin the debate tomorrow so that we can bring it around to third reading as soon as possible. Do you have any news from Montreal?'

'Yes,' Montarval replied. 'Very bad news. As you know, I bribed one of the archbishop's servants as soon after the disaster as I could. He was just about to get hold of the files when he was caught, and of course they fired him. It would be easy enough to suppress the archbishop, but what good would that do? It wouldn't give us back our files and if he were suppressed, even by a disease that I could have him contract, it would just upset people more. It was a tactical error to use a dagger to suppress Ducoudray. The imbecile I gave the job to misunderstood my instructions. I had told him to stab him *before* he could betray us; stabbing him afterwards only made things worse. We have so many other ways to get rid of traitors! I had taken steps to burn down the archbishop's palace in the hope of destroying everything, but just when we were about to carry it out, I found out that the old bishop was faster than I was: he had had all the principal documents photographed. By now every bishop in the country has a copy and probably some other people too.'

'How do you explain the silence of the Archbishop of Montreal?' Sir Henry asked.

'I'm not really sure,' Montarval replied. 'Perhaps he's just waiting so that he and his colleagues can all strike at once. I know there has been a lot of travelling back and forth in the past few days. And then perhaps I've managed to frighten him.'

'How could you do that?'

'I have one scheme that I'd kept as a last resort. Wherever we have a follower or an instrument, in every part of the country, I've had an anonymous letter addressed to the bishop saying that if he reveals any of the secrets that Ducoudray told him, or if he uses them in any way, every priest will be murdered within twenty-four hours. I even sent several trustworthy agents to deposit these letters in the most out-of-the-way post offices, in the unlikeliest places where our society couldn't possibly have taken root.'

'But what if someone were to denounce you? What if someone refused to write the anonymous letter you asked for?'

'It's not that at all! I'm not asking anyone to write; I said I was having these letters addressed to all the bishops in every part of the country. I should have said *mailed*. In fact, every letter has been written, sealed, addressed, and stamped by me, put into another envelope and sent to an associate with a note telling him to put it in the mail. We can ask the least advanced of our friends for this favour, even the ones who don't know the real goals of our organization and think we're an insurance company.'

'Brilliant! a true stroke of genius!' Sir Henry exclaimed, his face aglow. 'You really are a clever fellow!'

'It's our last hope. Right now the bishop's table must be literally covered with these letters. Ducoudray's death should convince him that it isn't a hollow threat; that is one of the great advantages to be gained from suppressing a traitor by violence. Perhaps he will come to the conclusion that he should keep his mouth shut. I was very careful not to threaten him personally: on the contrary, in fact, several of the letters state formally that he will not be touched, that we will keep him alive so that he can contemplate the corpses of his priests.'

'Perhaps that is a stroke of genius,' said Sir Henry, 'but if I had been in your place I should certainly have threatened the archbishop himself.'

'Well, Marwood, you know a lot about men of the world, but I know more about those who adore our Enemy, Jesus Christ. It's always dangerous to give them the opportunity to become martyrs. You never know what excess of self-sacrifice the one they worship might suggest to them. If I had threatened the bishop, there isn't the slightest doubt that by now everything would have been uncovered. By threatening the priests, I hope at least to make him hesitate long enough so that we can win here, in Parliament. Once the bill has been passed, it doesn't matter what happens. We'll have a *fait accompli*, which is always a very powerful weapon.'

'I have to tell you,' said the Prime Minister, 'that your plan is nothing short of marvellous. Your talent is truly extraordinary.'

'If this plan fails, though,' Montarval replied, 'I have to admit that I am at the end of my resources. We would have a total disaster on our hands. While we await our fate it is absolutely essential that we speed the adoption of the bill, but without pushing the House so much that people will be suspicious.'

At about the same time the two conspirators were having this conversation, Lamirande and Leverdier were walking along one of the long avenues between Wellington Street and the Parliament buildings. It was a fine day, almost mild, toward the end of February. The setting sun turned to gold and purple the small fluffy clouds that drifted lazily here and there in the blue sky. Something indefinable in the air announced that winter was nearly over, and you could almost smell spring in the air. But the two friends were not in harmony with nature's profound calm. Both were troubled, worried, and preoccupied and Lamirande's broken heart had not yet mended. Christian virtue is not insensitive or indifferent or stoical; it reacts keenly to suffering, tolerating it with patience and resignation, in perfect union with the suffering of man and of the Mother of Sorrows.

They were walking sadly past the building where the destiny of their race was being decided. They were unaware of the splendours of the setting sun, the softness of the air.

'Is it possible,' Lamirande asked, 'that we could have been so wrong? The papers that poor Ducoudray gave the Archbishop of Montreal were certainly important. They must contain undeniable proof that this constitution is a direct product of the Masonic lodges and that we are confronting a truly infernal conspiracy to prevent New France from taking its place among the nations of the earth. And yet the Archbishop of Montreal is silent! I don't understand at all and if I didn't have invincible faith in the promise of my patron saint I would be tempted to despair.'

'That's the second time in two days you've referred to a promise. When you heard about Ducoudray's conversion and his tragic death you said, "The promise is being fulfilled." What does all this mean?'

'Forgive me, my friend, it was a slip of the tongue. I cannot say more, even to you whom I love like a brother. Later you will be told everything.'

And as he remembered his heavy sacrifice and his beloved whom he had given up for patriotism, his eyes filled with tears and he could not repress a sob.

'My poor friend, how you must suffer.' Leverdier murmured.

The two companions continued to walk for some time in silence.

'It's true,' said Leverdier at last, 'that this lack of word from His Grace is most discouraging. Like you, I was firmly convinced that the documents he was given must contain weapons that could help us save our position if we received them at an opportune time. But the Archbishop of Montreal must have serious reasons for his behaviour.'

'I am absolutely convinced of that too. I'm sure he will eventually answer the letter I wrote the day after he testified. As you know, I asked if there was anything in Ducoudray's papers that could help us.'

Just then one of the Commons' pageboys came up to the two men and handed Lamirande a sealed envelope. He recognized the handwriting immediately – it was a telegram, or rather a letter written by telegraph, by the Archbishop of Montreal, in his own hand.

'It always happens,' said Lamirande. 'Speak of the angels and you hear the rustling of their wings. This is an answer to my letter.'
And he read:

Archepiscopal Palace, Montreal
22 February 1946, 5:00 p.m.
My dear Lamirande,
Can you possibly come to see me today? A number of my venerable colleagues are here and we wish to communicate to you some important and serious information that we cannot transmit in writing.
Awaiting the pleasure of meeting you, believe me your devoted servant in Our Lord Jesus Christ.
(signed) Archbishop of Montreal

'Good news at last!' Lamirande exclaimed. 'His Grace wouldn't summon me to Montreal unless he had found something important in those papers. He must want to pass something on to me directly.'
'Let's hope you're right,' replied Leverdier.
'What do you mean? Do you suspect something?'
'I'm afraid the solution may not be as simple as you think. I can't believe that the wicked men we have been dealing with can be at the end of their resources already. I'm afraid of some infernal machination — I can't be more specific, but I don't think that diabolical sect has been beaten yet. Did Montarval and Sir Henry seem as crushed as we expected the day after Ducoudray's murder?'
'I must admit that Montarval at least seems as haughty and impassive as ever; if he is afraid, he hides it well. Sir Henry seems more uncomfortable than usual — anyway, we'll soon know what's going on. There's a fast train at six o'clock. I have time to catch it and I'll be at the archbishop's palace before eight o'clock. I should be able to let you know the results of our conversation later tonight.'
The two friends then parted.
Soon the train, propelled by a powerful electric current that was transmitted by the rails to the wheels, was carrying Lamirande to Montreal at a speed of more than eighty miles an hour. Even this speed seemed unbearably slow to Lamirande, who wished that his body could be transported with the speed of thought. He did not share his friend's vague apprehensions, and the more he thought of the events of the last days the more he was convinced that the

dénouement was near, a dénouement that would be favourable to his patriotic hopes. The archbishop had proof of a Masonic conspiracy against the province; he had called together his colleagues and prepared a collective letter with supporting evidence; the letter would be communicated to him and, thus armed, he would conquer party spirit. Patriotism would win at last, the House would defeat the Government's evil project and New France would be born from the ruins of an anti-Christian sect.

This was the smiling image that made his heart rejoice, absorbed all his attention and made him unaware of external objects, the dizzying speed of the train, and the swirling of the woods and fields. The beauty of the landscape was not marred by the slightest thought of personal ambition, no matter how legitimate. In the past he might sometimes have thought of himself as the eventual leader of the new nation, even desiring the post in order that he might work for the glory of God and the fortunes of his country. Now, however, the great sorrow he had endured had further purified his soul, already so noble, so unselfish. His political aspirations did not contain the slightest element of personal advancement. When the great victory was won he would drop back into the obscurity of a life that would be modestly useful to his compatriots. His heart was filled with the memory of his dear Marguerite, the love of his child, the knowledge that he had made an enormous sacrifice for the love of his country. He would be happy to see others in the high post to which he had felt, in the past, that he himself was called. It was enough for him to consider that the position of leader of New France could never have existed if he had not sacrificed his greatest human love. For he saw as clearly as though it were written that Ducoudray's conversion was a payment for his own sacrifice; he was convinced that this grace had been Heaven's reply to his freely given sacrifice of his own happiness, and he could not doubt the effectiveness of the means chosen by Providence to bring about the country's salvation.

Thus he arrived at the archbishop's palace without a shadow of concern in his soul.

He was taken to the large salon where the archbishop was surrounded by his assistants and several bishops from Quebec and Ottawa, all obviously awaiting his arrival. Lamirande kneeled and asked the bishop's blessing.

'My dear child,' he said, in an effusion of paternal affection, 'may God bless you and give you the grace to bear like a Christian the great trial that is reserved for you.'

His words struck Lamirande like lightning. He rose to his feet, pale and unsteady. The room was spinning around him like an immense wheel and he had to lean against a chair to avoid falling.

'Your Grace!' he exclaimed, 'I beg you, explain what you mean! Is it possible that you have found nothing that will help uncover the infernal conspiracy that I am absolutely convinced is at work here?'

The prelate rose and formed a circle around Lamirande and the archbishop.

'Alas!' the old man replied. 'Far from finding nothing I have found far too much. It is frightful.'

He shuddered as though he were in pain. He was as much affected as Lamirande, who moved suddenly from despondency to joy.

'I understand, Your Grace, that reading the papers has horrified you; you must have felt that you were facing the jaws of Hell. But the more diabolical we show the conspiracy to be, the easier it will be to make it fail.'

'My poor friend,' the bishop replied, 'you cannot possibly imagine the truth. I asked God to give you the grace to bear a great trial like a Christian. This is the trial that I spoke of: in the papers that M. Ducoudray gave me I found everything that you might suspect and more, but I cannot allow you to use it.'

'But why, Milord?' Lamirande exclaimed, intrigued but not at all discouraged.

'Come and see,' said the bishop, leading him to a table covered with letters.

'Here are some letters,' he went on; 'read some — just take a few at random.'

Lamirande obeyed and he in turn murmured, 'This is monstrous!'

'There are 537 like the five you have just read,' said the bishop, 'and they all say the same terrible thing. Look at them: they come from every part of the country. I received the first one the very day that Ducoudray died, from Montreal and around the city. Then, as the news spread, they began to arrive from everywhere. I received some today from the farthest parts of the Gaspé and Abitibi. Some are badly written and misspelled and others don't contain a single error. Some are typed, others are written in pencil. There aren't two that are written by the same hand or on the same kind of paper and no two envelopes are alike. There is nothing to indicate that it is a hoax and God knows that my venerable colleagues and I all suspected such a hoax and have been searching for proof of one. But the more we looked the more we found proof to the contrary. We finally had to admit that the letters really have come from all over the country.'

'Yes, Milord,' Lamirande sighed, 'they were undoubtedly *written* in many different places, but as the result of an order sent from Montreal!'

'That is quite possible, even certain, but think carefully and you will realize that this order, far from diminishing the horror of the situation, only adds to it. We have proof of the existence of a terrifying organization with ramifications in all parts of the country, directed by one person.'

'But is it possible that the demon has such control over our country?'

'Alas, alas, there is the proof,' replied the prelate, pointing to the pile of letters. 'If an angel had suggested such a thing to me a week ago I should not have believed it; but now we must accept the evidence of these terrible letters. My God! My God! What a tragedy this is!'

And heavy tears fell down the holy bishop's wrinkled cheeks.

'But Your Grace, do you and your venerable colleagues really believe that the authors of these threats will dare to carry them out? Do you really believe that your priests would be murdered if you use the information you have?'

'Ducoudray was stabbed in the middle of Saint Catherine Street, practically under the eyes of the police. Does that not answer your question?'

Lamirande could not argue against such a reply. They were all silent for several minutes.

'If only he had threatened me along with my priests, with the grace of God my decision would have been easy,' said the archbishop. 'I could have said, "Here is a great duty for us to carry out; it may cost us our lives, but let us do it all the same and may God's will be done." But see how infernally clever these wretched people are! Not one of the letters contained a threat against me personally;

on the contrary, many say that they would avoid harming me so that, seeing my priests die one after the other, I could be fully aware of the extent of the disaster I had caused.'

'But Your Grace,' Lamirande exclaimed with all the strength of a drowning man clutching at a straw, 'do you not see that this unanimity in the threats is a clear indication that they all come from the same source?'

'Yes, replied the bishop sadly, 'a single head gave the orders, but that head directs a thousand arms.'

'It isn't possible!' Lamirande exclaimed. 'It's just not possible that in this province there could be a thousand assassins like the one who struck Ducoudray, or five hundred or one hundred or fifty or even twenty-five!'

'But you must admit that there are three at least, because poor Ducoudray was followed by three men. Only one man struck him but surely you cannot doubt that the other two were equally ready to act. Three assassins like them could shed great quantities of blood. Even if they could not assassinate all the priests they could kill a large number, and I could not condemn a single man to die while I myself was condemned to live.'

'But what about our country, Your Grace? Does your silence not condemn our country to death? You are convinced, like me, that if the constitution, the fruit of that dark conspiracy Ducoudray revealed to you, is imposed on us, our province is handed over once and for all to the infernal sect. It will be both prey and victim. What will be the state of the Church after a few years if this Masonic constitution is adopted? What will be the state of our faith and our customs? If you are so horrified at the thought that your revelations could lead indirectly to the death of a few priests, just think, Your Grace, try to imagine the effect if your silence were the direct cause of the eternal loss of God knows how many souls!'

The old bishop wept.

'Ah!' he murmured. 'If only I could die myself.'

'Your Grace,' Lamirande replied, 'sometimes the execution of one's duty requires sacrifices that are infinitely harder even than death which, for Christians after all, is only the painful passage-way to a better life.'

'But if I exposed my priests to death while my own safety was assured, I would loathe myself forever.'

'That is why I said just now that death is not always the greatest sacrifice that God can ask of us. For men of conscience, making oneself loathsome to oneself and others is a thousand times more horrible than simply dying. But if it is one's duty, Your Grace!'

'If I were certain that I would not at the same time become loathsome in the eyes of God! If I were certain that my duty is as you see it; if I could at least hope that my revelations would free us from the Masonic yoke that threatens us! But I have no such hope. I have considered everything you have said, my dear Lamirande. My colleagues and I have examined the situation; we have counted all the MPs. If we were to suppose that my revelations would turn all the Catholics against the prime minister he would still have a majority. A weak one, but large enough to pass the bill. Have you considered that?'

Lamirande had not. He was silent for a moment.

'But these revelations,' he began, 'would surely cause a number of non-Catholics to break away: my friend Vaughan and his group, for instance.'

'You think, or at least you hope, that that is so, but you cannot be morally certain. While we are morally certain of the opposite. For we know from doctrine, and through long experience that confirms the doctrine for us, that true faith is the necessary basis for all true good. Where faith exists, there is a solid foundation. Faith can be hidden like a rock, by waves or mud, but you can reach it and build your edifice upon it. Building where there is no faith is like building on sand. We can reasonably count on all the Catholics, because they all have that faith. But we are not permitted to count on the non-Catholics, even those whose souls are naturally honest. So you see, my dear friend, the position I find myself in: first of all, I have the moral certainty that if I speak out I will expose my priests to death; and secondly, that this will serve no useful purpose for the country.'

Lamirande was silent, seeking some way out of the terrible impasse. The bishop spoke again:

'There is only one thing I can and must do. You yourself were horribly slandered by Ducoudray when he accused you of wanting to sell out to the government. He left no document on the subject but he begged me to state publicly that it was totally fabricated and the opposite of the truth; that Sir Henry tried to tempt you but that you nobly rejected the temptation. My duty there is quite clear.

Moreover, as it is but a single incident that is not fundamentally related to Ducoudray's revelations I hope the murderers will not carry out their threats for such a small thing.'

'Of course,' Lamirande replied, 'the slander hurt me deeply and it did great harm to the cause that I defend. Without it the elections might have turned out differently. But today my personal rehabilitation is quite secondary. It won't change a single vote in the House. And perhaps the author of the threats would judge this revelation differently from you, perhaps he would strike. I beg you, Milord, don't say anything about it. I don't want to expose anyone to the slightest danger for the sake of my reputation, especially at a time when that reputation is of no interest to the public anyway.'

'You have a noble heart,' said the bishop, very moved.

A long and painful silence followed. Something told Lamirande that he was right, but he found that he could make no reply to the archbishop's contradictory reasoning.

'Is your mind firmly made up, Your Grace?' he asked finally.

'Yes, my child,' the archbishop replied affectionately. 'It is my duty, my painful duty, for I have no illusions about the fate that is reserved for us. God is my witness that I would gladly sacrifice my own life if it could save our country. But it is a dreadful thing to sacrifice the lives of those who are dear to us.'

'It is indeed,' Lamirande murmured, almost to himself; 'but with the grace of God it can be done.'

'Could you do it, M. Lamirande?'

'Yes, Milord; in fact I have already done so.'

'What! You have! What do you mean?'

Then, choking with emotion, his voice breaking into sobs, he told the bishops, in all humility, of his great sacrifice. Their tears mixed with his own. One after another, unable to speak, they came to embrace him.

'Could you not do what I have done? My wife is dead because I willed it, and I am still alive.'

'The position is not the same, my child,' said the archbishop. 'Your noble wife agreed to die.'

At these words Lamirande's face was suddenly illuminated by a celestial glow. He had found the escape he sought. He threw himself to his knees.

'Thank you for what you just said, Your Grace. It holds our country's salvation. Give me your blessing, for I am leaving.'

He rose, bade farewell to the august assembly, and went away, leaving the bishops amazed.

The good shepherd lays down his life for the sheep.
JOHN 10:11

22

THERE WAS A TRAIN FOR OTTAWA at a quarter past ten, and Lamirande had just enough time to catch it. He arrived in the capital at midnight. Leverdier, not expecting him until morning, had already gone to bed, but Lamirande did not hesitate to wake his friend. He told him everything that had happened, except for the incident at the end of the interview, saying only,

'To cut short my story, it's clear to me that there is only one thing that will persuade the archbishop to reveal the secrets he possesses: that is to ensure that all the members of the clergy will say unanimously, "Speak, Your Grace. We accept the consequences of your revelation, no matter how terrible they may be for us." I have enough faith in the clergy's patriotism to believe that if the situation is clearly presented to them they will respond nobly and with a single voice.'

'And I share your confidence,' the journalist replied simply.

'Let's get to work then!'

The two friends began to compose a circular letter. In an hour their task was finished. Here is what they wrote:

House of Commons, Ottawa
28 February 1946
Dear Father,
You have no doubt heard of the conversion of Charles Ducoudray and of the tragic but Christian end to his life; and you have read the testimonies of the Archbishop of Montreal and Father Grandmont, given at the coroner's inquest. You know, too, that Ducoudray was murdered for having communicated to the religious authorities the secrets of the occult society of which he had been a member. The press has written at length of all these extraordinary events, but there is more to the story than the public is aware of. Until now there has been only conjecture as to the nature of the secrets given to the Archbishop of Montreal by the heroic convert.

For some time now all those who are involved in politics have suspected the existence in this country of a dark and truly demonic organization that works in the shadows but with dreadful efficacity for the ruin of our beloved province. Superhuman efforts are being made to repress our patriotic spirit and to prevent French Canada from becoming an autonomous nation at the very moment when Divine Providence makes possible the realization of this project. These efforts, along with the cleverly treacherous constitution that the government wants to impose on us, seem to indicate clearly the existence of an anti-clerical and anti-French conspiracy that has been planned by the Masonic lodges.

It was because I was convinced that this was true that I wrote to Milord the Archbishop of Montreal the day after Ducoudray's death to ask if he had found any proof of such a conspiracy in the records of the sect. His Grace was silent for ten days. Last night he finally asked to see me. I went to him filled with joy and confidence, expecting I would soon have weapons strong enough to allow us to carry off a decisive victory over the sect. Imagine my sorrow when His Grace told me that I was condemned to an enormous disappointment. "Have you found nothing in Ducoudray's papers?" I asked him. "On the contrary," he replied, "I have found too much." Then he showed me a table covered with anonymous letters from every part of the country threatening all the priests with death if the bishop revealed the secrets Ducoudray had given him or if he used them in any way. I was unable to examine all the letters myself, but His Grace assured me that he had studied them with his episcopal colleagues, and that he had found nothing to suggest that it is merely a hoax; nor does Ducoudray's murder permit us to think that these are hollow threats. If the wording of these more than 500 letters is infinitely varied, the basis is the same: the priests are being threatened, but great care is being taken not to touch the bishop. I do not need to emphasize the infernal craftiness of this tactic, which makes it morally impossible for the archbishop to act. If only he himself were threatened, or if he had been threatened along with the priests, his decision would have been easy. But how could he decide to expose others to a cruel death while he himself is safe? The Archbishop of Montreal is incapable of such an action.

The uniformity of these threats indicates clearly that they issue from a single mind, even if several hands wrote the letters. But that does not improve the situation; far from it. For this single head that directs so many murderous hands horrifies His Grace, and for good reason. An organization that can strike a man with impunity in the heart of Montreal can commit many other similar crimes; there is no reason to deny that.

In order to point out the entire situation I must add that there is another reason why His Grace hesitates to reveal the secrets he possesses; he is convinced that to do so would be useless. Suppose, he says, that these revelations about the Masonic influence on the bill currently before the House could bring all the Catholic MPs to vote against it. Even then there would still be a majority, albeit a weak one, in favour of the government policy. I can add little to that, for the figures certainly show that His Grace is right. I only hope that such revelations will inspire a number of non-Catholic members of the government party who have sufficient honour to vote with us and give us the majority. His Grace does not share my optimism; at least, he finds the shred of hope too feeble to justify endangering the lives of his priests. If it were a question of his own life, I am absolutely convinced that he would not hesitate for a moment to expose the machinations of the sect, even if he were convinced that it would not even bring about the defeat of the bill. For he would tell himself, "Do what must be done, come what may."

And that, Father, is the situation in all its horror. It would be an insult to your patriotism, to your devotion, and to your intelligence if I were to add the slightest comment or make the least request.

Please accept my sincere compliments.
Joseph Lamirande, MP

The two friends spent the night making copies of the letter and addressing them to all the priests in the province. At nine o'clock in the morning all was ready. They were nearly dead with fatigue.

'Come on,' said Lamirande, 'let's mail these letters and then rest a bit. The sooner they're on their way the better.'

'Are you planning to mail them here in Ottawa?' Leverdier asked.

'Why not?'

'Because Montarval must have followers all over, especially in the post office, and he would simply tear them up. I'm absolutely certain that if we mail them here, not one of these letters will reach its destination.'

'You may be right; I hadn't thought of that. And it wouldn't be any better to mail them in Hull or any other city in the area. If he keeps an eye on the postal service in Ottawa he must do the same thing in Montreal and even in Quebec. What shall we do?'

'I have an idea!' the journalist exclaimed. 'It's unlikely that the Toronto post office is under surveillance. I'll go and mail them there.'

'It's a good idea, but only in part, because Montarval must be watching us even more closely than the post offices. I'm sure he knows every move we make. You remember the famous Duthier, Sir Henry's servant who is now one of the ushers in the House of Commons. Well, he was on the train to Montreal last night and he was also on the train that I took back here. There is absolutely no doubt that he was following me. He'd be right on your trail if you went to Toronto. But I think I have a solution: Vaughan can take the letters to Toronto. He could go there without arousing any suspicions. Let's go and find him.'

Ten minutes later the two friends were at the home of the young English Canadian, who was just preparing to go out.

'Vaughan,' said Lamirande, 'will you do me a great favour and not ask any questions about it?'

'Of course, if I can.'

'It's quite simple. I'd like you to be good enough to take the ten-thirty train to Toronto.'

'But that's exactly what I was about to do anyway. What can I do for you in Toronto?'

'I'd like you to mail several hundred letters.'

'Why not do it here?'

'You weren't to ask any questions!'

'Quite right! But where are the letters? That's another question? But it is permitted, isn't it?'

'They're at Leverdier's place. Forgive me for being so mysterious. I'll tell you all about it later. For the moment, I can only say that there are very serious reasons to believe that if I were to mail these letters in Ottawa, they would never reach their destination.'

'That's reason enough for me. Of course, I'm burning with curiosity about the story that must be behind all this, but I'm reasonable enough to wait for the explanation you've promised.'

'Thank you, my dear friend,' said Lamirande.

'Let's go then,' said Vaughan. 'It's almost time for the train.'

He picked up a small suitcase and went to the door.

'Don't you have a bigger valise?' Lamirande asked. 'We can't put a quarter of the letters into that little bag. But wait, I have another idea. That bag will be fine. Let's go.'

They went out. In the street, near Vaughan's apartment, they met Duthier.

'Did you see him?' Lamirande asked Leverdier in a low voice. 'He's right on our trail.'

Back at their boarding house Lamirande and Leverdier put the letters into a valise that Leverdier picked up. Lamirande took down another, empty bag.

'What are you going to do with that?' asked his companion.

'Play a trick on that spy Duthier! We're allowed a bit of fun after the fatigue and emotional upsets of the last eighteen hours, and I need to relax.'

Vaughan was waiting for them outside. When he saw them come out, each carrying a suitcase he uttered an exclamation of surprise. Lamirande gestured to him to speak quietly. Duthier was stationed on the other side of the street in front of a store, absorbed in a handsome display of neckties.

'Are there enough to fill two suitcases?' Vaughan asked in a low voice.

And as Lamirande smiled instead of answering, he said, 'Of course. I keep forgetting that I'm not supposed to ask questions.'

'That question was permitted,' Lamirande replied. 'There's nothing at all in the trunk that I'm carrying. It's just to prove to Leverdier and myself that we're not imposing a senseless burden on you.'

'The burden is nothing; it's the mystery surrounding it that I'd like to understand. What you just told me is just another riddle.'

'You'll have an explanation in the next issue.'

'As long as we don't have to wait too long for it!'

The three friends arrived at the railway station. The bell had just sounded five times.

'Right on time!' said Vaughan. 'Goodbye for now!'

'We're coming with you,' said Lamirande.

The two friends got onto the train with Vaughan and sat down with him like ordinary travellers. Vaughan was very puzzled, but he had promised to ask no more questions.

An instant later Duthier boarded the train and took a seat near the three friends. He unfolded a newspaper and began with great interest to read the news of the day.

'Be prepared,' said Lamirande to Leverdier in a low voice.

He had barely uttered his warning when the bell rang twice and the conductor shouted the traditional 'All aboard!' The train shook and got under way. Then Lamirande took the empty suitcase that he had put onto the rack along beside the other one and quickly saying goodbye to Vaughan, who was more and more puzzled, leaped out of the train with Leverdier following close behind. They were able to jump onto the platform without difficulty. Duthier, completely taken by surprise and in fact more or less reading his newspaper, did not realize that the men he had been ordered to follow had left the train until they were on the platform. He in turn left his seat and ran towards the door, but unfortunately at the same moment a very fat woman, carrying a child and a number of packages, decided to leave her seat because the sun was in her eyes. She blocked Duthier's passage.

'Let me by,' he shouted, furious.

The poor bewildered woman arranged herself as best she could, and the usher passed through, knocking over a hatbox and a tin of biscuits.

It had been only a slight delay, but the train had picked up speed. The luckless Duthier hesitated for a moment on the runningboard, but the sight of Lamirande and Leverdier standing on the platform where the train had already passed by made up his mind for him. He jumped. But he obviously did not excel at jumping from moving trains. He executed a superb pirouette and rolled in the sand alongside the track. He got up in a very bad mood, and noted that the only harm done was to his coat and trousers. He would have liked to avoid the station and the people standing around there who had witnessed his misadventure, but he remembered that if he had risked life and limb it was so that Lamirande would not get out of his sight. So he cleaned himself off as well as he could and went to the station. He was greeted by ill-concealed smiles, and as Lamirande came to meet him he remarked, 'Be sure they pay you what you've earned.'

All this time the train was taking Vaughan to Toronto, at full speed. The young politician was lost in conjectures on what had just happened. Lamirande had given him the key to the remaining suitcase. He took it down from the rack, opened it and noted that the letters that filled it were all addressed to priests. However, he was far from suspecting that the answers to these letters would determine the destiny of an entire people.

Do not prattle in the assembly of the elders.
ECCLESIASTICUS

23

THE HOUSE OPENED THAT DAY, and the galleries overflowed with spectators, for word had spread that the government was about to open fire and propose first reading of the bill entitled 'Act to provide for the establishment of the government of the Republic of Canada.' The general expectations were not disappointed. A few minutes after three o'clock, when the House had disposed of a variety of minor 'petitions,' 'reports,' and 'motions,' Sir Henry rose. There was applause from the government side, while among the French Canadians a certain reserve, even concern, could be noticed.

The prime minister's speech, very plausible, very literary, at times even attaining eloquence, increased the enthusiasm of his supporters and seemed to reassure many of the French Canadians. Sir Henry gave an account of the political events of the last few years. 'Canada,' he said, 'is an exceptionally fortunate country because it has at last attained autonomy and complete independence, smoothly, without upset or revolution or bloodshed. Like a fine ripe fruit, it has gently and naturally detached itself from the tree that produced it. We must not spoil the admirable work of the force we call the Supreme Being, who has arranged to allow us to found a great nation, spreading from one ocean to the other and occupying half of an immense continent. There are narrow-minded, disturbed people who would like to destroy this great work, break up this vast empire and disunite this great people under the pretext of the existence of different languages and religions among us. But these differences constitute an argument in favour of union rather than separation, for they will provide a pleasant variety within our unity. They will create healthy rivalry among the various elements that comprise our people; and they will allow the exercise of a great civic virtue that is essential to national prosperity: tolerance. The first bill that the government had the honour to submit to the House was misunderstood. Without daring to say so formally and without being able to prove it, some people have insinuated that the bill was the fruit of some dark conspiracy against the language and religion of some of the inhabitants of this country. There has been vague talk about secret societies, Masonic or other kinds of lodges plotting behind the scenes to destroy certain ideas and institutions. People claim to have found traces of this occult work in the bill itself. It is very painful to record that in the middle of the twentieth century there are still people who defend such worn-out old ideas. We cannot deny that appeals to the national and religious prejudices of a third of the population at first produced a certain amount of excitement: one of our colleagues even felt it his duty to abandon us to follow the movement that was created. But calm and reflection worked wonders. Today everyone, or almost everyone, agrees that what seemed to be a great peril was in fact our salvation. The silence of those who are particularly responsible for safeguarding the religious interests of the Catholics should prove to even the most timid and suspicious that the constitution submitted to the House for ratification is not hostile to any religious belief. It is a purely political work that does not threaten anyone's religion or nationality, and it should be judged according to sound practical principles, not according to racial or religious prejudices or fanciful puerile fears.'

Sir Henry's wily and treacherous speech went on for more than an hour.

Lawrence Houghton replied to him. The English-Canadian Leader of the Opposition declared that, following parliamentary procedure, he would not ask the House to vote on first reading of the bill, which is only a formality. 'But,' he said, 'I want it understood that my colleagues and I intend to fight this bill to the end, using every means that Parliament puts at our disposal. Because they seem blinded for reasons I do not understand and do not wish to qualify, the members from Quebec, with the exception of a small minority, seem willing to accept the proposed constitution, if we are to judge their intentions by their enthusiastic applause of the honourable prime minister. I am not trying to appear more French-Canadian than the representatives of the province of Quebec or more Catholic than those of my colleagues who profess the Roman cult. But I cannot help seeing and saying that this constitution, whether it was formulated in a secret lodge or in the prime minister's office, has but one goal: the strangling of the French element and the Catholic religion. Perhaps I will be told that if the French and the Catholics want to be strangled by the central government, what does that have to do with the English and the Protestants? It is true that we must not claim that we have a mission to protect the French and the Catholics despite themselves. But we know that sooner or later Catholic French Canada will realize its error, awaken from its strange sleep, and shake off this hypnotic trance into which it has been plunged. It will bitterly regret having entered this union that was not made for it; it will want to leave, and there will be long, exhausting, disastrous battles, leading perhaps to civil war. We see all this quite clearly. It is in our interest as well as in the interest of French Canada for us to seek to prevent the disaster the government is preparing for us through this union of elements that can live in peace only if they are independent of one another. We hope that English and French Canadians can get along like neighbours, joined by a simple customs and postal treaty. They will never get along together if we try to unite them through this bill that is, after all, only ill-disguised legislative union. There are too many basic differences between the two races who inhabit this country to be able to make them into a truly united nation. To achieve union, one of three things would be necessary: the peaceful fusion of the two elements into one; the equally peaceful absorption of one by the other; or the violent destruction of one of the races. The first two solutions are obviously impossible. One has only to study a little history to realize that peoples are never fused together without injustice, violence, conquest, and oppression. We often say that the English people themselves are the product of a fusion of Anglo-Saxons and the Normans. True; but the Normans conquered the Saxons and who can say what hatred, curses, and bitterness preceded and accompanied this fusion? Who can tell all that the Anglo-Saxons suffered before they formed a single and united people along with those by whom they had been conquered? We are not inclined to attempt a similar experiment. This country is large enough to contain several peoples, several nations. Providence has placed most of the French of America in the north-eastern part of the continent. It is the cradle of their race. Today their numbers are sufficient to form an autonomous nation. And so they should. At this time they do not appear to understand their national destiny, but, as I have said, they are truly hypnotized. This sorcery cannot last much longer. When they come out of this unnatural slumber, when patriotism takes hold among them again, we do not want them to find themselves at the bottom of the pit that is being dug beneath their feet. I repeat: it is in our own interests as well as theirs that we want to prevent this.'

This speech, so true, frank, and luminous, made a vivid impression on the House. More than one French member felt ashamed to be forced to admit that the English Protestant had just taught the French-Canadian members a lesson that was as terrible as it was well deserved.

Montarval rose to reply. There was slight applause, and a strange malaise was felt in the House.

The minister realized that it would take very little to cause real panic among the French supporters of the cabinet. He could read on their faces the doubts and hesitations that were tormenting them. He understood in a moment what remedy the situation required. Before he began to speak, he leaned towards his colleague, Sir Henry, and whispered a few words in his ear. The prime minister appeared surprised, but Montarval made a gesture that meant, 'That's that!' Then the prime minister wrote a note and went out into the corridor behind the Speaker's chair. Duthier was waiting there. Sir Henry signalled to him imperceptibly and the usher came over to the prime minister without appearing to see him. When the two men met Sir Henry slipped the note he had written into his employee's hand. Two minutes later Duthier had a page deliver it to Saint-Simon.

Montarval restricted himself to a few rather vague observations. 'Our goal,' he said, 'is to develop the work of Confederation that was begun nearly eighty years ago; it is to bring together, unite, and cement the various elements scattered across the surface of what was British America and what will be Canadian America; it is to make of all these elements one nation. There has been talk of founding a New France. That would a national disaster. Instead of tiny republics let us found one great and beautiful country. It is true that Caesar said he would rather be first in a village than second in Rome, but that was the voice of selfish ambition, not an expression of patriotic sentiment. The true patriot is concerned not with the post he will occupy in his country but with the place his country will attain among the nations. As far as I am concerned, I aspire simply to be a citizen of a great country.'

When Montarval had finished his speech, the Speaker waited a few moments, then put the question to the vote. Before he had time to say 'Carried!' Saint-Simon was on his feet.

'Mr Speaker!' he exclaimed harshly, 'this constitutional project is so odious it should never have been presented. I propose that it be given first reading not now but in six months' time.'

'The honourable member must have a seconder,' said the Speaker.

'As an act of courtesy,' said Montarval, 'I support the honourable member's motion, so that he can find out immediately that the House does not share his opinion.'

The proposal was thus put in order. The member for Quebec made an extremely violent speech, flagellating the government, the English and the Protestants, but being very careful not to use any solid argument against the ministerial project. It was a furious diatribe against everything that was not French and Roman Catholic. After this mild harangue, which went on for half an hour, the government policy had not received a single scratch while the blatant insults addressed to the ministers had returned to them the sympathy of their partisans, which had been temporarily shaken by Houghton. The House made no attempt to hide the profound disgust this speech had caused.

'Mr Speaker,' Lamirande began as soon as Saint-Simon had taken his seat, 'I have only two words to say: one word of thanks and one of protest. From the bottom of my heart I thank the Honourable Leader of the Opposition for his noble words. If New France awakens from her lethargy in time to overtake the freedom that is escaping her, she will owe him an eternal debt of gratitude. She will erect statues, and on the pedestals will be inscribed: "To Lawrence Houghton, English Protestant statesman, from a grateful French Catholic nation." And if she does not awaken, if she succumbs to her enemies' embrace, history will speak of her in the words the Latin poet put into the mouth of Hector when he announced the imminent fall of Troy to Aeneas:

> Si Pergama dextra
> Defendi possent, etiam hac defensa fuissent.*

But I hope that history will not have to record this cry of pain: I still hope that the present intrigues' (and as he said this Lamirande gave

---

* If a mortal man could have defended Pergamon, certainly that arm would have defended it.

Montarval a look that made him turn pale) 'these abominable intrigues and iniquities will not prevail and that New France will live.

'And now, Mr Speaker, my word of protest, which is addressed to the member from Quebec. With all the strength I can summon I condemn the despicable sentiments that he has just expressed. In the true patriotism that is recognized and approved by the religion of Jesus Christ, there is no sentiment but love of one's country. There is no room for hatred of other races. The patriot who is not content to love his own country but hates that of others is a false patriot, and sooner or later he will betray the cause he claims to defend, if he has not already done so.'

Saint-Simon's motion was put to the vote. Not a single government member wavered. Like one man they all voted on the first reading, which was given a strong majority.

'There they are, all formed into regiments,' Montarval whispered to Sir Henry. 'They've voted once in favour of the bill. Now it would take a dreadful blow to prevent them from voting the same way on second and third reading. In any battle the important point is to arrange for your troops to fire the first shot under conditions that are as favourable as possible.'

'You are unquestionably a genius,' said Sir Henry.

In honour and dishonour, in ill repute and good repute.
II CORINTHIANS 6:8

24

LAMIRANDE, LEVERDIER, HOUGHTON, and several other opposition members met as they were leaving the House.

'My dear Lamirande,' said Houghton, 'what are we going to do? What can we do? Good sense, justice, honour – all the good things in the world are on our side, but there are big battalions against us. This iniquitous project is bound to pass second and third reading with another huge majority, unless the province of Quebec wakes up – and there is nothing to indicate that that is near.'

'Nothing on the outside,' Lamirande replied, 'but I still have hopes – not just a vague feeling, but something based on the solid foundation of devotion, patriotism, and the spirit of sacrifice of our clergy. In a few days it is possible that something will happen that will awaken the province of Quebec as a country has never been awakened before.'

'If you are that optimistic,' said Houghton, 'we must organize ourselves to gain time. We must delay second and third reading as long as possible.'

Next day the battle began. Both sides had to display great skill. The government, while it pressed for the adoption of its evil bill, had to be careful to avoid any unseemly haste which could arouse suspicions and offend anyone's feelings. A good many of the government members wanted to speak on this highly important question, and their speeches had long been prepared. To silence them would have been as imprudent as turning off the safety valve of a steam engine. The opposition could criticize and fight the measure, but if it were seen to be openly filibustering it would give the majority a pretext for using the drastic means of closure to end the debate.

To the government proposal 'that the bill be read for the second time' Houghton and Lamirande moved the traditional opposition amendment: 'not now but in six months.' Then the speeches began.

The opposition attacked with such vigour and logic that the ministers and other government leaders had no choice but to reply.

If they had remained silent, as they had intended to do, the bulk of their army could have begun to grow demoralized. For five or six days, then, there was a running fire of questions and answers. However, everything is ultimately exhausted here on earth, even a parliamentary debate. The chief speakers for the opposition had shot all their arrows, and repetition of the same arguments by second-class orators provoked only occasional brief replies from the ministerial side. During the first days of the debate every speech made on the side of the House to the Speaker's left caused three or four government members to rise, burning with eagerness to reply, but now the opposition members were now obliged to follow one another.

At the start of the afternoon session on the seventh day, Lamirande, Leverdier, and Houghton were meeting to discuss the situation.

'It has been going on for a week now,' said Houghton to Lamirande, 'and we're at the end of our resources. Do you have any news?'

'Not yet, and I don't really expect anything for another four or five days.'

'Then wouldn't it be better to have the vote on second reading and then go back to discussion in general committee and finally on to the third reading?'

Leverdier was inclined to agree with Houghton, but Lamirande did not.

'I cannot agree,' he said, 'to have the vote on second reading now, because something tells me that we shall all need the delays we can obtain in general committee and on third reading later. Perhaps it's only a foreboding, but it's strong enough and persistent enough that I don't want to make light of it.'

'I respect everything about you, my dear Lamirande,' said Houghton, 'even your forebodings. But I really do not see how we can prolong the debate on second reading for another four or five days. Tomorrow, perhaps even tonight, they are going to want to apply closure.'

'I know,' Lamirande replied, 'so we must provoke some incident that will force suspension of debate for several days.'

'Yes, but how? I don't see any incident on the horizon,' said the leader of the opposition.

'I'm going to create one at this evening's session.'
'How?'
'I'm going to launch an accusation against the secretary of State and demand an inquiry.'
'Do you have any proof against him?'
'At the moment I don't have anything I can use.'
'You really amaze me; in fact I find it hard to understand you. You are never the one to make slanderous accusations against an adversary, even if you are sure of winning the most just battles by doing so.'
'You're quite right. "The end justifies the means," no matter what anyone says, is a doctrine that the Church condemns. We should never do harm even when we are convinced that it will lead to a great good. Theology teaches us that if it were possible to empty Hell by committing a single venial sin, we should not commit it. Besides, I didn't say that I was going to bring a *false* accusation against M. Montarval. On the contrary, I am as certain that it is true as I am that you are standing in front of me right now.'
'If you are so certain that your conscience is at ease,' Houghton replied, 'I understand. But you must realize that it is not enough to *know* that an accusation is true; you have to prove it too. And you said just now that you have no proof!'
'No proof that I can present to a committee.'
'Then how can you consider bringing this accusation against him?'
'The proof may appear any day now.'
'And if it doesn't?'
'I will be ruined forever, politically and socially.'
'At least you're going into it with your eyes open! You know exactly where this may lead.'
'Exactly!'
'Are you behaving wisely, my friend?' asked Leverdier, who had been silent until now.
'In human terms it's mad. In human terms I should wait to act until I have all the proof. You know as well as I do that it exists.'
'But you must not endanger your reputation. It doesn't belong just to you; it belongs to your friends and your country.'
'You admit that my reputation belongs to me at least as much as my life. Man is entitled to endanger his own life to save the lives of his fellow men, and we have the same right to court certain death in

order to accomplish a great act of charity. It's a question of saving an entire country, so surely I am entitled to endanger my own honour!'

'For a sensitive man,' said Houghton, 'honour is more precious than life. And you want to endanger yours! That is a truly heroic act, that I would certainly recoil from myself, although I admire it.'

'But is this terrible risk necessary or even useful?' Leverdier asked. 'Would it not be better to allow the vote on second reading, since we can hardly delay it any longer through ordinary means, and prolong the debate in committee and on the third reading as long as possible?'

'Something that is not natural, something solemn and imperative, tells me that we will need more delays later than these phases of the discussion can give us,' Lamirande replied gravely. 'It is a warning I cannot ignore. Both of you believe in the supernatural, in the existence of spirits and their power to communicate directly with the soul. Very well, I am obeying a message from on high. My God! If you knew all that I know, my dear friends, you would not try to detract me from my duty.'

All three were visibly moved. They were silent for some time.

'Besides,' said Lamirande, continuing as though he were talking to himself, 'what use would my own honour be if this man's iniquity triumphs? The loss of my reputation would be only one more drop in the sea of bitterness and desolation that would drown our poor country if God permits, because of our own crimes, that this infernal plot succeed. By exposing my honour and offering to sacrifice it, perhaps I can gain the few days I need to shed light on all this. And if the light does not appear, if our country succumbs, the burden will not be so hard to bear if I can testify that I sacrificed everything for it.'

'My mind is definitely made up,' he said, addressing his two companions. 'When the debate resumes tonight at eight o'clock I shall burn all my bridges.'

At the evening session, when it seemed that all debate was finished and that the vote on second reading was about to be taken, Lamirande rose. There was total silence, for everyone seemed to understand instinctively that something very serious was about to happen.

'Mr Speaker,' he began, 'to use the barbarism that has been consecrated by long usage, I rise on a point of privilege to make the following statement: I accuse a member of this House, the Honourable Aristide Montarval, member for Quebec Centre and secretary of State, of having conspired and plotted with various persons to deceive this House and this country as to the nature of the constitutional bill now before us. And I add that this constitutional bill is the fruit of plots and conspiracies that are contrary to the public interest, to order, and to peace. And I further accuse the Honourable Aristide Montarval of using illicit means, including threatening letters, to prevent this House from learning of the true nature of the constitutional bill it is being asked to vote on. I therefore ask that a special committee be appointed to examine this accusation, hear the proof, and present a report.'

It is hardly necessary to say that these strange words, uttered in a strong and penetrating voice, caused great excitement in the House and in the galleries. The earlier silence was replaced by muffled murmurs. As Lamirande spoke, even though his remarks were addressed to the Speaker in accordance with parliamentary custom, he had looked directly at Montarval who, despite his boldness, could not bear to look back. He was visibly terrified. He soon recovered, however; his unusual intelligence allowed him to understand what was happening. 'Lamirande *knows* everything,' he told himself, 'but he hasn't an ounce of proof. My threatening letters had their effect: the archbishop refused to turn over our files to him. He's brought this accusation against me to gain time and in the hope that the archbishop will change his mind.'

As soon as the House was calm again, Montarval rose to speak.

'The honourable member from Charlevoix,' he said with his evil smile, 'has forgotten one essential point: he has not volunteered to prove his accusation, which is even more vague than it is serious. Is this merely an oversight or is it a deliberate omission?'

And he took his seat as though waiting for a reply.

'Mr Speaker,' Lamirande began, 'when a member of this House makes an accusation against one of his colleagues, he is bound to prove it. And if I do not prove the accusation I have just made, the House can punish me in whatever way it deems suitable; I could be expelled if it is found that I have acted maliciously, without sufficient cause; and I will be dishonoured forever as a result. The honourable ministers know that I am perfectly aware of what awaits me if I do not prove my statement. My honour, which is as important to me, I suspect, as that of the secretary of state is to him, carries with it the duty not to neglect any means at my disposal to establish the truth of my accusation.'

'Very well!' Montarval replied, 'I shall be brief. Quite simply, I deny the accusation, and I deny it in the broadest and most formal manner; I deny it *in toto*. I declare that it has no basis in fact, that it is entirely and absolutely false and does not contain a single grain of truth. To prove that I do not fear an enquiry, not only do I accept the proposal that a special committee to be named, but I leave to my accuser the task of forming this committee to his own liking. Even if it is composed entirely of his friends and enemies of the government.'

'We shall leave the choice to the Speaker,' said Lamirande.

'Fine!' Montarval replied. 'And the committee must meet as soon as possible. Now, let's get back to serious business.'

The government wanted to have the vote on second reading immediately, but Houghton interrupted to point out that it would not be convenient to have the vote, even on second reading, as long as the House had not decided on the validity of Lamirande's accusation. The ministers, guided by Montarval, were inclined to ignore Houghton's observations and have the vote called. But, because of his personal friendship for Lamirande, Vaughan, who led a fairly large group within the government party, asked for a delay. Several French ministerial members who had noticed Montarval's reaction to the accusation were worried. 'After all, it may be true,' they said. They too insisted on the need for delay. These debates occupied the entire sitting and the government was forced to yield.

This was Lamirande's first success; he had gained some time, but at what a price!

It was Thursday evening. The committee was to meet the following day. Without appearing too demanding, Lamirande could request that he be given until Monday to prepare his case. But on Monday he would be forced either to proceed or to declare that there was no proof! It was not only expulsion from the House and political dishonour that awaited him. He would become the laughing stock of the entire country. He would be a fool in the eyes of the world.

Ordinary courage is sufficient to confront the ill will, anger, or hatred of one's fellow men; but to expose oneself deliberately to ridicule requires heroism. And Lamirande felt overwhelmed by a moral anguish. When he returned to his rooms after the sitting he opened his heart to Leverdier.

'Pray for me, my friend, as you have never prayed; for I am tempted as I have never been before. Pride and self-love are the most difficult feelings the human heart can be called upon to overcome. I am terrified by the thought that my compatriots will take me for a madman who should be in the Longue-Pointe asylum. Our Saviour was called a madman at Herod's court. May He give me the grace to accept this humiliation in union with Him.'

'It certainly is indeed an unenviable position' said Leverdier, 'and you have all my sympathy. If only I could diminish your suffering by sharing your sorrow!'

'Thank you, my friend, thank you! Do you know what temptation I fear I may succumb to?'

'I have no idea, unless it is despair.'

'I fear that at the last minute, seeing myself with my back to the wall and obliged to choose between ridicule and abuse of confidence, I may be weak and choose the latter, telling the committee: "Call the Archbishop of Montreal." It is certain that the holy bishop has told me about the proof he possesses in the strictest secrecy, so I cannot reveal what he has told me. But I am afraid I might do it anyway, from cowardice and pride, in order to escape ridicule. That is why I ask you to pray for me.'

The two friends stayed together, praying humbly, for some time.

The Speaker had appointed to the committee that would enquire into the accusation brought against the secretary of state seven MPs, among them the most serious and best placed of the different groups. Houghton, Leverdier, and a third member of the opposition, a member of the cabinet, and three ministerial members, including Vaughan, made up the committee, whose chairman was the minister. The committee met at ten o'clock on Friday morning; Montarval was present, insolent and provocative. The chairman read the accusation and invited the accuser to furnish proofs and witnesses. Lamirande, very calm, asked the committee to allow him a delay of two days.

'That is a most unusual request,' the chairman observed. 'As a general rule an enquiry of this kind must begin as soon as the accusation is made. It is customary for the member who believes he must denounce one of his colleagues to wait to do so until he has his proof before him.'

'That is quite true, Mr Chairman,' said Lamirande, 'and it is as an exceptional favour, not a right, that I ask the committee's indulgence in postponing this examination until Monday. I beg the members of the committee to believe me when I say that I do not act lightly in these circumstances.'

'Mr Chairman,' said Montarval, 'I have no objection at all to my accuser's extraordinary request. Not that I am indifferent or not anxious to see the end of this great hoax – for that is what it is, rather than an accusation – but because I want to give my adversary as much latitude as possible. I do not want him to be able to say later, "Ah, if the committee had given me just two days I could have produced my proof." The honourable member is the victim of a hoax, I repeat. By all means let us give him until Monday, so that he has time to realize his errors.'

All this put Montarval in a good light. His moderate, plausible words were contradicted, however, by the evil smile that wandered across his lips and did not extinguish the sinister light in his eyes. Lamirande, for his part, despite the bad position in which he already found himself, had an expression that was so severe, so composed, that all those present were struck by the contrast between the two men. Anyone who had only heard the accused and his accuser would have decided in favour of the former, while anyone who saw them could not have the slightest sympathy for Montarval.

'Very well,' said the chairman, 'since the chief interested party agrees to an adjournment, the enquiry will begin on Monday evening at eight o'clock. The House will probably not sit after six o'clock, so it will be possible for us to begin at eight o'clock. M. Lamirande, that means that next time you must come fully prepared.'

'I shall certainly not ask for another adjournment, Mr Chairman.'

What kind of preparations was Lamirande making?

For weeks he had been asking every community in the land to pray for him and his cause. Now he telegraphed all those he could reach, exhorting them to double their efforts. He visited the houses of all the religious orders in Ottawa, soliciting their spiritual aid. Then he spent three days, from Saturday to Monday, with the Capuchin Fathers, fasting and praying. He had arranged to meet Leverdier in the parliamentary library at half-past seven on Monday evening.

When he saw his friend he asked, 'Well, is there any news from the Archbishop of Montreal?'

'Not a word,' Leverdier replied sadly.

'May God's will be done.'

'My poor dear friend, how you must suffer! I share your suffering!'

'I thank you for your sympathy, it is very dear to me. But you are mistaken. I am not suffering at all. I have never been more calm and have rarely been happier.'

'But the other day you seemed terribly afraid of the great trial you soon must undergo.'

'I am no longer afraid. It is true that the flesh recoils from humiliation, but with the grace of God the soul can control the flesh and so experience an unspeakable joy.'

They went together to the room where the committee was meeting. It was already filled with curious spectators. At exactly eight o'clock the chairman opened the session with the usual formula, 'Order, gentlemen.'

'M. Lamirande,' the chairman went on, 'are you now prepared to produce documents or witnesses in support of the accusation you have brought against the honourable secretary of state?'

'I regret, Mr Chairman, that I must admit that I am not yet ready,' Lamirande replied.

'Then I assume that you will withdraw your accusation?'

'I cannot do that, because I know that it is well founded.'

'You say that it is well founded, but you can produce no proof.'

'That is precisely the position in which I find myself.'

'I need not tell you, M. Lamirande, that such a position is untenable. You must realize that.'

'I understand perfectly, Mr Chairman.'

'And yet you persist in refusing to withdraw your accusation?'

'Yes, Mr Chairman.'

Whistling could be heard from the back of the room. The chairman ordered silence. Montarval's smile was unusually wicked.

'If the committee decides that its dignity and the dignity of the House permit it, I am ready to allow my accuser another day's delay.'

His words provoked applause that the chairman silenced immediately.

'The committee will deliberate *in camera* and make known its decision.'

The spectators left the room, and fifteen minutes later the doors were reopened to the public.

'The committee has resolved,' said the chairman, 'to report immediately to the House on everything that has happened. The House will then decide what action will be appropriate.'

'My poor Lamirande,' said Vaughan as they left the committee room, 'I just don't understand you. Your expulsion from the House is inevitable, you are courting political dishonour and, need I add, ridicule, which is worse than all the rest.'

'But you must think that I am intelligent enough to understand something so obvious.'

'Then why are you acting like this?'

'For reasons you'll approve of one day.'

'If you weren't so calm I'd advise you to see a doctor. But your brain doesn't seem to be suffering any fatigue.'

'It has never been in better condition – but never mind that. Vaughan, I want to ask you a question and I want you to answer in all sincerity. If I could produce proof for my accusations, would you still support the government bill?'

'Yes, my friend, I would.'

'You would vote for that constitution even if it were proved, as clear as day, that it is the fruit of a black conspiracy and that its true goal is the eradication of the French race and the Catholic religion!'

'Yes, even under those conditions I would vote for it, because as you know I am in favour of a united Canada, strong and imposing. And you also know that I have no hatred for the French race or the Catholic religion. Far from it: I admire your heroic efforts to preserve them. But if the Catholic religion and the French race cannot accommodate themselves to a Canada that extends from one sea to the other, so much the worse for them!'

'But do you think that a country can be truly grand, truly prosperous, truly happy, if it owes its beginning to a conspiracy woven of racial and religious hatred? Would it not be true that its national life would be poisoned at the very outset?'

'My reply is the one that Protestants give to those who reproach them for the sins committed by the founders of their religion: the work is good, despite the faults of those who have done it.'

'And do you find that a satisfactory response?'

'Not when it is a matter of founding a religion, for a good religion can not issue from an impure source. That is why I have always said that if there is one religion that is true and good it is the Catholic religion, for it is the only one with a Founder one can love and respect. But it seems to me that when it is a matter of purely political project, we should not judge it according to the vices of its authors but according to its intrinsic merits.'

'But He who you say is worthy of love and respect has said that a bad tree never yields good fruit!'

'Ah!' sighed Vaughan, becoming pensive. 'If I had your faith perhaps I would see everything as you do, even politics.'

Then the two friends parted.

Lamirande noticed that already several of his colleagues were avoiding him as if he had the plague, and that others looked at him as though he were an object of curiosity, or simply crazy. The latter were the more charitable. They did not accuse him of unspeakable motives but they were convinced that their poor colleague was the victim of an *idée fixe* and would soon be in a mental hospital.

'My career is finished,' thought Lamirande. And anguish as heavy as a boulder struck against his heart and crushed it. He nearly cried aloud; but his heartache, although it was very great, could not trouble his soul, which remained closely tied to God.

For to such belongs the Kingdom of God.
MARK 10:14

25

LAMIRANDE WITHDREW INTO THE WINDOW RECESS to read the following letter, which he had received that morning.

Beauvoir Convent, near Quebec
6 March 1946
Dearest Papa,
I am very sad and I have to tell you why, because you are the only one who can make me feel better. You know I had my eighth birthday more than two months ago. I know my whole catechism and I understand all of it except for some words that are too big for me to understand. I will tell you in my own words what the catechism tells us to show you that I understand it. There is only one God and He is a pure spirit. A spirit is something that we cannot see. There is a spirit in every one of us and it is called the Soul. Our souls are joined to our bodies but God has no body. That is why we say that He is a pure spirit. In the beginning God was all alone. Then He created or made out of nothing many other pure spirits that were not as great as He and we call them the Angels. God can make something out of nothing. Some of the angels rebelled against God. They must have been very wicked because God is so good that He could not have made them unhappy. The leader of these bad angels is Lucifer, or Satan, whom we also call the Devil, and they were chased out of Heaven by the good angels whose leader was St Michael. The bad angels fell down into a horrible place called Hell. Then God created Adam and Eve, the first man and woman, to people the earth. Adam and Eve and the other humans were to take the places that had been left empty in Heaven after the fall of the bad angels. Lucifer was jealous, and he wanted to make Adam and Eve go into Hell with him, so that God would be unhappy. Lucifer took the form of a serpent and talked to Eve and told her to eat an apple that God had told them not to eat. Eve listened to Lucifer. When she was created she was all grown up, but I think she must have been really young like me because a real woman like my dear Mama or the nuns wouldn't have listened. Then Eve made her husband eat the apple

too. Adam listened to his wife instead of God, which was very wicked of him. I am sure that my dear Mama would never tell you to listen to her instead of to God and that you would never have acted like Adam even though you loved Mama as much as Adam loved Eve. God was very angry because Adam and Eve had disobeyed Him, and He made them leave the beautiful Garden where he had put them. They deserved to be sent to Hell because they had listened to Lucifer instead of God. They had lost the right to go to Heaven and they could not give this right to their children, because when you lose something you can't give it to somebody else. Because of the transgressions of our first parents all humans would have to belong to Lucifer. That is what we call "original sin." But God would not allow all humans to go to Hell because it would have made Lucifer too happy. When He sent Adam and Eve out of the Garden, He promised a Saviour to console them, someone who would come to repay the debt that men owed to God. For four thousand years people waited for the Saviour. The people who believed that He would come were saved. Finally the Saviour appeared on earth. He was Jesus Christ, the son of God and of the Blessed Virgin, both God and man. That is what we call the mystery of the Incarnation. I don't understand that very well but I believe in it because it is in our catechism. You told me to learn my catechism, the sisters teach it to me and Father Grandmont explains it. The catechism is approved by the bishops and by the Pope who is the leader of all the bishops and of all Catholics. I believe everything the catechism says because you and the sisters and Father Grandmont and the bishops and the Pope would never teach lies to little children. Jesus Christ is equal to God His Father because there is God the Father, God the Son, and God the Holy Ghost. They are not three different Gods, only one. They form the Holy Trinity. That is another mystery I don't understand very well. I suppose they are not three because they love each other so much that they form one. It's a little like it was when Mama was still alive. You and she and I loved each other so much that we were one. Our Saviour Jesus Christ was a little child like me, very poor and unknown. He lived in hiding because some bad men wanted to kill Him. When Jesus Christ became a man he began to teach people how to get to Heaven. He performed many miracles, I mean things that man cannot do by himself, to prove that He was really our Saviour. There were a lot of people who believed in Him, but many others wanted Him put to death. The people who did not love Jesus, who was always so good to everybody, must have been bad angels, not men, because real men had to love Him because He had come to save them. If the wicked people who did not love Jesus were real men, that is another mystery that I don't understand. Three years later a wicked judge named Pontius Pilate condemned Our Lord and He was horribly mistreated for a whole night and then they nailed Him to a cross where He died. He offered His suffering and His death to repay the debt that men owed Him which they could not repay. Jesus must have loved people very much to have suffered so much to repay their debt so that they could go to Heaven. That must be another mystery because I don't understand how Jesus loved mankind. If all the men and women were like you and Mama and the sisters and Father Grandmont I could understand a little, but they say that there are wicked people and that Jesus loved them like the others and wanted to save them too. After He was dead, they put Him in a tomb but because He was God as well as a man He could not stay dead for long. On the third day He was revived, I mean He came out of the tomb alive. He spent forty days on earth with His mother, who must have been very happy to see Him alive, and with His Apostles and disciples. Then He went to Heaven, where He took the first place next to His father. And one day He will return to judge us all. The good people will go to Heaven with Him and the wicked will go to Hell with Lucifer. A few hours before He died, Jesus performed the greatest of His miracles. He changed bread and wine into His body and blood and gave the bread and wine to his Apostles. That is another mystery, which we call the Holy Eucharist. And he gave his Apostles the power to perform the same miracle and told them to give the power to others. They had to give it to others too, and so on until the end of the world. That is why there are still men — bishops and priests — who have this power. And before He went to Heaven, Jesus, who had come to save all mankind, founded His Church so that man could continue to be saved. He couldn't stay on earth forever because I imagine His father wanted Him in Heaven with Him. Jesus put St Peter at the head of His Church. He was the first pope and the Apostles were the first bishops. Bishops have priests to help them. The Pope, the bishops, and the priests carry on the work of Jesus, saving men. They do this by baptising them in the name of the Father and the Son and the Holy Ghost. This takes

them away from Lucifer and gives them to Jesus Christ, by nourishing their souls with the Holy Eucharist and forgiving their sins. When someone is baptised, he belongs to Jesus Christ, and in order to go to Heaven he only has to do what Christ has commanded. That must not be very difficult because Jesus was too good to make rules that were too hard. It can't be any more severe than our rules here in the convent. Jesus would not have taken the trouble to suffer so much to save mankind unless He had wanted to make their road easier. But they say that there are a lot of men who do not want to do the simple things that Jesus asks them to do. That is another mystery. There is one thing above all that Jesus wants us to do, that is to receive Holy Communion. I have heard a reading of the Gospels, that is the story of what Jesus Christ said and did when He was here on earth, and I am sure He said that in order to go to Heaven it is necessary to take communion, to receive the Holy Eucharist. And He said it in a tone that was almost angry because there were wicked men who did not want to take communion. That's not the way it's told in the Gospels, but I'm sure that's what it means. And that, dear Papa, is what makes me sad. I wrote you this long letter that took me six days to write so that I could talk to you about it. I want to do everything that Jesus Christ told us to do, because I want to go to Heaven, not Hell. When I talked to the sisters and asked them if I could take my first communion next May they told me I was too young to understand it and that I would have to wait at least a year and maybe two. And if I happened to die, I would not go to Heaven because Heaven is only for baptised children who die before they know what Jesus Christ ordered, and for those who were old enough to know what He wanted and did it as well as they could. But I am old enough to know that He wants us to take communion and that is what makes me so sad. I often wake up at night, and I'm afraid. I wrote you this long letter to show you that I understand my catechism and to ask you to write and ask Mother Superior to be good enough to let me take my first communion this year. Then if I died I would be sure of going to Heaven and I wouldn't be afraid of going to Hell. You will write to Mother Superior, won't you dear Papa, because I'm sure you want your little girl to go to Heaven where Mama is and where you will go yourself. I think you would be sad if I weren't there.
Your daughter who loves you very much,
Marie

I am adding this to tell you that I showed Mother Thérèse the first copy of my letter, because she teaches me how to correct my mistakes in French. When she read it she cried. Why did she cry, Papa? Is there something in this letter that could have made her sad? I only cry when I am sad.
Love again from your little girl.
Marie

'My God,' Lamirande murmured, putting the letter, onto which some gentle tears had fallen, into his billfold, 'I can bear anything as long as You leave me this child.'

On the wicked he will rain coals of fire and brimstone.
PSALMS 11:6

26

LEVERDIER MET LAMIRANDE AS HE WAS LEAVING the Parliament Buildings.

'My dear Lamirande,' he said, 'there is a ray of hope!'

'What is it?'

'There's a report in the latest edition of the *Ottawa Herald* that all the bishops are meeting in Montreal again. If His Grace has changed his mind, all is saved!'

'Whatever it is,' Lamirande replied, 'may God's will be done!'

Around eight o'clock the next morning Duthier came to look for Montarval in his private office in the Parliament buildings.

'Master,' said the usher, 'I have some news. Lamirande has just received a message from the Archbishop of Montreal, and he's getting ready to leave on the nine o'clock train with Leverdier.'

'Very well, follow them to the bishop's palace. When they leave, observe them very carefully. You're intelligent enough to know by looking at a man what kind of mood he's in, happy or annoyed. Watch Leverdier particularly. It's easier to tell the state of his soul from the expression on his face than it is with Lamirande. If Leverdier looks very happy when they leave the building, and if they are both heading for the Canadian Pacific station to catch the one o'clock train, send me these four words by telegram: "Fine weather, one o'clock." If Leverdier looks sad and dejected there won't be any need to telegraph.'

'What if he doesn't look either happy or sad?'

'Impossible! Now before you leave for Montreal remind your two companions to be ready by eleven o'clock to receive orders from me.'

Around eleven o'clock Lamirande and Leverdier were walking up the steps of the archbishop's palace in Montreal. They were excited, their hearts pounding as though they had just run a race. 'Come as quickly as possible': that was all the archbishop's message had said, but it was enough to rekindle some hope in the hearts of the two friends.

'That can mean only one thing,' Leverdier had exclaimed; 'His Grace has given in to the pressure the priests have brought to bear on him, and he's changed his mind and is going to give you Ducoudray's files.'

'I'm sure that's it too,' said Lamirande, 'but I'm afraid of one thing: that even this proof won't be enough. I'm afraid His Grace's prediction will come true and that despite everything the government will still have a majority. Last night Vaughan told me straight out that even if my accusation is proven he will still support the government bill. And you know there are seven or eight MPs who follow every move he makes. Of all the non-Catholics, I was counting on Vaughan most of all, but I've lost him. It's so true what they say, if the faith is absent so is everything else. His Grace pointed that out, and I realize now how right he was.'

'But at least if we have the documents you'll be able to rehabilitate yourself in the eyes of the House and the country.'

'Alas! what would that petty satisfaction be worth if we miss the main goal?'

They had exchanged these remarks while preparing to leave for Montreal.

When they entered the archbishop's salon it was a moment of veritable anguish. All the bishops and archbishops were there. The Archbishop of Montreal came to greet his visitors.

'You were quite right, my dear M. Lamirande, to count on the devotion and patriotism of the clergy. You have won. I had you come here so that I could give you something I refused you the other day.'

Lamirande could only stammer a few unintelligible words. The archbishop continued:

'I know what you have done. I have seen your letter to the clergy, and it had exactly the effect you might expect. For the past week my table has once again been hidden under a pile of letters; but these are not anonymous, and they fill me with as much joy and consolation as the first lot filled me with despair. Everyone had the same idea and they all wrote or came to see me. All, old and young, secular and regular clergy, said the same thing: "Speak, Your Grace;

reveal the secrets you possess, and think not of us but of the Church and our country." Not one expressed a different idea. And faced with this sublime movement I can no longer hesitate. I am going to give you everything, along with a collective letter signed by all of my venerable colleagues. No Catholic MP will dare to vote for the government bill after you have revealed what you know.'

'I am truly delighted, Milord,' Lamirande replied. 'I bless God and I thank Him for this great consolation. However, I still have one dreadful doubt. I fear these revelations will be useless and that the government will still have a majority. You were right, Your Grace, when you said that the faith is at the basis of everything.'

'We shall do what we can,' said the archbishop. 'We shall carry out our duty to the end. God will take care of the rest. After such devotion I am certain He will work a true miracle to save us — at the last minute if necessary.'

Then the prelate gave Lamirande photographed copies of all the documents that Docoudray had given him, along with a letter signed by all the bishops.

'I shall keep the originals,' he said, 'but if someone wants to consult them, I'll make them available.'

The two friends left the prelates. Leverdier was beaming. At the thought that his friend would no longer be an object of scorn, his soul was filled with an unspeakable joy that the least attentive observer could have read in his eyes. Thus Duthier thought he should add one word to the formula. He telegraphed to Montarval: *'Weather very fine, one o'clock.'*

'Idiot!' the minister muttered as he read the despatch. Then he rang, and two individuals who had been waiting in an anteroom for half an hour were shown into his office.

'Do you understand your instructions completely?' he asked them.

'Yes, Master,' one of them replied.

'Very well, then. Get going.'

They left, and Montarval locked the door behind them. Then he began to pace back and forth in his office, gripped by a horrible emotion, a violent, satanic rage. His fists were clenched and his mouth was foaming.

'He's winning! He's winning!' he repeated in a choked voice.

He grew more and more enflamed and called on the fallen angel:

'Eblis! All-powerful God, will you always let yourself be beaten by your eternal enemy? We had almost won, and now everything is in danger of crumbling. Let this final attempt succeed, at least. Let the fanatical worshipper of our Enemy be pulverized so that even his mother wouldn't recognize him!'
Suddenly he stopped.
'Ah! How forgetful I am!' he exclaimed. 'Poor Duthier will likely take the train with them, and I still need him.'
He then sent the following telegram:
'To the station-master at Mile End, to be delivered to M. Duthier on the one o'clock train from Montreal to Ottawa: Important message. Do not take same train as two friends.'
He gave the telegram to a commissionaire with the order to send it immediately.

Lamirande and Leverdier had taken the one o'clock train. Duthier was still following them, but they hardly noticed him, so absorbed were they in examining the documents given them by the Archbishop of Montreal. The horrifying plot surpassed their wildest imaginings. It was Satanism, pure and simple.
At Mile End, the train stopped for a few minutes. A crowd of workmen and idlers on the platform had formed a circle around a man who was stretched out on the ground.
'What is it?' Lamirande asked, opening a window.
'He got an electric shock,' someone replied.
Lamirande excitedly passed on to Leverdier the papers he had been examining. Now he was not thinking of the grave political problems that had preoccupied him earlier: he was a doctor, and his only thought was to save the life of an unfortunate man. In a moment he was on the platform. He made his way through the crowd and examined the stricken man.
'He may not be dead; please make room and let him breathe.'
The crowd moved back a little and Lamirande began to apply artificial respiration to the electrified workman.
Meanwhile the station master was shouting, 'Telegram for M. Duthier! Is he here?'
The parliamentary usher, who was among the crowd, went to pick up the message.

Leverdier had put all the documents into his travelling bag, which he held as he came to speak to Lamirande.

'We're going to miss the train,' he said.

In fact, at that very moment the call, 'All aboard!' could be heard.

'I can't let that man die,' Lamirande explained. 'For the moment my duty is here. Besides, the Great Atlantic has another train leaving for Ottawa in an hour.'

And he continued to care for the worker, who was beginning to show signs of life.

Duthier, who was standing nearby, had heard Lamirande's last words.

'My telegram warned me not to travel with those two,' he said to himself. 'The Master must have some reason for me not to arrive in Ottawa at the same time they do, but since they're taking the Great Atlantic there's no reason why I can't take the train I was going to.'

Just as the crowd was breaking up he jumped onto the platform of one of the cars and in a few minutes the train was heading for Ottawa at ninety miles an hour.

Duthier, who was something of a philosopher, started a conversation with a fellow passenger.

'Whatever they say, progress is a fine thing,' he began sententiously. 'Look how fast we're moving! Fifty years ago we would have said that the steam engine was the last work in progress. This very train did sixty miles an hour and everybody thought it was a marvellous thing — they talked about it in all the papers. Now that electricity has replaced steam, sixty miles an hour is all right for freight trains, but passenger trains do ninety. I've read that in the United States and England they even have trains that go a hundred miles an hour. We're always a little behind the times here.'

'When there's a derailment, I find eighty miles an hour quite fast enough,' the other man replied.

'Yes, but thanks to progress and vast improvements in the railways, there aren't nearly as many accidents as there used to be.'

'Perhaps, but they're more serious. Whenever there's an accident, it's a real disaster.'

'Are you against progress, sir?'

'Yes I am, when progress is against me.'

This rather enigmatic reply silenced the loquacious Duthier. He picked up his newspaper and began to read again.

It was a dull, foggy day, and you could barely see two hundred feet into the fields. The mechanic must have had trouble seeing ahead of him.

They had passed the last station before Ottawa, and the train continued to move like lightning. Suddenly there was a series of horrible shocks, a great shudder, and a sinister cracking noise. Then there was a pile of débris at the base of the embankment and the horrible cries of the dying tore through the fog.

Poor humanity had just offered a new holocaust to the God Progress.

And I will give you shepherds after my own heart.
JEREMIAH 3:15

27

THE HOUSE HAD MET AT THREE O'CLOCK. Near the beginning of the sitting the chairman of the enquiry submitted his report stating that Lamirande had produced no proof to support his accusation but that he still refused to withdraw it. One of the English ministerial MPs rose to propose that the Speaker invite the member from Cherlevoix to withdraw his accusation and apologize to the secretary of State. Vaughan and Houghton intervened, asking for a delay in adopting the proposal until Lamirande had returned.

'I have received a message from him,' said Houghton, 'announcing that he was taking the afternoon train from Montreal and would have explanations for the House when he returned. He could arrive any minute.'

Just then a telegram was handed to Montarval. Through a supreme effort he managed to look grave and concerned as he read the message:

'Unfortunately,' he said, 'we shall never hear our colleague's explanations. I have just received a message containing horrible news that the House will hear with deep sorrow.'

Then he read the telegram:

Pointe Gatineau, 12 March, 3:00 p.m.
A terrible catastrophe has just occurred two miles from here. Train number nine, which left Montreal at one o'clock, was derailed while travelling at a speed of ninety miles an hour. It fell from a considerable height and was completely demolished. It is not yet possible to list all the dead and injured, but there was a large number of victims. Only seven people escaped with slight injuries or were unharmed: Michel Panneton and George Bouliane of Aylmer, Pierre Fortin of Hull, John McManus and James Woodbridge of Ottawa, Thomas Miller of Toronto, and Andrew King of Montreal.

'As you see, Mr Speaker,' Montarval went on, 'our colleague's name is not on this list, so we have every reason to believe that he is dead or injured. This is most unfortunate, and I have no words to express my sorrow. It is true that our colleague had placed himself in a false position, but he always acted in good faith, and I am convinced that he was the victim of a cruel hoax and that he would ultimately have recognized his error. No one regrets his premature death more than I, if in fact he is dead; and no one offers him greater sympathy if he has been injured.'

As he spoke, like a skilful actor he had tears in his voice. One would have sworn that his sorrow was genuine.

The session was suspended to allow time for emotions to become calm. New dispatches only confirmed the first. Houghton, Vaughan, and several other MPs left for the scene of the tragedy. Around four o'clock the Speaker returned to his chair and the session continued. The prime minister asked for the vote to be taken on second reading of the constitution bill. 'Then,' he said, 'we shall adjourn.'

The Speaker was putting the question to the vote when a murmur, then an exclamation of surprise interrupted him. Montarval became livid. Lamirande and Leverdier had just entered the House.

Lamirande rose to speak as soon as he had reached his seat.

'Mr Speaker, before you put the question to the vote I request permission to make several observations. Or rather, so that I may be entitled to do so, I propose that the debate on second reading of the bill be adjourned. To begin, Mr Speaker, it seems that the House was surprised to see the honourable member from Portneuf and myself enter the House alive. I can understand your surprise, as I have just learned of the dreadful catastrophe that occurred to the train we were to have taken. We owe our presence here alive and well, rather than among the injured, to the aid of St Michael. No matter what the followers of Lucifer believe, he is stronger than Satan. We left the train at Mile End because of a providential event. I am even more saddened by the tragedy that occurred, because I fully believe that I unintentionally caused it. I mean that the calamity was the result not of an accident but of a crime. The last dispatches I read as I was entering the House state that it has been learned that the action was due to the fact that a section of rail had been moved and that a search is under way for two suspicious-looking men who were seen on the track not far from where the derailment took place. The dispatches add that among the dead is one of the ushers of this House, a man named Duthier. An unsigned telegram from Ottawa was found on his person that read, "To the station-master at Mile End, to be delivered to M. Duthier on the one o'clock train from Montreal to Ottawa: Important message. Do not take same train as two friends.'

Lamirande went on. 'This indicates clearly that someone in Ottawa had reason to believe that the train the two friends were to take was rather risky. Poor Duthier apparently misunderstood the warning and when he saw the two friends get off the train at Mile End he thought it would make no difference if he continued. His lack of perception cost him his life. The two friends in whose company it was unwise to travel were, no doubt, the honourable member for Portneuf and your humble servant. Since the death of M. Ducoudray, I have been constantly followed by the unfortunate Duthier. I couldn't take a step without tripping over him. Now why was it unwise to travel in the company of these two friends? Mr Speaker, when you know what is contained in the documents they were carrying, you will understand why the train they took was not supposed to reach its destination. You will also understand what must have inspired the two evildoers who moved the rail.'

The Members of the House and the spectators who filled the galleries were scarcely breathing. It was so silent you could have heard the buzzing of a fly or the scampering of a mouse. Lamirande continued.

'Now, Mr Speaker, still speaking to my motion that this debate be adjourned, permit me to read to the House a collective letter from the archbishops and bishops of the ecclesiastical provinces of Quebec, Montreal, and Ottawa, a letter that was given to me today by His Grace the Archbishop of Montreal.

Archbishop's Palace, Montreal, 11 March 1946
To M. Joseph Lamirande, MP, and to the other Honourable Members of the House of Commons, Ottawa
Gentlemen:
The House of Commons is currently debating a constitutional bill that is destined, if it becomes law, to establish a new Confederation of all the Canadian provinces. Many people believe that this projected constitution is far too centralizing, that it conceals a number of traps, and that it would be disastrous for the religious freedom of the Catholics and of the French-Canadian people because of the exorbitant powers it accords the central government. We do not intend to discuss this project in political terms, but we have a more

serious duty to perform. That is to disclose that the constitution you are studying was elaborated, clause by clause, not by the cabinet as you and your colleagues suppose, but in the depths of the Masonic lodges. No matter how unlikely this disclosure may appear to you, we can prove it by absolutely incontrovertible evidence.

You are well aware that a coroner's jury has declared that the journalist Ducoudray was murdered on the order of an occult society whose secrets he had revealed to the Archbishop of Montreal. In fact, on the night before his death, M. Ducoudray had been struck by divine grace and sincerely converted, and he had given to the Archbishop of Montreal all the files of the society whose secretary he had been for a number of years. There is no need to mention the sublime courage shown by this converted satanist; that story was told at the inquest. But what the public still does not know is the nature of the secrets that were confided to the religious authorities. The documents he gave to the archbishop — and their authenticity is unquestionable — establish the existence in this province of a dreadful sect, a society of satanists. It consists of men who invoke and adore Satan and have sworn undying hatred to the death of Our Lord Jesus Christ and of His Church. And it was within this society that the constitution which has been submitted to you was discussed, elaborated and adapted, line by line and paragraph by paragraph. This infernal society adopted the project because they saw in it the most effective way to destroy the Catholic religion in this country, as well as the French-Canadian nation which is the chief rampart of the Church in Canada.

We know that this will all sound unbelieveable to you. We have entrusted to M. Lamirande photographic copies of the documents. Examine them. You will find that they contain proof of all that we have said. The originals are at the archbishop's palace in Montreal, and you may consult them there. Among the documents is a list prepared by M. Ducoudray of the leading members of the satanic organization. At the head of the list are the names of M. Aristide Montarval and Sir Henry Marwood.

A number of the manuscripts given to the Archbishop of Montreal bear the signature "Grand Master." The archbishop has had these manuscripts examined by three experts who compared them with letters from M. Montarval, and all state that the handwriting is identical. Their expert testimony will be found among the relevant papers entrusted to M. Lamirande.

Finally, M. Ducoudray made a solemn declaration to the Archbishop of Montreal that the account published by his newspaper, *La Libre Pensée,* of an alleged attempt by M. Lamirande to sell his influence to the government was a black and abominable slander, invented by the leader of the society, M. Montarval; that, on the contrary, it was the prime minister who tried to bribe M. Lamirande.

Now, gentlemen, you will probably wonder why we have kept silent for so long. Here is the reason: just after M. Ducoudray's murder the Archbishop of Montreal began to receive anonymous letters threatening death to all the priests in the country if the secrets of the society were revealed. The letters were very careful not to threaten the archbishop himself. He had originally decided, therefore, to remain silent, not daring to endanger the lives of his priests and those of other dioceses. Ducoudray's murder was proof that these were not hollow threats. But when the priests were informed of the situation, they unanimously prayed and begged the Archbishop of Montreal to make known the plot that was being woven against the Church and the French Canadians, no matter what the consequences of the revelation might be for the clergy. Faced with their spirit of self-sacrifice, the archbishop decided that he could no longer remain silent. He summoned his colleagues and told them all that M. Ducoudray had entrusted to him. After a careful examination, we all agree that the documents are unquestionably authentic.

And that is the situation, gentlemen, described as simply as possible. It is hardly necessary for us to beg you to put aside all party prejudices, all personal or political considerations, and to join together to reject this satanic legislation. We are sure that you will understand that no Catholic Member of Parliament can, in conscience, vote for a project elaborated by an impious society with the express purpose of destroying the Catholic religion in this country. It is your most pressing duty to reject this legislation. We should be insulting your intelligence, your faith, and your patriotism if we insisted further on what must be done. We are convinced that not one of you will betray his role of Member of Parliament, Catholic and French Canadian. Not one of you will let himself be fooled by sophisms, no matter how plausible they may seem, that only invite you to forget that you are being asked to sanction a piece of legislation prepared by satanists with the goal of destroying the Kingdom of Jesus Christ among us.

'This document,' Lamirande added, 'bears, I repeat, the signatures of all the bishops and archbishops of French Canada. If I added a single comment I would only weaken what they have said. I shall be content, then, to propose that the debate now be adjourned.'

There had been total silence during the reading of the episcopal letter; now there was an outburst of exclamations, interpolations, and angry cries. All the Catholic members left their seats and hurried to Lamirande. They surrounded him and begged his pardon. Scarcely half an hour earlier they had been prepared to have him run out of the Parliament buildings, but now they recognized and acclaimed his as their leader. The four Catholic ministers left their colleagues, crossed the House, and went to join the group surrounding Lamirande. The scene was indescribable. The Speaker, realizing it was impossible to maintain order, declared the sitting suspended until eight o'clock and left his chair. At that moment Houghton, Vaughan, and the others who had gone to the scene of the accident returned. They were soon told all that had just taken place.

'Well, my dear Vaughan,' Lamirande exclaimed, 'the other day you told me that you didn't understand. Do you now?'

'Yes, I understand and I admire you!'

'I proved everything I put forward, didn't I?'

'And more!'

'And now that you have this proof are you still going to say that you will vote in favour of the constitution?'

'Yes, because despite its execrable origins I still believe it is a good constitution.'

'Then, my dear friend, it is my turn to say that I don't understand. And let me add that it would have been far less painful if you had voted to have me expelled from the House than for you to support this iniquitous work.'

Vaughan was visibly moved and embarrassed.

'It's still the same answer,' he said. 'You have faith and I do not. You believe that religion is the highest human good, and I still ask whether human life, like that of the animals, does not end with death. For you, the Beyond is a certitude, but for me it is a problem I cannot resolve.'

And the young English Canadian went away, pensive and sad.

The French and Catholic members, as well as Houghton and his partisans, went to the offices of the opposition to examine the documents and discuss the situation. Not one even thought of dinner.

'Everyone has answered the call,' said one of the ministers – or rather ex-ministers, as all of Sir Henry's Catholic colleagues had resigned forthwith.

They called the roll from a list of MPs someone had procured. Not one of the opposition MPs, nor a single Catholic was missing. Except Saint-Simon.

'I'm ready to bet my life that that scoundrel is with Montarval at this very moment!' Leverdier exclaimed.

Treacherous, reckless, swollen with conceit.
II TIMOTHY 3:4

28

HE WAS, IN FACT, WITH MONTARVAL, who, taking advantage of the confusion following Lamirande's revelations, had slipped out of the House. As he left, he gestured imperiously to Saint-Simon to follow him. The latter hesitated briefly. His conscience shouted to him, 'Do not obey him, you wretched man.' He heard this cry despite the noise. He would have heard it in the midst of a storm, at the height of a battle, for this feeble inner voice dominated all other outside sounds, no matter how overpowering they might be. Instead of following Montarval he took two steps towards Lamirande. Then it occurred to him that Montarval could ruin him. 'Why irritate him unnecessarily?' he asked himself; 'there's no harm in going to see what he wants.' And he followed his temptor. He had just rejected the last grace, trampled it underfoot. From this moment on the inner voice could no longer be heard and Saint-Simon descended into the abyss with no further resistance.

'As you see,' Montarval told him, when they were in a private office reserved for ministers, 'the situation is critical. We must show that we are in control. Until now your role has been easy; but that role is finished and now you must play an entirely new one.'

'You don't mean that I must speak out in favour of the constitutional bill that I condemned so violently?'

'You won't speak at all if it bothers you. Words are useless now anyway. But you will vote with us.'

'Vote for this constitution that I have denounced so strongly at the very moment when my compatriots are indignantly rejecting it! But you must realize that that would be impossible. I would be dishonoured forever!'

'And if you do not vote, you will not only be dishonoured, but ruined too.'

'What do you mean?' he stammered.

'This. You know I can prove that you sold yourself to the government and that I can throw you into the street. And I'll do both if you don't vote the way I want you to.'

'But that is a senseless form of cruelty. One vote more or less won't change the results. I won't vote against; that should be enough for you.'

'It's not, because a single vote can swing the balance. I'm sure the Speaker is against us, so both needn't be equal. All the Catholics will vote against us and when I was leaving the House I saw several non-Catholic ministerial MPs with Lamirande. Your vote could determine the result: I need it! Now do you understand?'

And Montarval hurried away, leaving poor Saint-Simon the victim not of remorse which can save, but of rage and despair, which lead only to perdition.

At a meeting of MPs opposed to the government, it was decided to bring things to a head by insisting that the vote on second reading be taken as soon as the sitting opened at eight o'clock. 'If we are to have a majority,' said Houghton and Lamirande, 'we'll have it this evening, before Montarval has time to weave more intrigues.'

The House was filled to capacity. There were 243 MPs, not counting the Speaker who, of course, votes only to break a tie. If all the MPs voted, there could not be a tie.

The public galleries were overflowing. Everywhere there was feverish agitation. It was a stormy gathering. The Speaker took his seat, and it was with some difficulty that he restored a measure of order and silence.

As soon as the sitting began, the well-known cries, 'Question! Question! Call the vote!' burst out. No one rose to speak. The ministers seemed to have their backs against the wall. Sir Henry, usually so adept at discerning the sudden formation of dangerous currents in meetings and then directing them while seeming to follow them, appeared nonplussed. Even Montarval, with all his resources, was at a loss. They seemed to be waiting for the end, totally in despair. And the shouts of 'Question! Call the vote!' increased. Finally Vaughan rose. There was immediate silence.

'Mr Speaker,' he began, 'I cannot allow the vote to be taken on second reading without giving a word of explanation and telling what I believe our position to be. I have examined the documents given to my friend the honourable member for Charlevoix by the Archbishop of Montreal. It is unquestionable that they are absolutely authentic, so that it is definitely established that the constitution bill the House is debating is the work not of the cabinet but of an occult society, of which the Secretary of State and the prime minister are the principal leaders. I detest secret societies of this kind and their shadowy, truly criminal workings. I am stating as clearly as I can that I no longer have any confidence in the prime minister or in his secretary of state, and that the present government must go. At the same time, even though the behaviour of those two ministers fills me with disgust, I shall vote for the constitutional bill because as a political work, despite its evil origins, it seems to me to be sound. One cannot deny that the authors of the bill intended to use it to harm the Catholic Church and the French element. They acted through hatred, through passion. I condemn their motives but as for the result of their work, I can only approve of it. I am now, as I have always been, in favour of a great Canada with a strong government; of the fusion of the races; of a united people speaking a single language, English.

'As for the Catholic Church, I am certainly not hostile to it. If any religion deserves respect and recognition, it is the Roman Catholic, which is the only reasonable and logical one. But I am basically of the opinion that the interests of our country, of the great Canada I want to help to establish, must come before the interests of any religious group, no matter how respectable it may be. If the Catholic Church is uncomfortable with the proposed régime, I sincerely regret it, but that is not sufficient reason for me to reject this constitutional bill. Of course, I should think and speak otherwise if I were a fervent Catholic like my dear good friend the honourable member for Charlevoix, whom I know I am causing considerable pain. But I am not a Catholic. I believe in material greatness. I cannot raise myself to the higher region of which I can catch a glimpse but which is just as impossible for me to attain as it is for the inhabitants of a chicken coop to follow the eagle's flight towards the stars. The political régime that is being proposed offers me everything I can understand and believe: the political greatness of my country. I accept it, though I despise the hand that offers it to us.'

This curious speech, which contained all the doubts, weaknesses, contradictions, and vague hopes of this poor soul for which God and the devil were disputing, made a profound impression on the House. There was a moment of silence. Montarval leaned toward Sir Henry and whispered something in his ear. The prime minister smiled; he had found how to do what he wanted. Without suspecting it Vaughan had tossed a rope to the drowning ministers.

'Mr Speaker,' said the prime minister, 'I sincerely thank the honourable member who has just spoken. I thank him for the patriotic attitude he has shown at this moment of crisis. It pains me, of course, to note that he no longer has confidence in the cabinet, but I am delighted to see that he can distinguish between the mistakes they may have made in preparing this constitutional bill and the bill itself. I admit that there have been indiscretions, that the documents which have been produced and whose authenticity I do not dispute cast some doubt on my own conduct and on that of my secreatry of state. But I am certain that the authors of the collective letter that was read this afternoon greatly exaggerate our guilt – although I confess that in our perhaps too ardent desire to assure the success of the great political task we have undertaken, we were not prudent in our choice of means. Accordingly, we have decided to submit without complaint to the punishment we deserve for this excess of zeal, this fault if you prefer. We intend to resign from the leadership as soon as we can do so without betraying our patriotism. But before we leave, we want to see this constitution adopted; we want to see the establishment of a united Canada, a great Canada. We do not seek a vote of confidence from the House. We ask only that the members remain faithful to themselves and do not denigrate themselves because of the imprudence of two ministers; that they do not reject a bill they had declared to be good just because there were discussions about it outside the cabinet. We do not ask them to spare us, but we are sufficiently confident of their patriotism to believe that it will not be harmful to our country if they wish to strike us. Let them put the final touch to the establishment of a united Canada by voting for this constitution, and there will be no need for them to ask for our resignation; we shall leave of our own accord, happy that we need reproach ourselves only for an excess of zeal in support of a great cause. Of course, if we listened only to our personal feelings we could retire immediately and leave to others the task of following the bill to its conclusion. That would be dangerous, and hardly patriotic behaviour on our part. A ministerial crisis just now could add complications that we should regret later. Once again, let us ensure the future of our country by endowing it with the constitution that has already been ratified once by an enormous majority in this House; the members will thereby fulfill their patriotic duty. Then we may fulfill our own, by submitting our resignation to His Excellency the Governor-General.'

This crafty speech had a marked effect on the English-Canadian members from Sir Henry's party, except for a small number. Under different circumstances, the French party members might have let themselves be caught in the prime minister's snare. Today, however, the veil had been completely torn away. Sir Henry's sophisms were powerless to blind them once again.

Sir Henry and Montarval realized the state of their minds and realized that they had done everything possible to strengthen their position.

'It's a throw of the dice,' said Montarval to Sir Henry. 'It will be a very slim majority, whichever way it goes. We have nothing to gain by delaying.'

And he too began to cry, 'Vote!'

The Speaker first put to the vote the traditional amendment proposed by Houghton and Lamirande: 'That this bill undergo second reading not now but in six months' time.' 'Will all those in favour of the amendment rise?' asked the Speaker. Never had a vote been taken under such emotional conditions. One after the other the MPs who favoured rejecting the bill rose. They numbered 121. Saint-Simon, his hat pulled down over his eyes, had not moved. A shudder ran through the ranks of the French members. A muffled groan could be heard.

'Order, gentlemen,' said the Speaker. 'All those who oppose the amendment will please rise.'

The assistant clerk called out the names of the voters, while the clerk recorded their votes. Among those who voted against delaying the vote for six months, against rejecting it, was Saint-Simon. There was an outburst of threatening whistles. The Speaker had trouble restoring sufficient order to allow the clerks to finish recording the votes.

Finally the task was completed. The chief clerk, visibly moved, announced the result of the vote.

'For the amendment: 121; against: 122.'

'The amendment has been rejected,' said the Speaker.

A stormy reaction greeted his words. From the government side the applause was frantic; from the opposition there were angry cries, whistles, and boos. This indescribable scene lasted for five minutes. It was Lamirande who was finally able to obtain some silence.

'The names!' he demanded. 'Give us the names!'

The clerk then read, in alphabetical order, the names of those who had voted against the amendment.

Once this formality was over Lamirande rose again.

'Mr Speaker,' he said, 'I note that the name of the honourable member for Quebec City is among those who voted against the amendment. As it is well known that the honourable member has already shown himself to be very hostile to the bill, I have reason to believe that he voted against shelving the bill in error.'

That was all the rules permitted him to say.

His appeal had no effect. The unfortunate Saint-Simon did not hesitate for a moment.

'It was no mistake,' he said.

There was a new outburst of boos and whistles, mingled with cries of 'Traitor! Sell-out!'

The Speaker completely lost control of the assembly. Again it was Lamirande who succeeded in re-establishing some order.

'Now,' said the Speaker, 'it is the principal question, second reading, that is put to the vote.'

The rules allowed some discussion. Saint-Simon rose, pale and haggard. There was complete silence, as everyone was curious to hear him explain his strange about-face.

'Mr Speaker,' he began in a false and peevish voice, 'I want to reply to the insults that have been directed against me and to give my reasons for deciding to vote in favour of the constitution I had formerly rejected. It is quite simply a question of choosing the lesser of two evils. I have vigorously opposed the constitutional bill and I still find it bad; but when I think that if the opposition succeeds in having it rejected the province of Quebec will fall into the hands of the member for Charlevoix and his supporters, I cannot allow such a misfortune to befall my country. The united Canada it is proposed to establish will no doubt, leave something to be desired, but the fanatic and intolerant New France, worthy of the Inquisition and the Middle Ages, that is envisaged by the member from Charlevoix and his friends, would be quite simply unacceptable. Thus I shall vote for this constitution, which I do not approve of, to spare our province even greater misfortune.'

His boldness plunged the assembly into astonishment mixed with stupor. The French MPs were so disgusted that they said nothing. The vote was taken on second reading, in total silence. The result, in any case, was already known:

'For, 122; against 121,' the clerk announced.

'The motion is carried,' said the Speaker.

The House then rose, and the MPs formed groups to carry on noisy discussions.

'All is not lost,' said Lamirande to his friends Leverdier and Houghton. 'this one-vote majority is due to betrayal and bad will, and God cannot allow it to determine the destiny of a people forever.'

A man's mind plans his way, but the Lord directs his steps.
PROVERBS 16:9

29

THE DAY AFTER SECOND READING the constitutional bill began the most severe trial such a bill must undergo: the 'general committee' or 'all-party committee.' The Speaker left his chair and went to the clerk of the House to summon the MP designated by the promoter of the bill to preside over the committee. Sir Henry was careful to confer this important post on one of his own blind partisans.

It is in 'general committee' that a bill is discussed article by article, clause by clause, examined and turned over in every direction; amendments are proposed during this phase. Each MP is entitled to speak as often as he deems appropriate. The MPs rise to vote and the clerk records only the count, not the names of the voters.

For ten days the opposition, which now consisted of Houghton's party reinforced by the Catholic members (except for Saint-Simon) and several English-Canadian members who had previously supported the government, delivered a series of powerful but unproductive assaults on the government and the bill. For although the Speaker was acting as an ordinary member of the House and voted with the opposition, Sir Henry and Montarval, through God knows what unspeakable and criminal influences, succeeded in removing two English members of the army commanded by Lamirande and Houghton. Thus the opposition found itself reduced to 120, including the Speaker, while the government had 123, plus the vote of the chairman of the general committee in the event that a tie resulted from the temporary absence of three government MPs.

Lamirande and Houghton worked harder than ever to persuade Vaughan to vote against the constitution, or at least to agree to the amendments that would have removed some of the poison Montarval had injected into it. If they could convert Vaughan to their cause they would triumph, for he was recognized as the leader of a group of seven or eight, all ready to leave the government party if Vaughan gave them the signal. But none was willing to do so without the permission of the 'captain.' Thus it was Vaughan who held the key to the situation. He remained deaf to Houghton's arguments, to Lamirande's prayers and pleas.

'If I believe in the Catholic Church as you do,' he explained to Lamirande, 'no one would oppose this bill more vigorously.'

'And what prevents you from believing in the Catholic Church as I do?' replied his friend.

'It's as though there were a band over the eyes of my intelligence, a veil hiding the light from me. If only I could rip it off.'

'No human power can remove this band or tear it off. It is very real, not at all imaginary. We Catholics know, and the Church knows, because on the solemn day of Good Friday the Church asks God to remove this band from the Jews: *"Ut Deus et Dominus noster auferat velamen de cordibus eorum"* Do you *really* want this band to be removed – not from your mind, because that is not where it is, but from your heart, *de corde tuo*?'

'Of course I should like it!'

'Ah! You would like it! But I want you to say "I want." You know as well as I do that "I should like" and "I want" don't mean the same thing at all. "I should like" has never shifted a single straw, but "I want" has moved mountains. There are thousands of people who have gone to Hell repeating all their lives, "I should like to be saved"; and that, my friend, is the difference between "I should like" and "I want".'

'It's a great difference, I realize that. And from now on I shall say "I want to believe," not "I should like".'

'Very well! If you really want to believe, you can take measures to do so. Faith is a gift freely given by God. As you said the other day, *"Spiritus ubi vult spirat."* But we must not take unfair advantage of this text. It does not absolve us of the need for all effort. The Spirit of God breathes where it will, but it breathes on those who show themselves to be worthy of it. Free will and grace, the role of God and the role of man in the work of salvation – these are profound mysteries. One thing is certain, however: in order to be saved, you need both grace and receptivity to grace – God's help, without which man can do nothing effective, and man's effort, his declaration "I want", without which the grace of God will be ineffective. For as St Augustine said, God, who created us without our help, does not save us without our co-operation. And even though He does not give the same grace to everyone, He gives everyone enough to save him if that is what he wants. Right now He is giving you the grace to say, "I want to believe." You must respond to that grace by asking for faith. You already know the prayers of the Church. Promise me that you will recite, every day from now on, three "Hail Mary's" and the *"Salve Regina"* to obtain faith in Our Lord Jesus Christ, the Son of Mary."

'Do you think that will be enough for me to obtain faith?'

'I know that repeating the prayer with the intention of being worthy of the grace that God has given you will obtain a new grace for you. I am certain of it. But I do not know in what form the new grace will appear, or when. All I know is that any grace for which there is response on our part draws a new favour to us, infallibly. Be careful, for example, not to resist this new grace when it is offered. It may happen quite suddenly, or pass before you never to return.'

'If only I could see some miracle, some supernatural manifestation.'

'But you could see a dead man revive without obtaining faith.'

'Still, such a remarkable event would at least prove the existence of the supernatural to me.'

'There are proofs of the supernatural all around you, and you don't believe in it! Miracles don't always produce converts. Remember the curse of Our Lord! "Woe to you, Chorazin! woe to you, Bethsaida! for if the mighty works done in you had been done in Tyre and Sidon, they would have repented long ago in sackcloth and ashes." Witnessing a miracle does not always lead to faith — at least not to the faith that saves, fertile faith that is accompanied by a changed life, good works, sacrifices, and devotion. On the contrary, thousands have believed without seeing any miracle except the Church, that "sign raised among the nations," according to the words of the Vatican Council. My dear friend, do not ask for miracles; for they might rise up against you, as the miracles of Our Lord will rise up on Judgement Day against Chorazin, Bethsaida, and Capernaum, those cities that saw wonders and were not converted, and which will be treated more harshly than Sodom. Ask for the strength to live according to your Faith. For if you search to the depths of your heart, you will see that that is where the real obstacle is to be found.'

'You seem to think I already have faith!'

'Indeed, if faith did not carry with it a change in life, if faith in Our Lord Jesus Christ did not impose more moral obligations than belief in mathematical truths, would you call yourself an unbeliever? You think that two plus two always equals four because you can live as you wish while holding this belief; but if a corollary to this belief required you to forgive insults or give up certain pleasures or make some other sacrifice that is repugnant to human nature, you might wonder whether, after all, two and two always equal four.'

'Perhaps that is true,' Vaughan murmured.

'You may be certain that it is true. That is where you find the veil, the hand: on your heart. Take careful note of the words in the holy liturgy that I just quoted to you: *"Ut auferat velamen de cordibus eorum."* You see: *"de cordibus,"* not *"de mentibus".'*

'I am suffering terribly,' said the young English Canadian.

'I understand your suffering; a great struggle is taking place in your heart, between Satan and divine grace. I have been anxiously following the course of this strange struggle for some time now, and I think we are arriving at the decisive moment. If you want divine grace to triumph over Satan you must pray: three "Hail Marys" and the *"Salve Regina"* every day.'

Then, as though speaking to himself, he added, almost in a whisper, 'I feel, I *know* that the crisis this soul is passing through is intimately tied to the crisis of our dear country. If this soul succumbs, all is lost. O Lord, let it triumph! And if a new sacrifice is necessary, I am here!'

Vaughan was deeply touched by his friend's words.

'I shall do as you ask,' he said; 'I shall pray.'

For truly, I say to you, if you have faith as a grain of mustard seed, you will say to this mountain, 'Move from here to there,' and it will move; and nothing will be impossible to you.   MATTHEW 17:20

30

THEY HAD HAD THIS CONVERSATION on the evening of the tenth day after the beginning of the battle 'in general committee.' The next day it was impossible to prolong the struggle. The list of amendments was exhausted; all had been pitilessly rejected. The government had triumphed, and many members of the opposition were profoundly discouraged.

'There's no use continuing the resistance,' those who were discouraged said to Houghton and Lamirande. 'You know we've done everything that was humanly possible. It would be childish to persist in our opposition. We must submit to the inevitable. We shall try to get the best we can from the situation that will be created for us in the new Confederation.'

Houghton and Lamirande were forced to give in. The group that wanted to continue the combat was reduced to the two leaders, Leverdier, and two or three others. The greater part of the army was demoralized. If they tried to resist the enemy fire any longer, they would be exposing themselves to a total rout.

The general committee passed the bill without amendment, and the third and final reading was fixed for the following day, March 25. On the morning when the final struggle was to begin, the two opposition leaders met at the Parliament buildings.

'We must make one last effort on third reading,' Lamirande said to Houghton. 'We must delay the consummation of this iniquity as long as possible.'

'You're absolutely right,' Houghton replied. 'I've made up my mind to oppose, even obstruct as long as our people are willing to follow us. I fear it won't be long, for fighting without the slightest hope of success is not much fun, you must admit.'

'I have not given up hope completely,' said Lamirande.

'But where can we expect help to come from?'

'From Vaughan.'

'He's beyond conversion. You and I, my dear Lamirande, have exhausted every bit of logic on him and with no success.'

'But God can do in one instant what our arguments cannot accomplish in two weeks.'

'Of course God could do so. But will He?'

'I hope so. I hope that something great will ...'

He never completed his thought. He was handed a telegram. He opened it and read. A stifled cry escaped his lips and his features darkened with pain.

'My God!' Houghton exclaimed. 'What dreadful news have you just received?'

Lamirande could not utter a single word. He held out the fatal paper and Houghton read:

Beauvoir Convent, 25 March 1946
To M. Joseph Lamirande, MP, Ottawa
Marie taken ill. Doctor without hope. If you want to see her alive, come immediately.
Sister Antonin, Superior

'She's my only child,' said Lamirande, 'my only joy in this world.'

Houghton took his hand.

'My poor, poor friend.'

'My God!' Lamirande exclaimed, 'is this the new sacrifice you are asking of me? It is too much! Too much! You are asking for more than my own life.'

And the poor man burst into sobs.

In a few moments he was able to control his emotions so that he could speak.

'There's a train leaving for Quebec soon. I'll take Vaughan with me. I need someone and you may need Leverdier. Hold on as long as you can. We don't know what may happen a few hours from now. Only God knows if a double tragedy awaits us. May His holy will be done.'

He went to look for Vaughan and soon found him.

'What is it?' Vaughan asked when he saw the look of anguish on his friend's face.

Lamirande handed him the horrible yellow sheet. Vaughan could only repeat what Houghton had said a moment earlier.

'My poor, poor friend!'

'Will you come with me?' asked Lamirande. 'I need a sympathetic friend; if I'm alone I fear my heart will break.'

'Of course,' Vaughan replied. 'I am only too happy to be able to give you some sign of my affection for you.'

'I shall be eternally grateful.'

It was noon, and the train left for Quebec at one o'clock, arriving at six. During the trip the two friends barely spoke. One was absorbed in his sorrow, the other preoccupied and tormented more than ever by the struggle that was going on in his heart. One prayer kept coming to the lips of the afflicted father: 'My God, I offer you my sorrow if it will obtain the conversion of this soul.'

Outside all was bleak. Rain fell in torrents from a leaden sky and angrily slashed at the windows. In the fields there were patches of snow alternating with pools of water wrinkled by the wind. The roads were filled with mud and dung-covered ice. The only sign of life came from the crows that noisily disputed winter's accumulation of rubbish. Nothing is less picturesque or less poetic than our Canadian countryside during the spring thaw. The earth's white mantle is torn and soiled while the green carpet of spring has not yet been laid down.

As the train moved towards the north-east at a dizzying speed, the countryside took on a different character. There were more patches of snow, and they were wider. Finally, near the Saint-Maurice River, which is the line of demarcation between the eastern and western parts of the province, only winter's presence could be seen.

At Trois-Rivières the train made a brief stop. A young clerk from the telegraph office got on to the train and ran from car to car shouting in a nasal voice, 'Telegram for M. Lamirande.' These simple words fell like an avalanche on Lamirande's soul. The wretched man felt crushed, completely destroyed. He gestured to Vaughan to take the telegram. What terror, what anguish one small piece of yellow paper can cause! Vaughan did not dare hand the telegram to Lamirande, who was looking at it with horror. For this insignificant slip of paper was indeed a terrifying object.

'Open it and read it,' he said at last. 'My God,' he added, 'give me the strength to submit to this new trial like a Christian.'

Vaughan opened the envelope, his hands trembling. He read:

Beauvoir Convent, 2:00 PM
To M. Joseph Lamirande, Trois-Rivières, on the train from Ottawa

Marie is in Heaven. May God console you.
Sister Antonin

Although it was not unexpected, it was still a terrible blow. The good sister's prayer was not granted: as a further trial for His faithful servant God gave him no consolation. On the contrary, He allowed the most bitter waves of human sorrow to engulf his so tender and loving heart. He could think of only one thing: now he was alone in the world. His most important earthly possession had been taken away forever. For a few minutes he would see a poor little corpse, then nothing more of the child he had loved so dearly: never another caress, never another smile. He was not thinking of his daughter's happiness, nor did he remember that in terms of eternity the separation brought about by death is a temporary one; he saw only the fearsome wound inflicted on his father's heart, and he was sorely tempted to complain against divine Providence, to call it unfair, to protest that he did not deserve such an affliction. But God was only testing him; He had not abandoned him. And his soul, hurt and weakened as it was, had, with the grace of God, the strength to repel any thought of revolt.

Night fell as the two travellers set off along the long tree-bordered alley that led from the Chemin Saint-Louis to the convent at Beauvoir, perched on the cliff that dominates the great river. The rain was still falling dismally, and the wind was moaning in the naked branches of the maple and birch trees, in the pines and the sombre spruce. Since they had received the fatal message, the two friends had barely exchanged a word. Vaughan realized that Lamirande's sorrow was one of those great afflictions that words do nothing to assuage, that only silent, sympathetic waiting can relieve.

They were expecting Lamirande at the convent. Father Grandmont met him at the door and held him for a long time in a fatherly embrace.

'I saw her die,' he said. 'I gave her holy communion. I've never seen anything so beautiful. Despite your terrible affliction you should be proud.'

'Father, Father, I am in such pain!' was Lamirande's only reply.

Then, after a supreme effort to contain himself, he introduced Vaughan to the good priest:

'Here is a friend whose soul is overwhelmed as much as my heart is broken. Help us both with your prayers.'

They went to the death chamber. Four nuns were praying around the modest white bed where the child seemed to sleep. Only her death-like pallor indicated that it was not sleep. Lamirande fell to his knees beside his child, and raising his eyes and hands to Heaven, he cried in a strong and vibrant voice:

'Lord Jesus, who gave back to the widow in Nain her only son, have pity on me as You had pity on that afflicted mother. Her sorrow could not have been greater than my own. Her son was his mother's sole support; my daughter was my only joy on this earth. Without her son, the widow of Nain might have starved to death, and you gave him back to her.' Without my daughter my heart will break. Oh, give her back to me, all-powerful Jesus, infinitely good.'

Lamirande was still looking towards Heaven in a sort of ecstasy. Father Grandmont, Vaughan, and the four nuns were staring at the bed. A cry of astonishment escaped from all of them at once. Stupefied, they saw the child's waxen cheeks turn pink, her pale lips turn to crimson. She opened her shining eyes and, seeing her father, called to him softly:

'Papa! Dear Papa!'

At the sound of her beloved voice Lamirande started. He looked down, and seeing his daughter alive, her arms stretched out to him, a smile on her lips, he was near collapse. Mere words could not express his joy.

'My God, my God, how good You are!' he murmured.

Then the child threw herself into her father's arms, and they held each other in a long, silent embrace.

It was Marie who finally spoke.

'Dear Papa, I was really dead, wasn't I? It wasn't a dream. I've often dreamed of Heaven, but it was never like that. Oh, it was so beautiful in Heaven, Papa dear. Nothing on earth is like it.'

'Were you happy there?'

'Oh yes Papa, I can't tell you how happy I was with Jesus and the Blessed Virgin and Mama and all the saints and angels in a bright and shining light, brighter than a thousand suns, but it didn't even hurt your eyes. And I saw the place that's being saved for you, very high, but very close to me. It's hard to explain, but oh! there is such joy in Heaven!'

'And why did you leave this happiness, my child?'

'Because the Child Jesus said to me, "Marie, your father is calling you. Do you want to leave Heaven and go and see your father?" And I answered, "I am happy here, and I would gladly stay here forever; but if my father is calling me I must go to him. Keep my place here, gentle Jesus, so that I can come back when my father doesn't need me any more." And the Child, who is like the Master of Heaven, nodded His head and smiled at me. So I came back because you needed me, Papa dear. I shall try to be good and make you happy. Then we shall go to Paradise together.'

'And you aren't sorry about leaving Heaven, darling?'

'No, because I saw that it was what the Child wanted, and in Heaven the greatest happiness is to want what He wants. I don't regret it because it can make you happy.'

'But if you could go back to Heaven now, wouldn't that make you happy?'

'Of course, if it was what you and Jesus wanted.'

'Very well, my child, it is my wish that you return to Heaven, and I am sure that it is also the wish of the One you call the Child. It was selfish and senseless of me to interrupt your happiness. Go now! Go back to the Child and the Blessed Virgin and your mother and all the saints and angels and into the light of glory.'

He pressed a long kiss on his daughter's brow and placed her gently on her bed. Then the roses faded from her cheeks to be replaced once more by wax. And her crimson lips turned pale, but they kept their celestial smile.

Marie had gone back to join the Child and the Blessed Virgin and her mother and all the saints and angels in the light of glory, more brilliant than a thousand suns.

For where your treasure is, there will your heart be also.
MATTHEW 6:21

31

LAMIRANDE, FATHER GRANDMONT, VAUGHAN, and the four nuns kneeled around the bed for some time. Lamirande was the first to come back to himself. He rose and touched Vaughan lightly on the shoulder. The young English Canadian started — it was as though he were in a kind of ecstasy. Lamirande's hand brought him back to the reality around him.

'My friend,' said Lamirande, 'you wanted to see the supernatural. You've seen it now. Do you believe?'

'Yes.' Vaughan replied. 'I believe. But it wasn't the miracle that gave me faith. At least, it was not the miracle that converted me, that changed my heart and tore aside the veil. Of course, when I saw your daughter come back to life, all the doubts that had been haunting me about the reality of our future life vanished instantly. But even that was not what saved me. As the light entered my mind, my heart seemed to harden and the veil become thicker. If your daughter had stayed alive, I should have left here as much a *believer* as you, but still not a *convert*. But your renunciation of the happiness of keeping your child with you required a flood of grace to sweep over you. And that I felt! It was as though a torrent had filled your heart and overflowed into mine, pulling me along. Even so, I could have resisted; but my heart softened, the veil was torn, and now I am not only a believer but a convert. I see Heaven and I want to attain it. God used your sublime sacrifice as His instrument to make me a disciple of the One who granted your prayer and to Whom you sacrificed your last happiness on earth.'

The two friends embraced. Father Grandmont came up to them and Vaughan, said, 'Father, I repeat the words the Ethiopian said to St Philip on the road from Jerusalem to Gaza: "What is to prevent my being baptised?" '

'And I,' replied the priest, 'reply with St Philip, "If you believe with all your heart, you may." '

'I believe that Jesus Christ is the Son of God,' Vaughan replied, just as the minister of Queen Candace had replied two thousand years before.

Father Grandmont questioned the young English Canadian and soon realized that he was already perfectly instructed in the Catholic religion.

In the convent chapel the venerable priest poured the holy water of baptism on the convert's forehead. Lamirande was godfather to his friend and Sister Antonin was godmother. It was a most touching sight: God's minister, his splendid face framed in silver hair, beamed with joy; the two men, thoughtful and mature; the nuns in their stalls, motionless in their vast white veils; the altar, where a thousand candles burned as on a holy day – it made a picture worthy of the brush of Raphael.

It was almost ten o'clock at night when the ceremony was finished.

'And now,' said Vaughan, 'we must go back to Ottawa as quickly as possible. I have an important duty to perform and great wrongs to set right.'

'Must I leave my child so soon?' Lamirande asked. 'I should have liked to spend the night by her side. We could take the first train tomorrow morning. My soul is rent by emotion. I need a few hours, not for sleep but for prayer.'

'So be it,' replied his friend, 'but I must send Houghton a telegram.'

He went to a nearby office and wired the Leader of the Opposition:

'For the love of God do not allow third reading before our return.'

Then he returned to the convent, and the two friends, along with Father Grandmont, spent the night in prayer and pious conversation. Vaughan edified his two companions with his outbursts of faith, his fervour, and his gentle, confident, childlike piety.

Early next morning Father Grandmont said mass. Lamirande and Vaughan received holy communion from his hand. Vaughan was radiant, transfigured.

'How great is the goodness of God!' he exclaimed to his friend. 'How powerful is His grace. Only a few hours ago my heart was filled with ice; now it is afire. In the past I saw nothing beautiful, nothing great beyond material and human things; now all that is terrestrial seems small and insignificant. Before, Heaven was far away and even more uncertain. Now the life of the future seems to me to be the true life, life par excellence, and our real homeland is above us.

Before today I never experienced true happiness; true joy was unknown to me. Now I have completely changed, and everything appears changed to me. I see everything differently, I understand differently — life, death, the world, mankind, events, the past, the present, the future. And it is divine grace that has wrought this tremendous change in me. How powerful is this grace, and how good is God!'

Lamirande was overjoyed to hear his friend praise his happiness so enthusiastically.

'Yes,' he replied, 'God is infinitely good and His grace is infinitely powerful. But His goodness is not always presented in the same fashion, and His grace, while it is always powerful, is not always sensitive. Your soul is inundated with delight — it is truly a foretaste of Heaven. No doubt God is granting you this favour to confirm you in His service. But do not be surprised or hurt or discouraged if, some time later, the delicious fervour you feel today is replaced by a distressing aridity, a horrible disgust; if the Heaven that now appears so near and smiling grows distant and stony-faced; if your soul, now so full of unction and noble thoughts, becomes arid as the desert; if prayer which today is a natural and spontaneous outpouring of your heart to God becomes a veritable burden, more painful than the hardest labour. Our Lord often puts his most faithful servants to the test in this way and such a test may be reserved for you. If it does happen to you, do not let it discourage you. Pray, even when you no longer find satisfaction in prayer, even when you think that you no longer love God and that God is no longer interested in you. For the prayer that is offered in the wilderness can be more pleasing to Heaven than orisons soaring effortlessly from a heart plunged deep in fervour. It is on arid rocks, not fertile ground, that the most subtle, delicately perfumed flowers are to be found.'

Their conversation was interrupted by preparations for their departure. Lamirande, accompanied by Vaughan and Father Grandmont, went one last time to the room where Marie had died. Lamirande looked for a long time at his beloved daughter. Nature claimed its due: he wept copiously, though without bitterness. Then, overcoming this last weakness, he exclaimed,

'I thank you, God, for the blessings You have bestowed upon us. In return for one small sacrifice, You have granted the conversion of my friend, and, through his conversion, assured the future of our beloved country. In fact, to a faithful soul, the sacrifice is a slight one, even though it wrenched my heart most painfully. My daughter is infinitely happy with You, and even though our separation is painful, in terms of eternity it is brief. And to repay me for a few years' suffering which I freely accept, You are removing the last infernal obstacles that have prevented our people from attaining its Providential destiny. You guarantee the freedom of Your Church in this country; You thereby facilitate the salvation of millions of souls still to be born. And You grant all these uncountable blessings because one human heart has had the grace to sacrifice itself for love of You. I thank You God, and bless You.'

Lamirande and Vaughan left Quebec for Ottawa, and Montarval was told of their departure almost immediately, for he had spies everywhere. The late lamented Duthier had not been alone in the service of the satanist leader. The news of their sudden departure and the knowledge of the sad event that had motivated it, cast Montarval into a strangely troubled state. He had a foreboding that the dénouement was near, and that it would be fatal to him; this trip seemed related in some way that he could not learn or even suspect to the impending ruin of all his projects. An hour before the sitting was to begin he shut himself into a secret room in his house, a room no one ever entered, for any reason whatsoever. The walls were covered with red hangings; it was a satanic temple. The hideous emblems of the infernal cult adorned the room. Montarval, the victim of a desperate agitation, went before a kind of altar where incense was burning and began a horrible invocation:
'Come Eblis! God of infinite desolation and boundless despair; Inspirer of all revolt against the cruel laws of Jehovah, of all hatred of abject virtue and infamous holiness; sublime author of all pride, all crime, all sins, all sorrow, death and everything called evil by the priests of Adonai; valiant destroyer of eternal tyranny; implacable enemy of Christ, His Church and His priests; indefatigable liberator of the human race; Thou turnest men away from the humiliating joys of Heaven and preparest them for the harsh delights of thy kingdom of fire and liberty: come, oh spirit of vengeance, oh ever-persecuted, eternal rebel. The supreme hour is at hand! I, thy faithful servant, can no longer see what road to follow. Darkness

surrounds me, I am assailed by hesitation, pursued by dark forebodings. Come. Reveal to me the actions of this mortal who combats our project so relentlessly; come and show me how to win success at last.'

As he spoke a glacial wind filled the room. Then, in the midst of the white smoke from the incense, a vague gigantic form appeared, and a voice that seemed to come from far away began to speak:

'A power that is stronger than my own prevents me from communicating freely with you. I will conquer this hostile power one day; I will deliver the entire universe from it. But now it holds me cruelly in its grasp. I can tell you only this: Do not lose a minute; hasten the events.'

The voice was suddenly silent and the form vanished.

Debate on third reading of the constitutional bill began when the sitting opened at three o'clock. The prime minister expressed the hope that since all topics for discussion had been exhausted, the House would not delay any longer in carrying out the formality of third reading; it would only waste time if all the arguments for and against the bill were to be repeated. He made it clear that the government would oppose adjourning the sitting before the vote was taken.

Houghton, Leverdier, and the other opposition leaders were not taken in by Sir Henry's sophisms. They were determined to prolong the debate until Lamirande returned, no matter what the cost. Except for Leverdier, none had the slightest hope of winning, but they loved and respected their colleague too much to deny him their last mark of sympathy and esteem. Because the government's majority was so slim, they no longer had to fear the arbitrary application of closure; Vaughan's group, even though it favoured the bill would not allow it. Debate began again, more bitter than ever. But strict silence was imposed on the ministerial side: not one member on the Speaker's right rose to reply to the debaters from the left who had once again to bear the burden of the debate.

Around ten o'clock at night Houghton received a message from Vaughan. He showed it to Leverdier and to three other French MPs whom he knew to be perfectly discreet.

'Be very careful not to breathe a word about it to anyone at all,' he told them.

'Why not?' Leverdier asked. 'It's natural to encourage our friends; this message says quite clearly that Vaughan has suddenly changed his mind and is coming over to our side.'

'And it is precisely because his message says quite clearly that Vaughan is with us that I beg you to keep it absolutely secret. I showed it to the four of you because you won't be tempted to weaken even for a moment. But once again, for the love of God, don't breathe a word to anyone, because if certain people hear this news – people you can see from where we're sitting – there will most certainly be another tragic railway accident. And this time it will come closer to success.'

'Do you really think so?' asked one of the four.

'Absolutely,' replied the leader of the opposition. 'The only thing that could prevent another accident, if a certain person were to learn what we already know, is that the two people who are suspected of being the authors of the recent catastrophe have just been arrested in Montreal. Even so, there may be others like them. In any case, keep the contents of this message secret, if you love Lamirande and Vaughan and want to serve our country.'

'Don't worry,' they replied. 'But if these two wretches have been caught, they may name the instigator of their crime.'

'Perhaps. Provided that he doesn't open the door of their prison with a key of gold – or something else of a less precious metal.'

At midnight Houghton moved that the House be adjourned, saying that the sitting had gone on long enough, that it was unreasonable to force the members to speak indefinitely on such an important question without giving them time to reflect – one day's delay would not endanger the country. As leader of the opposition he would undertake to guarantee termination of the debate at the end of the next sitting, if the government, for its part, would consent to adjourn the House. But the ministers rejected his proposal, declaring that they would not consent to adjourn the House until after the vote on third reading.

This haughty and brutal refusal had one excellent result; it was the last straw for the members of the opposition. Their spirits rose and they were determined to prolong the session indefinitely. This was exactly what Houghton and Leverdier wanted; now Lamirande and Vaughan would have time to return. The opposition organized its forces for the rest of the night.

As the government had opposed adjournment, it was incumbent on them to maintain a sufficient number of MPs to allow the House to sit. The opposition had only to supply speakers for the twelve hours from midnight to noon. Houghton had no trouble finding twelve of his partisans who were prepared to speak for an hour. He expected Vaughan to return around noon; if not, he could find other speakers to prolong the session until evening.

Who has not witnessed one of those sessions where the minority, to protest what it considers an unjustice, a tyranny on the part of the majority, decides to sit indefinitely? There is a comic, even a grotesque element to such scenes. The governmental MPs, obliged to remain in sufficient numbers to prevent adjournment, assumed postures and stances completely lacking in poetry or dignity. Some sink deep in their chairs, their hats pulled down over their eyes, or half-asleep on their desks, snoring. Others, with no false shame, order in steaks or chops, and fight against boredom armed with knives and forks. On the opposition side the benches are empty; everyone goes to rest in his office. Only those responsible for continuing the debate are left, along with two or three others in case some accident occurs. If the one who is speaking is accustomed to this parliamentary game, he knows how to conduct himself. He begins by speaking very slowly, wandering as far as he can from the subject without exposing himself to a call to order. He will quote at length and on every subject from the inevitable Todd, the inescapable May, the unavoidable Bourinot, those classic authors on the Canadian parliament from the end of the nineteenth century who are still authorities in the middle of the twentieth. Reading a few pages of these authors rests the speaker's mind, if not his audience, by excusing him from the trouble of seeking his own phrases or ideas. If the few friends who remain notice that he is floundering too much and that the Speaker is about to ask him to be silent they will find a way to bring about some incident to give him time to pull himself together. And when he has finally come to the end of his resources another will take his place and start again the same moving quotations from Todd, May, and Bourinot. Gradually minds will relax, and eventually a compromise will be reached. This is the usual ending to those sessions that are prolonged *ab irato*.

The memorable sitting of the last parliament of the Canadian confederation which had begun at three o'clock PM on March 25, 1946, was to end not with a compromise but with a triumphant defeat for one side and victory for the other.

The animated debate went on all night: it was not yet purely factitious. Several French-Canadian MPs, including Leverdier, still had something to say, and they spoke heatedly.

March 26 dawned grey and mournful. The rain had stopped but a thick fog enveloped and penetrated everything. As the morning went on the atmosphere in the House became depressing. The floor was strewn with crumpled newspapers, scraps of notes, and blue books. Each speaker was obviously marking time. Around eleven o'clock Houghton received a message from Vaughan, dated at Saint-Martin; 'Hold tight, arriving Ottawa half-past noon.' Now there was nothing more to fear. It was impossible for the enemy to plan a new railway accident. The opposition leader showed the message to his colleagues quite freely now. It was passed from hand to hand.

'Just keep at it a bit longer,' said Houghton, 'help is at hand.'

Montarval did not fail to notice the animation that greeted Vaughan's message on the Opposition side. Montarval had scarcely left his seat since the previous night. He was shaken by a dark and impotent rage.

The news that Lamirande and Vaughan were arriving and that Vaughan now opposed the bill spread rapidly; excitement was at its peak. The galleries were filled and the MPs took their seats. There was a kind of fever in the air. Everyone realized that the dénouement was at hand.

Finally, a few minutes before one o'clock, Lamirande and Vaughan entered the House. They were greeted by a long burst of applause. Then a number of MPs came to offer their condolences to Lamirande; it was known that his daughter had died, although the extraordinary circumstances surrounding her death had not yet been disclosed. Everyone was struck by the change in Vaughan. He was no longer laughing, carefree, and slightly sceptical, but grave, though without a hint of sadness. On the contrary, a kind of tranquil joy marked his features; they radiated a sweetness, a nobility, a greatness that had not been evident before.

The MP who had been speaking when Lamirande and Vaughan entered the House realized that there was no need to continue his speech. He ended it abruptly, sparing the House several pages of May that he had been preparing to read. The precedents no longer interested anyone. Now they were curious to know the future.

'Mr Speaker,' said Vaughan, as soon as he was able to speak, 'I now propose to vote against this constitutional bill that I previously supported so stubbornly. But first I wish to tell the House, in a few words, the reason for this radical change. A profound moral transformation in me has completely changed my political opinions. You may say what you will, but religion, the bond which unites us with God, will always have a preponderant influence on politics, the bond which unites men among themselves. The man who truly believes in Jesus Christ, the Son of God, who descended into this world to redeem mankind and open the gates of heaven to us; the man who truly believes in the holy Catholic Church founded by Jesus Christ upon Peter and the Apostles in order to continue across the ages His work of redemption and salvation; the man who firmly believes in these great fundamental truths cannot envisage politics in the same way as one who does not believe. When I speak of politics, I speak of the real thing, not railways and navigation and commerce; I speak of the great problems whose solution will determine the future of mankind. Until now, during our discussion of the constitutional bill, I considered only the purely human aspect of the question. I saw only the material greatness and prosperity of the country. And it seemed to me that this greatness would be better assured by a close union of the provinces than by their separation. Now I see that even from an earthly point of view I was wrong – so true is it that we see the things in this world only rising above them. But now the material greatness of our country seems to me to be quite secondary importance. The first question I ask myself is this: "Is this constitution we are being asked to vote on not designed to hinder the activities of the Catholic Church, possibly to destroy those activities completely?" The information we were given the other day proves that this constitution was conceived in an atmosphere that was hostile to the Church and consequently to the salvation of souls. Yesterday I was prepared to vote for it even though I knew it would serve to oppress the Church and kill faith. I was prepared to commit this political crime because I was an insensitive, malevolent man with my eyes to the ground, and I attached more importance to transient things than to eternity, to questions of territorial extent and national prestige than to the loss of salvation of souls. Today, if that constitution were to assure us of the greatest, richest, most powerful empire in the world but endangered the salvation of a single soul, I would gladly sacrifice my life rather than sanction it with my vote. And if such a great change has been effected in me, if I see things so differently from the way I saw them yesterday, it is because I left here an unbeliever and I have come back a believer. I am a believer like my friend; the light that illuminates him shines on me too. All that he believes, I believe; all that he loves, I love; all that he adores and hopes for I too hope for and adore. You may ask how this great change came about; it is a subject that is far too intimate, too sacred for me even to touch on it here. Suffice it to say that no matter how extraordinary the effect may seem to you, it is far less so than the cause that produced it. And now, a word to those of my friends whom I may have blinded by my sophisms in favour of this evil bill. If they cannot see it as I do, from the supernatural point of view, I hope they can see it as the honourable leader of the opposition does, from the point of view of honour and reason. I hope they realize that this constitution is directed against the religion, the language, and the nationality of an entire people; that its object is to unite Canada by destroying what is most precious to a third of its population. May they realize that a political work with such a foundation can be neither stable nor fruitful. It is only through separation that we will find true greatness and prosperity, because in it we will find peace.'

The young English Canadian sat down, and there was a silence that was both solemn and filled with emotion, and more approving than the most thunderous applause. The House understood that any noisy demonstration would be inappropriate. Not one MP rose to speak. Everything had been said, everything had been done.

Houghton and Lamirande again made the standard motion: 'That the bill be given its third reading not now but in six months' time.' The Speaker put the motion to the vote. The result was not in doubt because it was well known that Vaughan controlled at least seven votes. The shift of eight votes put the government in the minority by eleven votes, 127 to 116 according to the figures the clerk read out.

As soon as the Speaker announced the result, the opposition, which had been silent after Vaughan's speech, broke into enthusiastic applause and a show of delirious joy. The MPs shook hands warmly, congratulated each other, laughed and cried and danced for joy; they pounded their desks, roared their delight, and threw into the air whatever they happened to have in their hands. For it is true that even the most serious men sometimes become true children when they are strongly moved. Only Lamirande remained calm in the midst of the storm.

> So the murderer and blasphemer ...
> came to the end of his life by a most pitiable fate.
> II MACCABEES 9:28

32

WHEN THE SPEAKER FINALLY SUCCEEDED in restoring some order, Sir Henry Marwood rose, pale and defeated, to move that the House be adjourned, and announced that the cabinet would resign immediately.

Montarval remained in his seat, seemingly unaware of what was happening around him. If his colleagues had not been so feverishly excited, they would have seen in his eyes a flame of rage and despair that expressed unspeakable horror. Lamirande saw it and shuddered.

The MPs dispersed, going into the corridors, the library, and outside into the alleys where the fog was still thick and penetrating. Lamirande, Houghton, and Leverdier walked together behind the Parliament buildings, away from the noisier groups. They felt the need to communicate their thoughts and feelings. Houghton had just said, 'Any religion that can bring about such a change in Vaughan is not a religion like the others; it must be the only true one and I am going to study it seriously myself.' As he spoke, one of the guards ran up to them, looking terrified.

'Gentlemen,' he exclaimed, 'something horrible has happened! M. Montarval has shot himself in the head.'

The four friends ran after the man. He took them to the most distant part of the grounds, to the section of the cliff above the Ottawa River that is called 'Lovers' Walk.' There they saw the unfortunate satanist lying in the mud, blood streaming from a bullet hole in his head, but still alive. As they arrived, he tried in vain to get up and reach his weapon which had fallen several feet from him. They picked him up and lay him on a bench. Lamirande examined the wound and declared that it was mortal. They carried him to a nearby pavilion, and the guard, at Lamirande's order, ran to bring a cushion, some water, and a stimulant. On the way, he met an Oblate priest who had been led there by some mysterious impulse. When the priest learned the sad news he too ran to the pavilion, where he saw a dreadful sight. Montarval was lying on a table, dying. His breathing was only a rattle, and from his right temple a thin stream of blood spilled, drop by drop, onto the floor. His eyes were open, glassy and staring.

'Is he conscious?' asked the priest.

'I don't think so,' Lamirande replied. 'He was when we found him here, but since we moved him he has given no sign that he recognizes us.'

The guard soon returned. They put the cushion under Montarval's head, and Lamirande wet his lips with a few drops of brandy. The stimulant had some effect; the dying man tried to turn over, and the others helped him. Just then a veil of fog was blown into the open doorway, wavered in the middle of the pavilion, and then slithered into a corner where it assumed a vague, indefinite shape. Montarval stared at it; Lamirande gave him a few more drops of brandy. The dying man gestured to the doctor to bend over, and said to him, with great effort,

'Lamirande, I hate you.'

'And I,' he replied, 'forgive you with all my heart and beg you to think of the terrible judgement of God, before Whom you must soon appear. For God is terrible, but He is also infinitely merciful. You can still throw yourself into his arms.'

'I hate your god!' the dying man gasped.

'How horrible!' murmured the Oblate, bringing his crucifix to his lips. 'My God, forgive him this blasphemy; he doesn't know what he's saying.'

Montarval had raised himself slightly on his elbow and was still looking at the cloud in the corner of the pavilion. Everyone instinctively turned in the same direction. Was it an optical illusion or was the wisp of fog really assuming a colossal human shape? If it was an illusion, they all shared it, for they all saw the shape, and they all felt the same terror that froze the blood in their veins.

'Eblis! Eblis!' the dying man cried suddenly. 'You have deceived me; you promised I would triumph, but I suffered a humiliating defeat; I am threatened by revelations that could send me to jail, perhaps to the gallows.'

He could not go on; his strength had left him. He fell back onto his cushion, but he was not yet unconscious. The priest came up to him and held up the crucifix.

'Here is the One who will never deceive you, either in this world or in the next. Satan, Eblis as you call him, is the Prince of Lies. He deceived you in this life, and he will do so in the future. Hell, his kingdom, is a place of terrifying horrors. Jesus Christ, our God, offers you forgiveness in Heaven. Renounce the demon before eternity swallows you up.'

The Luciferian got up again, sustained by a force that was visibly superhuman.

'Your God!' he spat out between clenched teeth. 'I hate Him! I despise Him. His Heaven is a place of humiliation and degradation. I want no part of it. I prefer Hell, whatever it may be!'

As he uttered these words of the damned he pushed away the crucifix with an angry gesture. It was his last act. A convulsive tremor shook him from head to foot; his eyes opened wide and assumed an expression of unspeakable horror. His limbs stiffened and he uttered a cry of despair that would be engraved forever in the minds of the six men who had witnessed the horrifying scene.

'We must leave at once!' the priest exclaimed. 'This place is evil; it is inhabited by demons!'

They all ran outside, their faces white with terror, their flesh trembling and afraid.

'Merciful God!' Lamirande exclaimed, 'if it is possible, have pity on him!'

> I have finished the race.
> II TIMOTHY 4:7

33

TWO DAYS LATER, AT MID-MORNING, Lamirande, Leverdier, and Vaughan, who had taken the night train from Ottawa, went to the convent at Beauvoir. The weather was delightful. The dismal rain was over, the fog had dispersed, and the wind no longer moaned in the great pines. It had frozen during the night and the frost-covered trees looked like gigantic plumes that cut through the brilliant blue sky to form a picture of such strange beauty no painter would have the audacity to try to reproduce it.

Although they were needed in Ottawa, Leverdier and Vaughan had not wanted their friend to go alone to attend the last rites for his daughter. Houghton, too, had wanted to accompany them, but it was quite impossible for him to leave the capital.

The fall of the government and Montarval's miserable death had produced a general upset. The country's evil genius had disappeared, the intrigues had ceased, and political affairs resumed their normal course. Separatism, which had earlier seemed to be only a dream, was now widely accepted. Even those who still did not approve of it accepted it as inevitable. Now it was just a question of executing the policy as quickly as possible. The task was given to Houghton, and he was working to put together a cabinet to liquidate the situation. He first approached Lamirande, who, while he did not refuse to enter the government which had to exist only long enough to effect the separation, had asked for three days of grace.

'When my child is in her final resting place,' he said, 'I will give you my answer. Meanwhile, work with Leverdier and Vaughan to form your cabinet, as though I did not exist.'

'It will be difficult,' Houghton replied, 'not to take into account the man who has been chosen by Providence to create the movement that now leads our country towards its new destiny.'

'Nevertheless,' replied Lamirande, 'you must get used to the idea. Some are called to begin a work, while others must complete it. He who sows does not always reap. Moses led God's chosen people out of the land of Egypt, but it was Joshua who brought them into the land of Canaan.'

'Moses had a moment's hesitation; that is why it was not given to him to lead his people across the Jordan.'

'And who tells you that I, like Moses in the desert of Sinai, have not doubted too?'

The nuns at Beauvoir had asked Lamirande as a special favour that Marie's mortal remains be entrusted to them. She was placed in the vault beneath their chapel.

Lamirande stayed for some time, kneeling on the cold stones. His two friends wanted to remain with him, but he gestured to them to leave. He wanted to be alone with God and his child. When he finally rejoined his two companions, they saw on his features and in his eyes the traces of copious tears and a celestial reflection, an indefinable light that they had never seen there before.

They set off together along the road to the town and the station. But when they arrived at the railway, Lamirande suddenly stopped, like someone who has just remembered some important business.

'Take the first train,' he told his friends. 'Houghton needs you now. I have some things to look after and some people to see here. I'll take another train.'

Then, shaking hands effusively with his two friends, he walked rapidly away from them. They were completely taken by surprise and thought neither to question nor to stop him. When they had recovered, he was already far away.

'Should we follow him?' Vaughan asked.

'I think it would be better to do as he asked,' Leverdier replied.

'Don't you find his behaviour rather strange?'

'Yes, it is strange, or rather it is new. But nothing about it worries me. Let's go.'

And they set out for Ottawa, firmly convinced that Lamirande would join them there soon. But they never saw him again, in Ottawa or anywhere else.

The fifth day after the funeral, there was great concern over Lamirande's disappearance. His friends were thinking seriously of going to Quebec City to look for him when Leverdier received the following letter:

New York, 2 April 1946
My dear friend,
I know you are all concerned about me. But be reassured, nothing is wrong. I am in perfect health, both mentally and physically.

I am leaving this world forever. Do not try to find me; it would be fruitless to look. I can hide myself so effectively that no one will ever find me.

My dear friend, it is not bitterness or misanthropy that led me to this decision. In my heart I still love the things of this earth. Legitimate happiness here still has a powerful attraction for me. I can imagine a smiling future for myself: an important position in this country; the esteem and recognition of my fellow citizens; new domestic ties that would unite me even more closely to you; an admirable wife; the blonde heads of children. Ah! do not think that I am indifferent to such a dream or that I renounce it easily! But when Father Grandmont tells you of certain events that I have concealed from you, you will agree that one who has received such extraordinary favours should not remain in this world. When a man has seen what I have seen, heard what I have heard, suffered what I have suffered, there is only one thing left for him to do on earth: to pray, while he waits to be summoned by God.

If I did not tell you and Vaughan of my decision before, it was because I wanted to avoid arguments that would likely have been painful and would certainly have been useless. Do not ask Father Grandmont where I am going, for even he does not know.

And now, I bid you farewell, I want to say one last word about politics and a word about business. Father Grandmont will give you what I call my political testament. Give it to our friends, especially Houghton and Vaughan. It contains what I might have been able to do to help you in the great task that is still to be accomplished: the separation of the provinces and the organization of New France. I think I have gone into both these questions in detail. Weigh it all, before God, and take from it what seems useful. Even if I had stayed with you, I could have told you no more. This document contains all my small baggage of knowledge, experience, and thoughts of the future. Besides, what is especially necessary is the intimate union of our compatriots within the Catholic faith. I feel that this union will take place more easily around my memory than around my person.

Along with my political testament Father Grandmont will give you power of attorney, which will authorize you to dispose of everything that belonged to me. I have only one object that is truly precious: the miraculous statue of St Joseph. I should have liked to give it to you, but Father Grandmont asked for it, and so insistently, for the chapel of Notre Dame du Chemin, that I could not refuse him. To you I give the leaf from the lily that was removed from the statue by St Joseph himself.

Let Houghton and Vaughan choose what souvenir they want, then divide my possessions into three equal parts: one for the poor, one for your sister Hélène so that she can give alms while praying for me, and one for the development of the task that you will direct.

Finally, give fond greetings to all my friends.

My brother, my friend! Farewell forever in this world; we shall meet again in the Heaven that Our Lord Jesus Christ has conquered for us at the price of His most previous blood. Amen.
Joseph Lamirande

I waited patiently for the Lord.
PSALMS 40:1

Epilogue

THE FOLLOWING ARTICLE WAS PUBLISHED in the February 15, 1977 issue of *La Croix* in Grenoble, France:

Saint-Laurent-du Pont, 13 February 1977
To the Editor:
Not far from here, at the Great Charterhouse, a life has just been extinguished: a humble life, its achievements carefully concealed, even mysterious, but a life which must have been great and glorious in the eyes of God. For the passage of this soul from earthly time into eternity was accompanied by celestial phenomena that were truly extraordinary.

Brother Jean is no longer in this world. Perhaps you have never even heard of him. Very few people in France ever saw him, and even fewer were aware of his existence.

More than thirty years ago a man arrived at the Great Charterhouse. He was about forty, well dressed, distinguished looking, speaking perfect French, and yet clearly a stranger to our country. He asked to see the abbot who at that time was Dom Augustin of blessed memory. Tradition has it that they spent several hours together, but no one knows what went on between them. The monks and brothers who were alive then recall that when the interview was over, the Father and the stranger appeared singularly moved. Both had shed many tears, but tears of deep feeling rather than pain. For their faces, although tear-stained, were beaming with great joy. That very day the stranger put on a monk's habit and assumed the name of Jean. Afterwards he never left the monastery except, in the last years, for certain errands in Fourvoirie, Currière, and Saint-Pierre. He even went to Saint-Laurent several times, guiding travellers on the Grand Som. Climbing this Alpine peak seemed to be his only real passion, if one may use the word. He carried out punctually, eagerly, and with perfect obedience all the other orders of his superiors, but when he was told to take visitors to the Grand Som his humble face and gentle eyes would be illuminated with a childlike joy. One day someone asked him why he was so fond of scaling this peak; he replied, 'It is so beautiful up there, and you feel so close to Heaven!'

Except for Dom Augustin, no one in the monastery knew who he was or where he had come from. He was obviously well educated, but he never wanted to be anything but a simple brother. For a long time, with the permission of the authorities, he never set foot outside the monastery and he never came into contact with any stranger. Fifteen years ago, when Dom Augustin was on his deathbed, he called all the monks to his side and begged them to tell whoever replaced him to respect Brother Jean's secret as he himself had done for so long. At this time the present successor to Saint Bruno, Dom François, knows no more than you or I about this modest brother who certainly must have played an important role somewhere in the world. And it must have been a role that was as salutary as it was remarkable, for Brother Jean was no great sinner come to take refuge in this solitude as a form of penitence. One had only to look into his calm and lucid eyes to realize that the soul of which they were the mirror had never been stained by crime or disturbed by remorse. He seemed like someone who had had a mission to accomplish in this world, who had accomplished it, and who had come here to these serene heights to await his entry into the celestial homeland.

I said that no one except Dom Augustin knew who he was. No one did know, but I suspected, and this is how I believe I unravelled the secret of Brother Jean.

Last August I went to the Great Charterhouse with two friends from Paris. One of them, Monsieur G, has travelled widely, especially in America, and he had spent several months in New France. As the weather was fine we wanted to climb the Grand Som, and Brother Jean was appointed as our guide and companion. Despite his seventy years, he outdistanced us easily. He had to keep slowing down for us to catch up.

We had been on the summit for twenty minutes or so, silently enjoying the magnificent sight, when we heard two voices speaking with great animation. Two young men of twenty-five or thirty were approaching the rock where the four of us were sitting, without noticing us. One of them shouted to the other, who was some distance away, 'Over here, Leverdier, here's a spectacular view!' I saw Brother Jean give a start and turn pale when he heard the name Leverdier; and my friend, Monsieur G., uttered a cry of surprise and delight. He got up and spoke to the two young men who were now quite close to us.

'I heard you mention the name Leverdier. I once knew a Paul Leverdier very well. He was the President of New France. Are you by chance related to him?'

'Yes, sir,' one of the young men replied very courteously, 'the man you knew was my father.'

Naturally they came to join our group, and we all began to speak. My friend G. asked the young man many questions about his father and his country.

'What delightful hours I spent with your father! He told me in great detail of the remarkable events, both painful and touching, that marked the foundation of the Republic of New France, now flourishing so happily. It was one of the most beautiful stories I have ever heard; I'm sure you know it as well as I.'

'As a matter of fact,' the young man replied, 'I often heard my father tell that same marvellous story.'

'And what about your father's friend Lamirande? According to your father, it was *his* sublime sacrifice that saved the country. Is his story still a great mystery?'

'Yes, it is. We are certain that he has retired to some European monastery but we have never heard from him. My father must have spoken to you about Lamirande's great friend Vaughan, who was present at the miracle in the convent at Beauvoir. M. Vaughan, as you may know, spent two years travelling in Europe after the political situation was straightened out. He visited every monastery and convent and retreat imaginable. He even went to the Holy Land. My father often spoke of his travels; but all his searching was in vain and the mystery was never solved.'

'And that wretched journalist – his name escapes me – who played such an odious role and sold himself body and soul to the leader of the Satanists – what happened to him?'

'You must mean Saint-Simon. He came to a sad end. He died insane, just last year, after spending I don't know how many years in a hospital. He was mad for wealth, and he always thought he was surrounded by pieces of gold. I saw him once, and it was a heartbreaking sight.'

'But tell me more about that good man Lamirande. Is your country properly grateful to him? Is his memory kept alive?'

'Yes, his name is blessed by all our people. He is revered as a saint and as the father of our country. Many young men were named Joseph in his memory. In fact, my own name is Joseph Lamirande Leverdier. My father must have told you about the miraculous statue of St Joseph. It is still in the chapel of Notre Dame du Chemin, which you have probably visited. The chapel has become a shrine visited by pilgrims from all over the nation, and thousands of souls find spiritual strength at the feet of the statue, especially the spirit of sacrifice and devotion, the strength needed for self-abnegation and for carrying out painful duties.'

'And tell me of your good Aunt Hélène. Is she still alive? Does she still expect Lamirande to return?'

'Alas, she does. It is the only point on which my dear aunt — how shall I explain it — does not see things as others do. She is a good angel for the poor, always gentle and kind. During that beautiful episode she must have experienced great heartache, which cast the only shadows on the events. It seems to me that instead of shutting himself in some convent M. Lamirande should have...

The young man was unable to finish his sentence. Brother Jean brought his hand to his heart and fell in a faint. We rushed to his side, and he soon regained consciousness.

'It's nothing,' he said. 'My heart is probably not as strong as my legs; this thin air sometimes bothers me.'

He went to sit down. After a few minutes he said he had recovered sufficiently to make the descent. My companions and the two young men found nothing remarkable in what had happened. They thought the fainting spell was simply due to fatigue. But because I knew something of the mystery surrounding Brother Jean and had seen his reaction to the name Leverdier, I was firmly convinced that his heart had been affected by emotion, not fatigue. I was positive that our companion was the hero of New France. And I must admit that I was strongly tempted to tell my companions. But I resisted the temptation. Why, I asked myself, should I reveal the secret that God had permitted him to keep for so long? Would it not be a kind of sacrilege? I had the strength to hold my tongue.

But I must finish. At the end of January Brother Jean fell gravely ill. He prepared for his death most admirably, with heroic resignation. His suffering must have been atrocious, but he never uttered the slightest complaint, nor did he show the slightest sign of impatience. Only a certain involuntary muscular contraction indicated the pain he must have suffered. The monks were filled with admiration. They realized that a true saint was about to leave them and they surrounded the bed of the dying man with profound respect. At the end, the abbot and several of the Fathers were at his side, reciting the prayers for the dying and repeating for him the names of Jesus, Mary, and Joseph. His eyes were closed, he was scarcely breathing, but his features, twisted by pain, showed that his life was not yet extinguished. Suddenly, an angelic harmony and an equally celestial perfume that no human language could describe filled the modest cell.

We knew immediately, the monks told me later, that the harmony and the perfume came from Heaven, because we perceived them first with our souls, which then communicated them to our senses, the opposite of what usually happens. It was truly something undefinable and indescribable. Then — I let the Fathers speak — the music and the perfume continued to fill the cell, not more intensely but more sweetly. Then we saw, at first through our inner eyes, so to speak, then through our corporeal eyes, a shape begin to form above the bed, like clouds of a dazzling whiteness. In the middle of the clouds there was the face of an eight-year-old child, a face with human features but one which bore a reflection of glory. And the child spoke, her words reaching our ears mysteriously, through our souls. 'Father,' she said, 'the Child Jesus has sent me for you. Come.' Brother Jean opened his eyes and rose slightly, spread his arms towards the celestial apparition and exclaimed, 'My child! At last! Thank you, God!' And like a luminous breath his soul left his body, which fell back onto the bed. We stayed, sunk in prayer, for some time. When we rose again there was nothing supernatural in the cell except the smile that illuminated the features of Brother Jean.

THE SOCIAL HISTORY OF CANADA
General Editor: Michael Bliss

1 *The Wretched of Canada: Letters to R.B. Bennett 1930-1935*
  Edited and introduced by L.M. Grayson and Michael Bliss

2 *Canada and the Canadian Question*
  Goldwin Smith
  Introduction, Carl Berger

3 *My Neighbor*
  J.S. Woodsworth
  Introduction, Richard Allen

4 *The Bunkhouse Man*
  E.W. Bradwin
  Introduction, Jean Burnet

5 *In Times Like These*
  Nellie McClung
  Introduction, Veronica Strong-Boag

6 *The City below the Hill*
  H.B. Ames
  Introduction, Paul Rutherford

7 *Strangers within Our Gates*
  J.S. Woodsworth
  Introduction, Marilyn Barber

8 *The Rapids*
  Alan Sullivan
  Introduction, Michael Bliss

9 *Philosophy of Railroads and Other Essays*
  T.C. Keefer
  Introduction, H.V. Nelles

10 *The Americanization of Canada 1907*
   Samuel E. Moffett
   Introduction, Allan Smith

11 *Rural Life in Canada: Its Trend and Tasks*
   John MacDougall
   Introduction, R. Craig Brown

12 *The New Christianity*
   Salem Bland
   Introduction, Richard Allen

13 *Canada Investigates Industrialism: The Royal Commission on the Relations of Labor and Capital*
   Edited and introduced by Greg Kealey

14 *Industry and Humanity*
William Lyon Mackenzie King
Introduction, David Jay Bercuson

15 *The Social Criticism of Stephen Leacock: The Unsolved Riddle of Social Justice and Other Essays*
Stephen Leacock
Edited and introduced by Alan Bowker

16 *A Dutch Homesteader on the Prairies: The Letters of Willem De Gelder*
Willem De Gelder
Translated and introduced by H. Ganzevoort

17 *The Tragedy of Quebec: The Expulsion of its Protestant Farmers*
Robert Sellar
Introduction, Robert Hill

18 *The Woman Suffrage Movement in Canada*
Catherine L. Cleverdon
Introduction, Ramsay Cook

19 *The Queen v Louis Riel*
Introduction, Desmond Morton

20 *The Writing on the Wall*
Hilda Glynn-Ward
Introduction, Patricia E. Roy

21 *By Great Waters: A Newfoundland and Labrador Anthology*
Edited and introduced by Peter Neary and Patrick O'Flaherty

22 *Saving the Canadian City.
The First Phase 1880-1920: An Anthology of Articles on Urban Reform*
Edited and introduced by Paul Rutherford

23 *The Magpie*
Douglas Durkin
Introduction, Peter E. Rider

24 *Report on Social Security for Canada*
Leonard Marsh
New introduction by the author

25 *A History of Farmers' Movements in Canada*
Louis Aubrey Wood
Introduction, Foster J.K. Griezic

26 *Social Planning for Canada*
League for Social Reconstruction
Introduction, F.R. Scott et al.

27 *For My Country (Pour la patrie)*
Jules-Paul Tardivel
Translation, Sheila Fischman
Introduction, A.I. Silver

Available in cloth and paper editions

www.ingramcontent.com/pod-product-compliance
Lightning Source LLC
Chambersburg PA
CBHW032032290426
44110CB00012B/773